American Government and Popular Discontent

Popular distrust and the entrenchment of government by professionals lie at the root of America's most pressing political problems. How did U.S. politics get to this point? Contemporary American politics got much of its shape from the transformations brought about from the 1950s to the 1980s. Presidential and congressional behavior, voting behavior, public opinion, public policy and federalism were all reconfigured during that time and many of those changes persist to this day and structure the political environment in the early twenty-first century.

Throughout American history, parties have been a reliable instrument for translating majority preferences into public policy. From the 1950s to the 1980s, a gradual antiparty realignment, alongside the growth of professional government, produced a new American political system of remarkable durability – and remarkable dysfunction. It is a system that is paradoxically stable despite witnessing frequent shifts in party control of the institutions of government at the state and national level. Schier and Eberly's system-level view of American politics demonstrates the disconnect between an increasingly polarized and partisan elite and an increasingly disaffected mass public.

Steven E. Schier is Dorothy H. and Edward C. Congdon Professor of Political Science at Carleton College in Northfield, Minnesota. He is the author or editor of fifteen books, most recently *The American Elections of 2012*, co-edited with Janet Box-Steffensmeier, and numerous scholarly articles. His analysis has appeared in the *New York Times*, *Washington Post*, *USA Today*, *Atlantic Magazine* and other publications.

Todd E. Eberly is an assistant professor of Political Science and coordinator of Public Policy Studies at St. Mary's College of Maryland. He specializes in the policy and political legacies of the Great Society and has published numerous scholarly articles. His analysis and commentary have been featured in the *Washington Post*, the *Baltimore Sun*, and on Public Radio.

American Government and Popular Discontent

Stability without Success

Steven E. Schier and
Todd E. Eberly

Routledge
Taylor & Francis Group

NEW YORK AND LONDON

First published 2013
by Routledge
605 Third Avenue, New York, NY 10017
4 Park Square, Milton Park, Abingdon, Oxon OX14 4RN

Routledge is an imprint of the Taylor & Francis Group, an informa business

© 2013 Taylor & Francis

The right of Steven E. Schier and Todd E. Eberly to be identified as author of this work has been asserted by him/her in accordance with sections 77 and 78 of the Copyright, Designs and Patents Act 1988.

Library of Congress Cataloging-in-Publication Data
Schier, Steven E.
American government and popular discontent : stability without success / Steven E. Schier, Todd E. Eberly.
pages cm
1. Political participation–United States. 2. Pressure groups–United States. 3. Right and left (Political science)–United States. 4. United States–Politics and government. I. Eberly, Todd E. II. Title.
JK1764.S358 2013
320.973–dc23
2012048684

ISBN: 978-0-415-89329-9 (hbk)
ISBN: 978-0-415-89330-5 (pbk)
ISBN: 978-0-203-80579-4 (ebk)

Typeset in Bembo
by Keystroke, Station Road, Codsall, Wolverhampton

For Helen Virginia Schier Drury
and
Abigail and Kathryn Eberly

Contents

Figures

Tables

Preface

This book is designed for use in American Government courses, from survey classes to more focused courses on the national political system, including classes on Parties and Elections, the Presidency, Congress, the Bureaucracy and Public Policy. In it, we place the operation of each of these national political institutions in broader systemic perspective.

Our book's theme will surprise some readers. Despite considerable political turbulence in national politics since the 1960s, we found much stability in the national political system over the last four decades, displayed with empirical evidence throughout our chapters. Two traits have simultaneously served to produce electoral turbulence but systemic stability during that time: widespread popular discontent with national government and the increasing dominance of occupational professionalism among the ranks of those who govern our nation. Popular discontent produces regular spasms of electoral turbulence, but professional government has remained a stable and defining characteristic of our national political system since the 1960s.

Our book originated with Todd Eberly's research revealing stable national electoral alignments since the 1960s. We further developed our book by drawing upon the path-breaking research of political scientists John Aldrich and Richard Niemi, who had previously detected the advent of a "Fifth Party System" in the 1960s. Our subsequent investigation of other national governing institutions revealed how they, like the party system, all had been transformed from 1955–1980. Key presidential, congressional, bureaucratic and judicial behaviors and traits remarkably have remained stable during the decades since then. A new American political system of paradoxical constancy had arisen from 1955–1980 and is with us still.

Acknowledgments

We wish to thank Saint Mary's College of Maryland and Carleton College, particularly Carleton's Dean of the College Beverly Nagel, for their support of our work. Richard Niemi helped us conceptualize our argument early, serving as an important contributor to our work. Steve Schier thanks his wife Mary for her ongoing support of many years. Todd Eberly thanks his wife Christina for being a constant source of support.

1 The New American Political System

An Overview

Barack Obama had good reason to be frustrated. As he ran for re-election in the fall of 2012, one of his landmark legislative accomplishments, the Affordable Care Act providing major reform of the nation's health care, remained controversial and subject to strong partisan divisions of opinion. An August 2012 survey found that though 64 percent of Democrats had a favorable opinion of it, only 35 percent of political independents and 8 percent of Republicans shared that favorable opinion (Kaiser Family Foundation 2012). Transforming American health care had been a goal of Democrats and liberals, beginning with Harry Truman in the 1940s. Obama saw this as the major legacy his presidency could deliver. Obama had proposed the biggest change in American health care since the passage of Medicare, federal health insurance for the elderly, in 1965.

The 2009–10 battle for passage of the health care bill was bitter and divisive in Congress and among the public. The administration had begun by cutting deals with affected interest groups—hospitals, doctors, insurance companies and the pharmaceutical industry—over the parameters of the legislation. Obama then let the Democratic-majority House and the Senate work on the legislative specifics, with only a tiny handful of GOP Senators willing to cooperate with the Democratic majorities. Out in the country, a protest against "government encroachment" began—known as the Tea Party. In the summer of 2009, lawmakers encountered irate citizens' concerns about a government "takeover" of health care. In January 2010, while Congress still worked on the legislation, Republican Scott Brown shocked the political world by winning a special Senate election to fill the seat of deceased liberal icon Ted Kennedy of Massachusetts.

Despite this political reversal, the Obama administration played "small ball" by making specific deals on particular aspects of the vast (2,000-plus pages) legislation (Johnson 2011, 157). Senator Ben Nelson of Nebraska got his state a higher Medicare reimbursement rate. Senator Mary Landrieu of Louisiana received more money for hurricane recovery. After months of negotiations among Democrats, Congress passed the law on March 25, 2010. The bill included many big changes in health care, including the expansion of Medicaid (medical insurance for the poor) eligibility, the establishment of government-run health insurance exchanges to facilitate the purchase of private insurance, and prohibitions on health insurers denying coverage due to pre-existing conditions. Public opposition to the legislation, however, did not recede. The Tea Party movement spawned several activist organizations that contributed to the GOP takeover of the House and gains in the Senate in the 2010 elections. Though Obama won a narrow re-election victory in 2012, his health care law remained unpopular with voters. National exit polls revealed that 49 percent of voters wanted the health care reform law fully or partially repealed but only 44 percent wanted the law to remain or be expanded (Schultheis 2012).

Obama's predecessor George W. Bush in 2005 had suffered an even worse fate with Social Security reform. After his 2004 re-election, Bush promised to spend his "political capital" on a major transformation of the nation's public retirement pension program. Though broad agreement existed that the program faced long-term financing problems, no consensus existed about how to alter its financing. Bush proposed that Social Security recipients receive "personal accounts," an approach strongly opposed by the Democrats. Bush embarked on a public persuasion tour, involving "60 stops in 60 days." Administration officials backed that up with hundreds of traveling stops and radio interviews as well.

Bush's proposal got nowhere. Though both Houses of Congress had GOP majorities, no committee took a vote on Social Security reform in 2005 or 2006. Public opinion polls showed no movement toward Bush's position (Edwards 2007, 262–263). Democrats and the American Association of Retired Persons, the nation's largest senior lobby, remained firmly opposed. With his grand initiative shelved, Bush then encountered great difficulties responding to the devastation of Hurricane Katrina. In the Fall of 2006, Democrats swept to majority control of Congress.

Both Obama and Bush pursued ambitious items dear to the hearts of the partisan and ideological followers, but that left many in the public realm cold. A strong protest against the presidents' partisan initiatives arose and produced a substantial electoral rebuke in mid-term elections. Our argument here is that such trends arise from the systemic environment in which Bush and Obama governed. Successful leadership is rare in this environment. As America's presidents attempt to command a government of career professionals in Congress and the bureaucracy, they frequently find themselves subject to tides of popular discontent.

The two presidents' frustrations are grounded in the core circumstances of America's contemporary political system. We define a *political system* as a social organization in which power is allocated among a small group of citizens who govern the greater community. Our present political system has several traits that serve to frustrate effective leadership, as Bush and Obama discovered. At present, America has no stable majority party that routinely wins elections and rules. Instead, power has fluctuated with increasing frequency between Democrats and Republicans in recent years. The public dislikes political parties and has low trust in government. America's fragmented media environment encourages acquisition of political knowledge by partisan and ideological activists who voice unceasing demands and agendas, while making it easier for far more citizens to tune out. Career professionals whose occupational welfare may not involve following presidential leadership populate the nation's bureaucracy. Federal courts increasingly engage in policymaking regarding issues that were previously the province of Congress and the president.

Seven Big Changes

When did these traits arise? Contemporary American politics got much of its shape from transformations from the 1960s to the 1980s. Presidential and congressional behavior, voting behavior, major media, public opinion, public policy and federalism altered during that time and many of those changes persist to this day. Several political scientists have noted aspects of this in scholarly articles.[1] In this book, we bring together these changes to form a composite view. We focus on the national political system as a whole and how many of the changes it underwent during the 20-year period endure to the present day.

Seven changes in America's politics and government originating from 1960 to 1980 are now central traits of our national political system.

First, the 1964 election marked the end of the Democratic dominance of the New Deal era—established with the election of Franklin Roosevelt in 1932—and the start of our present electoral era.[2] Political scientist Gerald Pomper first hinted at this in 1967 when his review of state-by-state election data revealed a tremendous electoral upheaval had occurred in 1964 (Pomper 1967). The upheaval hinted at by Pomper was significant and continued through the election of 1968. The electoral change witnessed during the 1960s was unlike any prior period in America and its impact has persisted into the twenty-first century. Chapter 2 features our update of Pomper's analysis.

Second, the end of the New Deal electoral coalition was not marked by the rise of a new electoral alignment in the traditional sense (Burnham 1970). Political scientists have identified certain elections, like those of 1860 and 1932, as realigning, creating lasting changes in party allegiances among the electorate. In the past, political realignments had resulted in the clear dominance of one party—that did not happen post 1964. Many scholars look to the 1968 election and the victory of Richard Nixon as the start of a "southern realignment" that brought Republicans to dominance in presidential elections and slowly moved them to parity in congressional elections—a trend that culminated in the mid-term elections of 1994 (Lawrence 1997). This, however, only tells part of the story. Because of Watergate, American politics was adrift until 1980 when Ronald Reagan sought to complete a Republican realignment, but it would be incomplete, and because of changes underway since the late 1960s, neither party would achieve dominance (Ladd 1997). So an *anti-majority party realignment* replaced the New Deal—not a shift in mass-party allegiance, but a decline in such allegiances among a significant portion of the public (Paulson 2007). This decline in allegiance continues to the present even as clear evidence demonstrates increased polarization among political elites. *Polarization* is increased partisan and ideological distance between the two major parties as they become extreme in their issue positions. Evidence of elite polarization, Morris Fiorina notes, is often mistaken as demonstrating increased mass polarization (Fiorina, Abrams, and Pope 2008, 2009). Still, Alan Abramowitz clearly demonstrates evidence of polarization among the most informed and politically active citizens (Abramowitz 2010). The seeming paradox of growing partisanship in voting at a time when the mass public shows little indication of polarization, may be explained by changes in the media and is explored in Chapter 4.

Third, American media has transformed in the present era. At the dawn of the New Deal Era in the 1930s, radio was the only source of broadcast media known to most people, and newspapers were the dominant source of information. Variety of programming was limited. The advent of television introduced a dramatic and new broadcast medium, but variety of programming remained minimal. As recently as 1970, most Americans had few television viewing options; the three major networks claimed 8 out of 10 viewers. Most homes had one TV and network or local news was an evening staple (Prior 2007). This began to change rapidly during the 1970s and 1980s as cable television and then satellite television became commonplace. Today, the major networks compete with hundreds of cable and satellite channels available in nearly 90 percent of homes. The internet has become a major new source for news and all manner of media exist for accessing information and entertainment. The media explosion of the current political era has been transformative. Those who are politically active have gained immeasurable access to news and information and the advent of partisan media has allowed for selective viewing. Individuals with less interest in politics enjoy an array of entertainment choices as an alternative to news. The result is an electorate that is more polarized than before. In this new media environment, partisans have their views and motivation to vote reinforced by the information explosion as more moderate voters tune out the world of politics (Prior 2007).

Fourth, since 1968, there has been a decline of party affiliation among Americans[3] even as partisanship among voters increased. In 1960, the authors of *The American Voter* wrote of the lasting attachment that most Americans had to one of the nation's political parties. Their loyalties helped to establish the stability of the party system. For many Americans, that stability is now more tenuous. Though partisan voters compose a growing share of the electorate, dissatisfaction with the two major parties, closely matched partisan allegiances, and occasional upticks in participation by less partisan voters have spawned in recent decades: (1) an increasing prevalence of divided party control of government (especially evident at the state level); (2) the Wallace, Anderson, Perot and Nader third party presidential candidacies; and (3) rapidly shifting alteration of the parties' control of government in the twenty-first century. Partisanship has increased among politically active elites but there has not been a corresponding increase among the mass public. Increased polarization and partisanship among politically active citizens, however, have resulted in significant party sorting. *Party sorting* refers to the increased fit between party affiliation and ideology and issue positions.[4] We explore the phenomenon of party sorting further in Chapter 4.

Fifth, since the 1960s, trust in government has declined and has remained at low levels. Along with declining party identification, low trust is an indicator of greater public disaffection with the political system. Why the decline in trust? Scholars have looked to Watergate and Vietnam as inducing "widespread popular mistrust of government" that has undermined the government's ability to enact policy (McQuaid 1989; Hetherington 2006). Social scientists have found widespread consequences issuing from the declining in trust since the 1960s. These include declining confidence in Congress and the presidency, more anti-incumbent voting, higher support for third-party candidates and less support for expanded federal domestic policies (Hetherington 2006; Chanley, Rudolph, and Rahn 2000; Levi and Stoker 2000). The decline in trust is a major force in American politics and we address its impact later in Chapter 3.

Sixth, the rise of more "professionalism" among governing elites has contributed to this mass volatility. Those in various professional occupations now dominate American government due the rise in education levels since the 1950s and the need for informed policy experts to carry out the ever-growing responsibilities of government. These governing professionals are an elite built on merit through occupational accomplishment. They now populate interest groups, the bureaucracy, the courts, the institutional presidency, and Congress. Even at the state level, there has been an increase in the number of professional legislatures since the 1960s. Many government professionals perceive little need to mobilize the public broadly the way parties did in previous eras. Three examples can illustrate this. First, candidates now narrowly target their appeals to likely voters. Second, unelected judges increasingly engage in policymaking behavior, previously the province of elected legislatures. Third, the great growth in professional interest group activity since 1970 has produced a proliferation of elite advocacy strategies. In an era of professional advocacy, policymaking need not involve the successful channeling of mass preferences, but instead what E. E. Schattschneider described as getting "results by procedures that simply ignore the sovereign majority" (1977, 189). Such elite behaviors have furthered the public's sense of disconnect from government and created a self-reinforcing chain. Elite "shortcuts" facilitate episodes of populist anger. The tax revolt of the late 1970s culminated in the "Reagan revolution." The anti-incumbent waves in the 1992 and 1994 elections resulted in the defeat of a sitting president and the first GOP Congress in 40 years. The turbulent elections of 2006, 2008, and 2010 saw party control of Congress switch twice as shifting partisan waves created an oscillating direction in national government.

Seventh, changing behavior in national institutions transformed governance. Congressional incumbents' electoral security contributed to legislative professionalism. Partisan polarization produced party voting in both chambers, strong majority party rule in the House and filibusters in the Senate. Presidents, for their part, were more subject to tides of popular disapproval than were more electorally secure legislators. In addition, bureaucratic activity grew in scale and federal courts asserted more expansive policymaking powers. Specific indicators tell the tale. Presidents suffered from lower levels of job approval. House and Senate incumbents gained more electoral security in the 1960s and 1970s. Party unity voting increased in both chambers. The support gap for presidents between rival congressional partisans grew. The majority party in the House increased its use of restrictive rules on consideration of bills and the Senate became far more prone to filibusters by dissenting partisan minorities. The number of federal regulations issued by the bureaucracy annually mushroomed. Federal court appointments became fronts of partisan battle because of the courts' increased involvement in policymaking.

America's national political system evolved during the 1960s and 1970s into a government of professionals with unstable mass allegiances. The public does not seem to like our regime of government by professionals. Satisfaction with government is at record lows, and, for decades, the majority of the public has harbored distrust that they can rely upon the government to "do the right thing" most of the time. Squire determined that the public holds a less favorable opinion of professional legislatures as compared to amateur, or citizen legislatures, but legislators in professional legislatures are more satisfied with their work than their weak legislature counterparts (Squire 1993).

The present system, however, has persisted despite sporadic populist eruptions for about 50 years. Its stability rests upon a paradoxical entrenchment of professionals in government and interest groups and a persistent popular disaffection with government and parties that prevents a reorientation of the system through party realignment. Previously in American history, parties have been a reliable instrument for translating majority preferences into public policy, as evident in the partisan realignments of 1860 and 1932. From the 1950s to the 1980s, a gradual anti-majority party realignment, alongside the growth of professional government, produced a new American political system of remarkable durability—one not defined by mass-based party allegiance. It has persisted despite witnessing frequent shifts in party control of the institutions of government at the state and national level.

Governance in the Present Era

In following chapters, we explore the impact of the changes in major elements of the present political era, partisanship, the electorate, institutions, on governance. Our initial inventory here reveals extensive impacts.

The People

As government has grown larger and more complex, public confidence in government has declined. Ever more Americans express distrust in government and a belief that they have little impact on the decisions made by government. These high levels of distrust benefit third party candidates (Wallace, Anderson, Perot, and Nader) and out party challengers in two-party races (Hetherington 1999). The electoral impact of declining trust contributes to the oscillating partisan control of government evident in the current era. Though few would deny the growing power and influence of political parties within the institutions of government, we demonstrate a clear decline in partisan affiliation among the mass public since the late 1960s and no changes in mass polarization. Yet there is evidence that politically active individuals compose a larger share of actual voters than in the past. Independent and apolitical individuals are participating at lower levels. Such voters have a moderating effect on elections and their decreasing presence at the polls has contributed to a more polarized politics (Prior 2007). There is reason to suspect that changes in media availability and greater ability to select content have contributed to the rising share of partisan voters as less partisan, potential voters, are voting at lower levels than in the past.

Political Parties

The rise in a closely matched partisan voter mix, combined with high levels of distrust and occasional upswings in participation by less partisan voters, has ushered in an era of highly competitive party politics. In the present era, neither political party has been able to claim the sustained allegiance of a majority of the voting public for much more than a handful of election cycles. The high level of partisan competition, coupled with declining turnout among more moderate voters, has served to discourage moderation and compromise as parties have become ever more reliant on their more partisan, activist bases. Tenuous holds on the institutions of government have encouraged parties in the majority to seek a "go it alone" strategy geared toward accomplishing as much as possible in a short time. For the minority party the motivation to obstruct the majority agenda overrides all other considerations. The result is often a game of partisan brinksmanship that simply serves to reinforce and perpetuate the major elements of the present era—declining levels of trust in government, declining levels of long-term partisan attachment, and an increased reliance on partisan base voters.

Congress

By 1980, the Democrats' long-established hold on Congress was weakening and with the election of Ronald Reagan and a Republican Senate, Republicans were no longer America's minority party. This new level of competition affected Congress in important ways. Republicans in the House responded to the era of competiveness by becoming more aggressive. The GOPers, taking advantage of House rules regarding debate and amendment, obstructed the majority party's agenda. Democrats responded by imposing ever more restrictive rules on legislation, bypassing committees and sub-committees. With such shortcuts, total days in session declined. The filibuster became a more common tool of minority party obstruction in the Senate. Republicans had employed it increasingly at the end of the 1970s, as did the Democrats once Republicans reclaimed control of the Senate in 1980.

Following the emergence of a unified Republican Congress after the 1994 mid-terms, America entered a now two-decade-long era of close partisan margins in Congress. The steady disappearance of a moderate voice in Congress can be linked to many other changes brought about in this era, including the rise of a more partisan mix of voters, closed primary systems that attract more activist voters, and high tech advances in congressional redistricting which have made safe seats the norm rather than the exception. Liberal Democrats and conservative Republicans now reliably dominate party primaries, which in turn produce candidates close to the divergent ideological poles of American politics. Shifts in party control from elections thus can have large ideological consequences in governance. In this era of intense competition, and, more recently, rapid oscillation in partisan control, a game of high-stakes legislative politics emerged.

The President

The absence of a stable dominant majority party coalition since the 1960s has made the president an independent agent dependent on short-term popular support for political success. A review of average yearly approval data from the Gallup Poll from Eisenhower to George W. Bush superimposed with a tally of the percentage of presidential initiatives approved by Congress reveals that a president's popularity often determines success in Congress. Simply stated, popular presidents enjoy greater legislative success regardless of partisan control of government. Given enduring public distrust of government, the best way for presidents to prevail is to be popular.

The downside to presidential authority premised on public approval, however, is that it tends to be a diminishing commodity. Gallup data also show presidential approval declines over the course of a president's term in office, and average presidential approval, regardless of president, has been declining since Eisenhower. This creates an authority problem for presidents, as the office has grown to require public support as an essential source of power. Simultaneous to this, there has been a rise in the gap between a president's approval rating by members of his own party and members of the opposition party. Opposition party members in Congress may be less inclined to oppose a president who enjoys the support of a significant share of their voters, but as that level of support falls, there is no downside to opposing the president. This helps to explain the rise in the partisan support gap in Congress for presidents.

The Bureaucracy

Congress in recent decades has made deals, not laws. By that we mean that the pressure to achieve policy goals and advance an agenda in a highly competitive and hyper-partisan era results in Congress passing laws with broadly defined goals, but often lacking in specifics. In an era of polarization and close partisan margins, compromise on well-defined policy statements is difficult to achieve. Congress defers policymaking details to the bureaucracy to bypass the obstacles faced within Congress. The ever-increasing number of pages published each year in the Federal Register offers evidence of this increased reliance on the bureaucracy.

Both parties have an incentive to defer the specifics of policy to the implementing agency because it offers at least three avenues by which they may influence the final direction of policy. The majority party could rely on control of Congress and its oversight authority to influence the implementing agency. The minority party may play the odds of obtaining control of Congress and exercising similar influence. The parties may look to the presidency as a means by which to influence the implementing agency through the power of appointments or executive orders. Another option for parties, and interest groups, is to use the courts to challenge an agency's interpretation or enforcement of laws. Regardless of the path chosen, the result is a politicized bureaucracy.

Most of the federal bureaucracy is comprised of career civil service employees and is not subject to presidential appointment or congressional approval. However, presidents and Congress still try to influence bureaucratic actions, Congress can use oversight or appropriations to influence the bureaucracy and presidents can use the power of appointment or executive order. Presidents have found that there are limits to what they can do with the bureaucracy unilaterally. The pursuit of new policies is especially difficult, but the obstruction of existing policies is easier to accomplish. In an era of divided government, or rapidly oscillating control of government, a new president may use his power and influence as Chief Executive to derail policy implementation or enforcement stemming from a prior or opposition Congress.

The bureaucracy finds itself in a precarious position during the current era; though staffed by a more educated and more independent class of civil servants than at any time in American history, it has been burdened with ever more responsibilities with regard to implementation and policy development. Concurrent with this expansion in responsibilities, it is subject to pressures that undermine its effectiveness. Therefore, as the responsibilities of the federal bureaucracy increase and the pages of the Federal Register grow, public confidence in the professional bureaucracy declines.

The Courts

In the present era, the courts have become far more involved in policy implementation and interpretation. This stems from the increased tendency by Congress to pass laws with broad goals, but ill-defined policies. The implementing federal agency assumes the responsibility of developing policy specifics in the form of federal regulations. Given the lack of clarity often present in federal legislation, the actual intent or meaning of a law may be open to various interpretations. Under the U.S. Constitution, the courts are the final arbiter on all matters of law. Additionally, the doctrine of judicial review subjects legislative and executive action to review, and possible invalidation, by the judiciary.

Progressive reforms enacted in the aftermath of Watergate increased public access to the courts and this enhanced access granted citizens and special interest groups a new avenue for challenging or shaping policy. As a result, in areas such as environmental protection and disability rights, the courts have become key players in the policy process. The parties and partisan activists have become more concerned with the make-up of the court, especially the Court of Appeals because the Supreme Court never reviews most Appeals Court decisions.[5]

The high level of partisan competition evident in the Sixth Party System has affected the courts in important ways. A successful confirmation was virtually assured for presidential nominees to the U.S. Appeals Court in the 1950s and 1960s, and the confirmation process, from nomination to confirmation, lasted less than four months. By 2008, a nominee to the Appeals Court might expect the confirmation process to last six months and the likelihood of confirmation is a 50/50 prospect. There is tremendous motivation for opposition party members in Congress to delay the confirmation process and play the odds that they may be the majority party in Congress or the White House after the next election. Over 10 percent of federal appellate and district court judgeships were vacant when Barack Obama assumed the presidency in 2009.

The Road from Here

The following chapters explore the implications of our post-1960 political system for national politics, institutions and policy. Chapter 2 establishes the emergence and stability of the present era. Chapter 3 explores the crucial intersection of declining levels of trust and the rise in the level of "professional" government. Chapter 4 explores the intersection of the public, the parties, and a changed media environment. Chapter 5 relates this electoral change to the behavior of America's professionalized and polarized Congress. Chapter 6 explains the post-1965 rise of a more bureaucratic and assertive presidency that suffers from unstable public support. Chapter 7 explores the impact of these changes on policymaking and bureaucratic implementation. Chapter 8 assesses changes in the composition of the federal judiciary and the rise of its expanded policymaking efforts since 1960. Chapter 9 assesses the "staying power" of the present system and the prospects for its future transformation. Our Afterword assesses the 2012 election's impact upon the stable system explained in the book.

2 The Current Stable System
A Data Portrait

In Chapter 1, we defined a political system as a social organization allocating power among a small group of citizens who govern the greater community. The contemporary political system in America emerged from changes occurring between 1968 and 1980, and the present system is quite stable. For many students of American politics, our discussion of the contemporary political system will be reminiscent of what others have termed party systems. A *party system* is best understood as a period "of a generation or more in which electoral politics differ distinctly from the periods before and after" (Aldrich and Niemi 1996, 87). Campbell writes, "American electoral history has long been characterized as a series of party systems and realignments. Party systems define normal partisan politics, and realignments are the change from one party system to the next" (2006, 359).

We agree with the many scholars who identify five demonstrable party systems in American history.[1] The First Party System existed from 1790 until the mid-1820s, the Second emerged and lasted until the Civil War in 1860, the Third lasted until the mid-1890s, and the Fourth ended with the Great Depression in the early 1930s. The emergence of the Fifth Party System is typically associated with the election of Franklin Roosevelt in 1932, often referred to as the New Deal Era. There is some dispute as to whether the Fifth Party System ended, though we and other scholars point to the critical era of the mid to late 1960s as the point at which the Fifth Party System collapsed and a new party system emerged (Aldrich and Niemi 1996; Campbell 2006; Paulson 2007). We demonstrate that collapse and emergence in the pages that follow.

Our focus in this book, however, is on America's political system that encompasses elements beyond partisanship and election outcomes. For example, the institutional relationships between the branches of government are a crucial element of a political system missed in a focus on electoral politics. This chapter reveals many connections between party systems and the broader political system. Examining the overall national political system provides a more complete picture of the dynamics of a given era. Data for many of the political system variables that we consider in the following pages, however, are not available for periods prior to the early 1950s. To remedy this gap in historical evidence, we include in this chapter two methods by which we demonstrate the existence of prior party systems and the emergence of the Sixth Party System—and the current political system—in the late 1960s. The first method updates a classic work on the collapse of party systems and the second updates a work that looked beyond just partisan electoral outcomes to explain the traits of our present party system.

The Six Party Systems

The Fifth Party System collapsed at the presidential level in 1964. The traditional Democratic coalition of the New Deal Era was gone, Lyndon Johnson's overwhelming reelection notwithstanding. Johnson's victory in 1964 witnessed declines in Democratic support in the once solidly Democratic South and increasing Democratic support in the former Republican strongholds of New England. A review of state-by-state Democratic vote share in successive elections provides evidence of the collapse.

Gerald Pomper (Pomper 1967) first examined continuity and change in presidential elections via linear correlation of state-by-state election results in paired presidential elections. Pomper was interested in identifying the cleavage points that precede the emergence of party systems. According to Pomper, such a cleavage would be evident via a "change in the parties' bases of support [...] the geographic distribution of each party's vote would be different from the past: traditional strongholds would fall, while new areas of strength would become evident" (1967, 539). Such changes or shifts in support would be evident in statistical analyses of the correlation between sequential elections. In short, a break in continuity, as demonstrated by a low level of correlation with preceding elections, suggests the end of a party system. Pomper (1967, 540) compared the Democratic Party's share of the total vote by state from 1824 to 1964[2] and identified five "electoral cleavages" in American history, cleavages that correspond to prevailing scholarship on American party systems.

To demonstrate the collapse of the Fifth Party System and the emergence of the Sixth, we updated Pomper's work through the election of 2008. We paired successive elections by comparing the Democratic share of the total vote by state. The state-by-state comparison generates a Pearson correlation coefficient with a low or negative value indicating a disruption or cleavage point and a higher positive value indicating continuity or electoral stability.[3] Figure 2.1 presents the results.

The first three cleavages identified by Pomper in 1967 are evident, but two subsequent cleavages are also apparent using correlations derived from data from the eleven presidential elections held since Pomper's original work. The most important element of Figure 2.1 is the trend since 1964 because it represents election data accumulated since Pomper's original work, inclusive of 2008.[4] The cleavage that Pomper noted in 1960 and 1964 is evident, and 1968 emerges as a crucial year as it was highly correlated with 1964. Likewise,

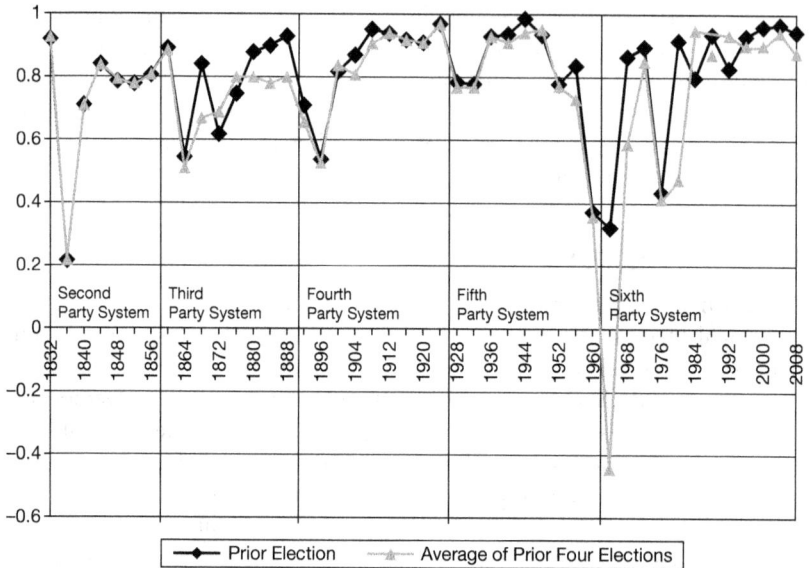

Figure 2.1 Correlation of successive presidential elections with prior election, 1828–2008, and the average of four prior elections, 1848–2008, graphed at latter year

Source: State-by-state election data retrieved from Leip (2010).

1972 was highly correlated with 1968. Remember, a high positive correlation indicates stability. Given that each election is unique, it is necessary to smooth out election-to-election changes that may cloud any study of electoral stability or change. This can be accomplished by correlating the results of a given election to the average of the prior four elections. Figure 2.1 demonstrates this approach and confirms the general findings. It is clear that the New Deal coalition, the Fifth Party System, met its end in the 1960s and a new, stable era emerged after 1968.

The results of the 1964 election were poorly correlated with the results of the 1960 election, but even more telling, the results were negatively correlated with the average of the prior four elections—suggesting an inverse relationship. The Fifth Party System ended and the parties' electoral coalitions had changed. A new era of stability emerges post 1968, save for the election of 1976 which witnessed the presence on the Democratic ballot of Jimmy Carter, a Southern Democrat who likely disrupted the Republican Party's emerging hold on the states of the Deep South. Indeed, the nomination of a moderate to conservative Southern Democrat to run against a moderate Republican, in President Gerald Ford, resulted in a one-time reemergence of the New Deal Coalition of states.[5] The election of 1976 was more highly correlated with the elections of 1932 through 1960 than with either 1964 or 1968. One might reasonably add the resignation of Richard Nixon, following the Watergate scandal, and his subsequent and controversial pardon by President Ford as another explanation for the discontinuity in 1976.

Barack Obama pieced together an impressive electoral coalition in the 2008 election that included traditionally Republican states like Indiana, Virginia, and North Carolina. Obama became the first Democrat since Lyndon Johnson in 1964 to receive more than 50.1 percent of the national popular vote. The Congressional victories by Democrats in the 2006 midterms coupled with Obama's election in 2008 led many to wonder whether a new political era, a realignment, had arrived. The demise of one political system and the arrival of a new era should be evident via a break in electoral continuity. Yet Figure 2.1 shows the 2008 election demonstrated a high degree of correlation with the election of 2004 and with the average of the preceding four elections. Preliminary data from the 2012 election support this conclusion (see Afterword).

The stability of the present era, evident in the state-by-state correlation analysis, ignores a crucial fact about American presidential elections. Rather than one election, every presidential election is in fact 51 separate elections in the states and the District of Columbia (DC). However, most states are not competitive. Nearly three-quarters of states and DC are relatively reliable members of either the Democrats' or the Republicans' electoral coalition. Indeed, a study conducted just prior to the 2008 election (Pollard 2008) determined that 20 states are reliably Republican and 19 (including the District of Columbia) are reliably Democratic.[6] Republicans are strongest in the South, the Great Plains, and the Mountain West, while Democrats tend to be strongest in the Northeast, the Great Lakes, and on the West Coast.

There are 39 states considered rather safe and neither party has a lock on the 270 electoral votes needed for victory so the true contest often focuses on so-called swing states. The *Oxford Advanced Learner's Dictionary* (2011) defines a swing state as "a state where none of the candidates running for president can be certain of getting the most support." As shown in Table 2.1, 12 states, that often proved crucial to electoral victory, had not been consistently in either party's victory column between 1988 and 2004.

Stability in the present era would suggest the presence of elections maintaining each party's geographic coalition. At first glance, the results of the 2008 election do suggest some reorganization of the geographic coalitions had occurred. Barack Obama won all 19 of the reliably Democratic states, but also carried six of the 12 swing states, and claimed four reliably Republican states (CO, IN, NC, and VA)—resulting in a 365 to 173 Electoral Vote victory. One test of stability would be to examine the degree of correlation between Democratic Party vote share in successive elections in states that have emerged under the current era as reliably Republican, reliably Democrat, or swing states.[7]

As shown in Panel A of Figure 2.2, the Democratic coalition has been the very model of stability since 1968, following the clear breakdown of the New Deal, or Fifth Party System, and the loss of the southern states in presidential

Table 2.1 Swing states prior to 2008 election and winning party by election

State	Election year					
	1988	*1992*	*1996*	*2000*	*2004*	*2008*
Arkansas	R	D	D	R	R	R
Florida	R	R	D	R	R	D
Iowa	D	D	D	D	R	D
Kentucky	R	D	D	R	R	R
Louisiana	R	D	D	R	R	R
Missouri	R	D	D	R	R	R
Nevada	R	D	D	R	R	D
New Hampshire	R	D	D	R	D	D
New Mexico	R	D	D	D	R	D
Ohio	R	D	D	R	R	D
Tennessee	R	D	D	R	R	R
West Virginia	D	D	D	R	R	R

Source: Compiled by authors.

elections. The Republican coalition has been less stable, but this is likely a reflection of the southern realignment that helped Republicans win seven of the 11 presidential elections between 1968 and 2008. The elections of 1976, 1992 and 1996 each featured a Southern Democrat on the ticket (Jimmy Carter and Bill Clinton, respectively) and in each election, the victorious Democrat was able to erode the Republican's southern support—despite this, the Republican coalition has been highly stable since 1996.

Correlation coefficients in swing states are much as expected, high in years of in-party reelection and low in years of out-party victory, though 2008 was highly correlated with 2004. The 2008/2004 correlation is an intriguing result because George W. Bush won 11 of the 12 swing states in 2004. The high degree of correlation likely reflects the closeness of the results in the five swing states won by Barack Obama in 2008 but won by Bush in 2004. It is at least possible that the high degree of correlation between 2004 and 2008, even in the presence of out-party victory, could indicate some changes taking place in swing states—a political reordering of geographic coalitions. Six swing states (AR, KY, LA, MO, TN and WV) have not voted Democratic since 1996; recoding those states as reliably Republican reduces the correlation for 2008 among swing states and only slightly reduces the Republican correlation (Panel B of Figure 2.2). The results appear to suggest that the southern realignment, a key component of the post-New Deal era, is complete as four of the six swing states recoded as Republican are southern states.

Figures 2.1 and 2.2 reveal the emergence and stability of the Sixth Party System. They also show a key characteristic of the contemporary political system discussed in the following chapters—the highly competitive nature

A: Election Correlations in Democratic, Republican, and Swing States

B: Election Correlations in Democratic, Reclassified Republican, and Redefined Swing States

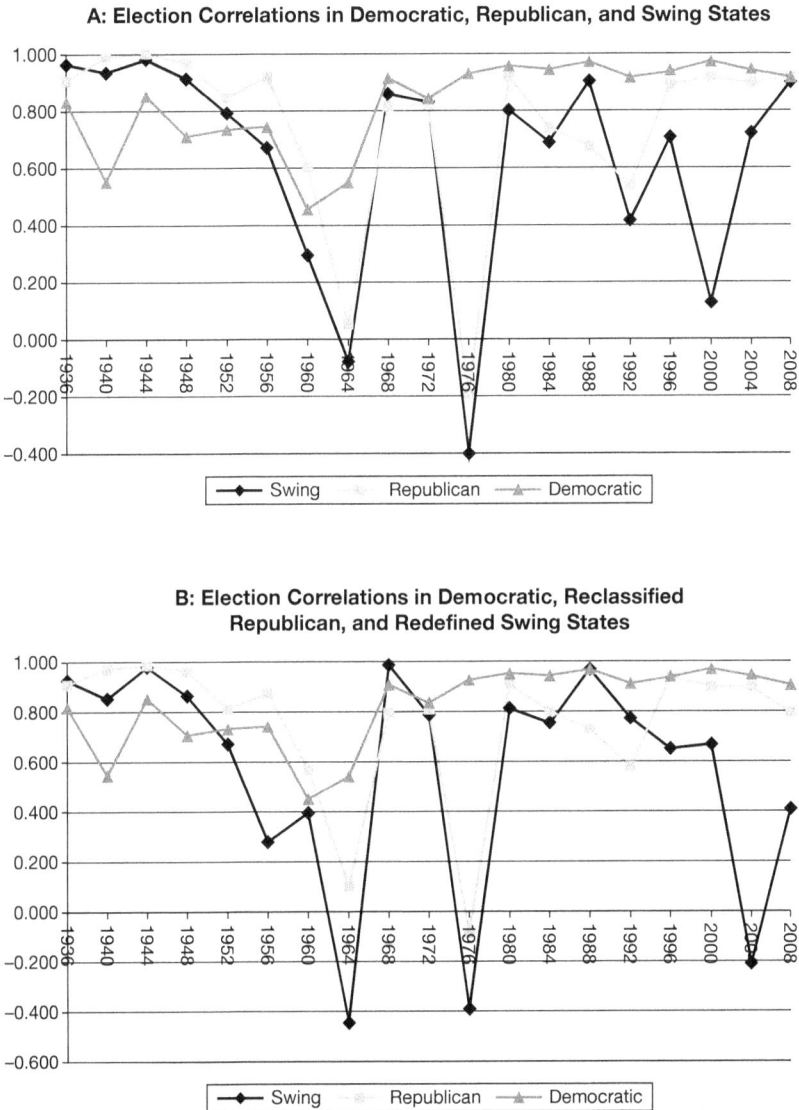

Figure 2.2 Correlation of presidential vote in designated years, with prior election by state partisan strength, 1936–2008

Source: Leip (2010).

of American politics. Only 12 of 50 states and the District of Columbia were swing states prior to the 2008 election. Including results from 2008 suggests a smaller constellation of swing states, perhaps as few as six. Even if one were to move the four reliably Republican states (CO, IN, NC, and VA) won by

Barack Obama into the swing state category (perhaps a very premature move), the evidence still suggests a shrinking electoral playing field with neither party claiming a reliable lock on enough states to claim the 270 electoral votes needed for victory. Simply stated, the battle for the presidency remains highly competitive.

The Contemporary Political System

In their work, *The Sixth American Party System*, John H. Aldrich and Richard G. Niemi (1996) demonstrated the emergence of the Sixth Party System that relied on variables other than election results. Aldrich and Niemi reviewed a number of election-related attitudinal and behavioral changes during the 1960s. They determined—via a variable-by-variable examination of attitudinal changes coupled with a collective review of the identified variables—that the Fifth Party System was disrupted during the 1960s, followed by a new and stable equilibrium that emerged by 1972 and was evident through 1992. The authors discovered "the origins of today's climate of popular discontent can be traced back to the 1960s. Specifically, a collection of items thought to measure trust or confidence in government revealed a dramatic loss of trust after 1964" (1996, 98).

Aldrich and Niemi identified 27 variables with values for all or most elections from 1952 to 1992. The variables captured voter level as well as systemic changes and included partisanship, party image, the balance between the public's focus on domestic and foreign policy issues, the linkage of issues to parties over candidates, turnout, split-ticket voting, presidential coattails, incumbent security and confidence in government. The authors considered these measures individually to discern micropatterns, but then standardized the measures to facilitate a collective, or macropattern, analysis.

Aldrich and Niemi argued the "critical era between party systems is a set of rapid changes in a broad range of crucial political variables." Changes that once made, endured. Their work concluded with the presidential election year of 1992. The mid-term election of 1994 saw the rise of a Republican Congress for the first time in 50 years and the culmination of a Republican Congressional realignment in the South. The election of George W. Bush in 2000 resulted in unified Republican government for the first time since the early years of the Eisenhower administration—but it would not last. The elections of 2006 and 2008 saw a resurgence of Congressional Democrats and the presidential election of 2008 suggested the potential for significant changes to the Republican and Democratic electoral coalitions—perhaps evidence of the "critical era between party systems."

To determine if the new and stable era observed by Aldrich and Niemi was still evident in recent decades, we replicated the authors' original work through 2008 using 26 of their original 27 variables.[8] Though not shown, our update to the original work produced the same results for the period

1952–1992. We then assembled evidence on additional indicators not captured in the original work. In addition to 26 variables identified by the two authors, we added 14 more that broaden our scope beyond the party system to include public opinion and institutional behavior.[9] The Appendix details these 40 variables and their sources. The addition of these new variables did not change the overall trend observed by Aldrich and Niemi— suggesting again the interplay of party and political system.

First, we examine trends in our specific indicators. The many "micro-patterns" in the partisan nature of the electorate, institutional changes in Congress, the presidency, and relationships between the branches, and mass electoral behavior do have a common shape, and we discuss them in greater detail in subsequent chapters. In aggregate, we find many elements of the present political system arose from the turmoil of the 1960s. They distinctly differ from those of the prior party system and there has been remarkable stability in the Sixth Party System since the early 1970s.

With regard to partisanship, or parties in the electorate, there has been a clear rise in black support for the Democratic Party and a corresponding and highly correlated decline in southern whites in the Democratic Party and a corresponding and highly correlated rise in the share of whites identifying as Independent (Figure 2.3). There has also been an increase in the share of all voters neutral toward both parties.

Institutionally, House and Senate incumbent security has grown, presidential legislative success in Congress declined, as did Appeals Court nomination success in the Senate (Figure 2.4). An ever-widening gap appeared between the level of support a president receives from members of his own party in Congress and members of the opposition party. With the rise in divided government, the changes in the presidential partisan support gap likely explain the lower levels of legislative success and the more difficult confirmation process.

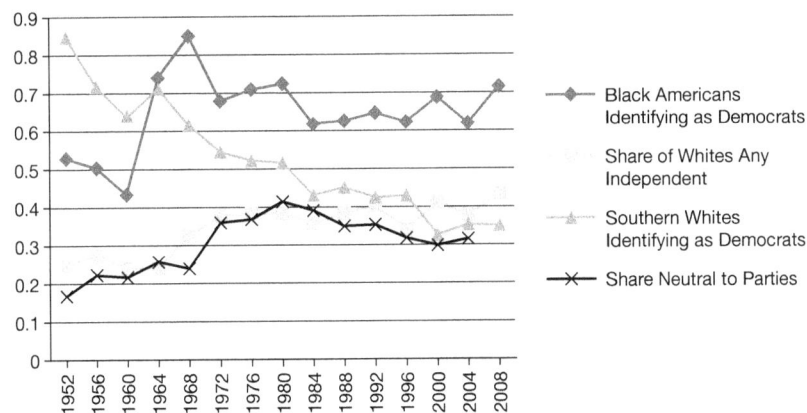

Figure 2.3 Trends for select partisanship variables, 1952–2008

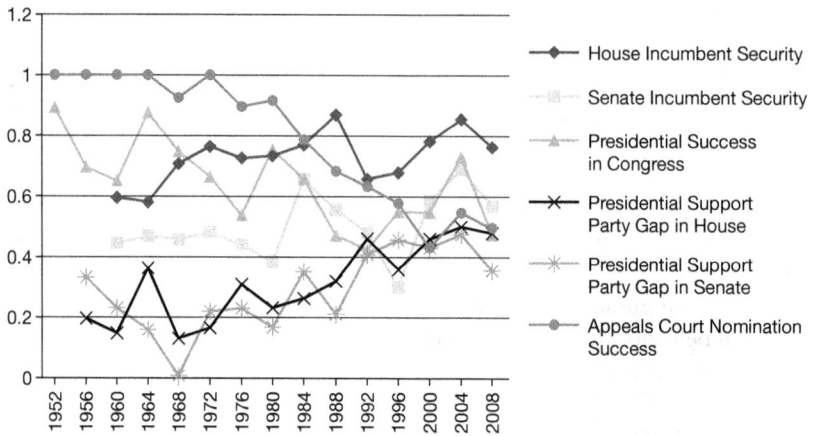

Figure 2.4 Trends for select institutional variables, 1952–2008

Concerning public opinion and the electorate, popular discontent has increased markedly. "Popular discontent" measures the percentage of the public since 1952 agreeing, "Public officials don't care what people like me think." It is highly correlated with nearly every other indicator included in our analysis. Along with the rise in popular discontent, turnouts for presidential and mid-term elections have declined. More ballot initiatives appear on state ballots, a means of policymaking that circumscribes the power of elected legislators and governors.[10] There has also been a reversal in the public's perception of the country's most important problem. With few exceptions (the second Iraq War), a clear trend exists toward the public labeling the most important problem as a domestic policy problem (Figure 2.5).

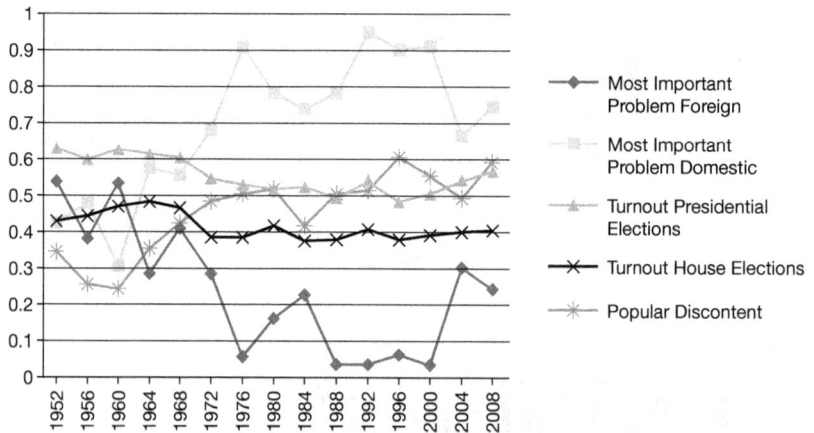

Figure 2.5 Trends for select electorate variables, 1952–2008

We next consider the "macropattern" among our indicators and in a manner that allows variable-by-variable comparison to determine whether the current system is one of stasis or change. Our update to the Aldrich and Niemi research includes 40 variables that represent key elements of any political system. These variables have different scales with results of varied ranges. As with the work that we are updating, we standardized the variables such that each had a mean of zero and a variance of one across the 15 election years studied.[11] We then set the polarity of each observation, multiplying the standardized variable by -1 where appropriate, so that negative values appear during the Fifth Party System (prior to 1964) and positive values appear during the Sixth Party System (post 1968). Values for 1964 and 1968, the "critical era" between systems, were left unadjusted. We then combined these standardized measures into a single variable with 538 observations (555 minus missing data).

Figure 2.6 presents the mean score of the combined, standardized measures for each of election years between 1952 and 2008. Its pattern strongly resembles the 1952–1992 trend discovered by Aldrich and Niemi.[12] Both tell the same story. The stability of the Fifth Party System ended in 1964 and 1968 and a new, stable system arose in 1972. In fact, the stability of the present system has been quite remarkable given the seeming evidence of instability. Divided government, a rising number of political independents, third party uprisings, and seesaw Congressional control have marked the current system. Our update to the Aldrich and Niemi data through 2008 clearly shows both the micro and macropattern stability observed during the 1972–1992 period persists. We are in a new American political system, and the partisanship

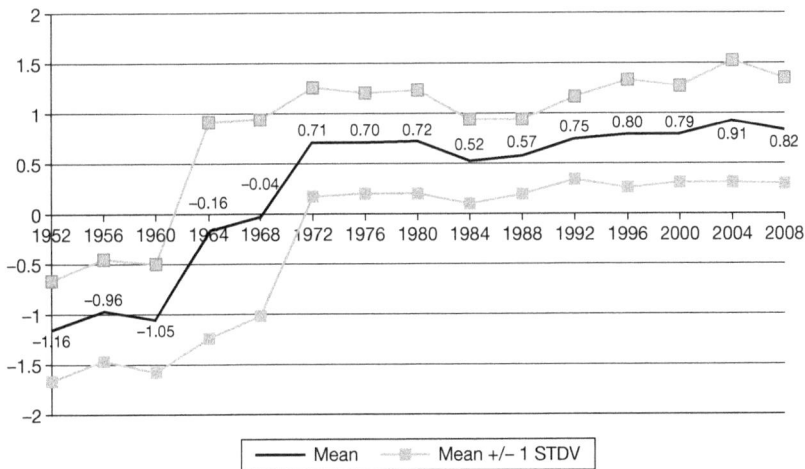

Figure 2.6 American political system macropattern, 1952–2008, averages and +/− 1 standard deviation of 40 standardized variables

Sources: See Appendix.

variables in our analysis, discussed below, reveal that the Sixth American Party system is still with us.

From Figure 2.6, it is clear that big changes in the 1960s and 1970s resulted in the stable traits of the current national political system. We disaggregated the overall trend into smaller trends involving partisanship, the electorate and institutional behavior. In these figures, the trend is the same as our overall pattern presented in Figure 2.6.

The trends revealed in an analysis of 17 partisanship variables, presented in Figure 2.7, indicate that we are still in the Sixth Party System, with stable features since the 1960s. Because of the anti-majority party alignment of that era, we have been in a "no party majority" system for several decades. The system is unique in American history in that there is no permanent majority party that dominates national politics, like the GOP from 1860 to 1932 or the Democrats from 1932 to 1968. The present stability reflects a highly competitive rivalry between the two major parties that translates into vacillating party control of individual branches of government. Variation in party control creates the impression of instability, but it is in fact a hallmark of the present stable era. Chapter 4 examines specific partisan trends in more depth.

The stability in the pattern of institutional variables, shown in Figure 2.8, reflects the current period's pointed competition in government between evenly matched parties, neither of which securely holds majority support from the public. Restrictive rules and cloture motions in the present era frequently are used to quash partisan and ideological rivals in Congress.

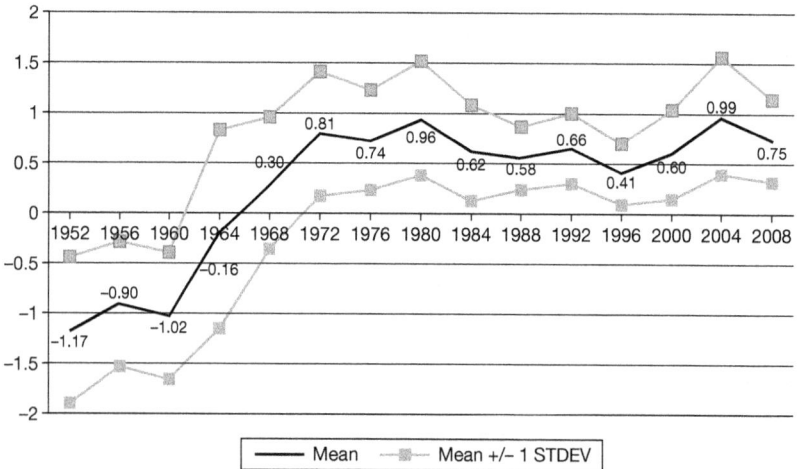

Figure 2.7 Partisanship micropattern, 1952–2008, shown are mean and +/– 1 standard deviation of 17 standardized variables related to the electorate partisanship

Sources: See Appendix.

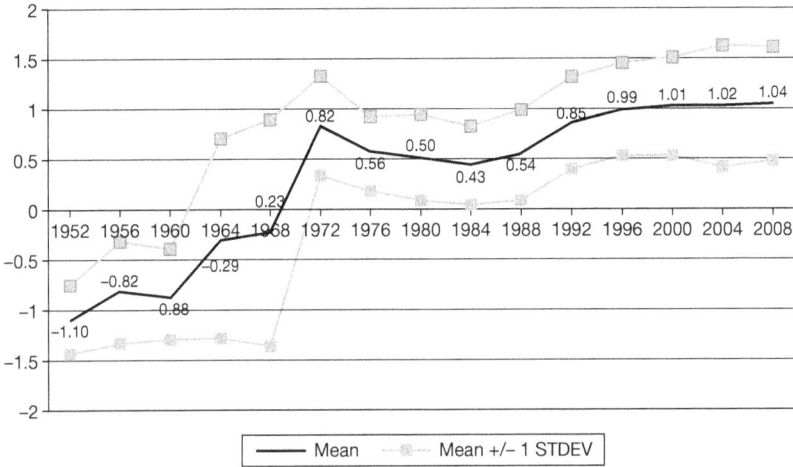

Figure 2.8 Institutional micropattern, 1952–2008, shown are mean and +/− 1
standard deviation of 14 standardized variables related to the institutions

Sources: see Appendix.

Presidential success in Congress increasingly hinges on party line votes. Federal appeals court nominations are more likely to invoke barbed partisan controversies in the Senate. In addition, executive government continues to expand with the growth of regulations. Chapters 5 through 8 further examine the institutional features of the present era and present many of the individual measures used in the macro- and micropattern analyses.

Figure 2.9 contains nine measures of the electorate and shows more volatile trends than do the institutional and partisanship figures. That is hardly surprising, given the turbulent electoral environment of recent decades, in which public support zigzagged between the parties. No president has served two full consecutive elected terms from 1960 to 1980, Republicans held the Senate for the first time in 30 years from 1980–1986, the first partisan turnover of Congress in 40 years occurred in 1994 and elections from 2006 to 2010 produced shifting partisan control of the presidency and Congress. Popular attachment to the party system had declined and a growing segment of the public lacked an allegiance to either party. Party sorting proceeded over the decades. Public distrust at times crested and manifested itself via populist uprisings. Populist uprisings are in fact an established aspect of the current American political system. The elections of 1974, 1980, 1994, 2006 and 2010—in which popular discontent led to major electoral shifts—are recurrent features of the current era's electoral pattern.

Overall, across indicators of the electorate, institutions and partisanship, big changes began in the early 1960s and resulted in stable patterns in electoral behavior, partisanship and institutional behavior since the late 1970s. But

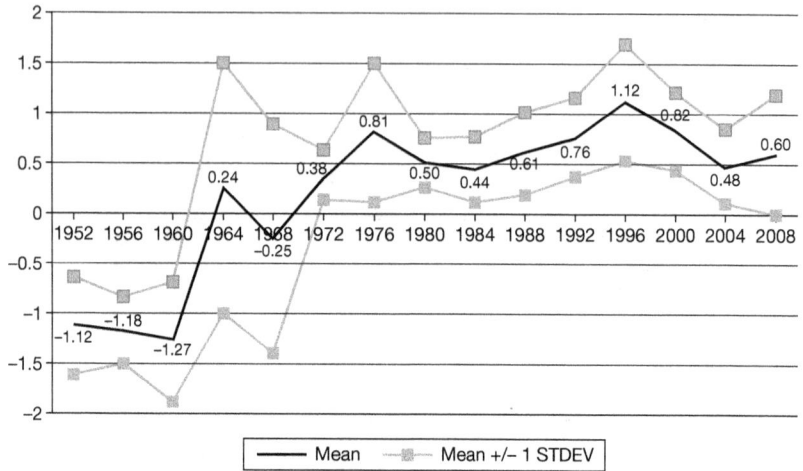

Figure 2.9 Electorate micropattern, 1952–2008, shown are mean and +/− 1
standard deviation of 9 standardized variables related to the electorate

Sources: see Appendix.

what do all these changes mean in practical terms? We can illustrate this by
comparing the traits of the pre-1964 system with the stable trend since the
1970s.

Before 1964, partisanship and party coalitions differed considerably in their
characteristics from the post-1972 period.[13]At the earlier time, a smaller
proportion of blacks were Democrats and more were apolitical. The large
percentage of apolitical blacks no doubt resulted from their widespread
disenfranchisement in the American South. Fewer whites were independent;
more were strong partisans. Southern whites had much stronger support for
the Democratic Party and the share of the Democratic coalition that was
working class was larger, as was the share of Democrats in the electorate. The
share of the public neutral about the parties was much smaller. Split ticketing
of any sort was less common. Voting for the presidential and Congressional
candidates of one's preferred party was more frequent.

Regarding the electorate and its views, Americans experienced the height
of the Cold War with the Soviet Union during the 1950s, so Americans
viewed foreign problems as most important much more than they did after
1972, as the Vietnam War and the standoff with the USSR began to wind
down. Turnout in presidential and House elections was much higher and
popular discontent with government much lower. Ballot initiatives, a reform
aimed at circumventing elected officials, were in less frequent use and fewer
passed into law.

Institutional behavior during the 1950s also contrasted with that of the
later period. Representatives and Senators were less electorally secure and
their careers in Congress were shorter. Party unity voting in the House

and Senate was lower because of the presence of large numbers of conservative white Southern Democrats and moderate Northern Republicans who have since disappeared from its halls. Presidential success in Congress was higher, and the presidential support gap between fellow and rival Congressional partisans was lower. Presidential approval ratings were higher, and the partisan gap in presidential approval was lower. The House majority party employed fewer restrictive rules and the Senate fewer filibusters. The bureaucracy issued far fewer federal regulations annually. In aggregate, our 14 institutional variables demonstrate considerable stability since 1972.

It is striking that among our 40 indicators, all but five of the changes described in the preceding paragraphs occurred between 1960 and 1980. Much ink has been spilled assessing the turbulence of the 1960s and 1970s, and our evidence reveals that trends then transformed the national political system. Five indicators did not have big shifts until the 1980s, but all of them were in accord with the many trends begun a few decades earlier. Three represented ongoing partisan polarization: marked increases in House party unity voting, a growing partisan support gap for presidents in the Senate, and a larger partisan gap in public approval of the president. Another, increased ballot initiative success spiked in the 1980s, reflecting another rise in popular discontent with political institutions that initially arose two decades earlier. In addition, Senators became more electorally secure in the 1980s as House members had in the 1960s and 1970s.

Conclusion

John H. Aldrich and Richard G. Niemi (Aldrich and Niemi 1996) demonstrated the disruption of the Fifth Party System during the 1960s, and the emergence of a new and stable equilibrium by 1972. The 1964 election marked the end of the New Deal era and the start of an electoral era that continues to perplex political elites.[14] Political scientist Gerald Pomper first hinted at this in 1967 when his review of state-by-state election data revealed a tremendous electoral upheaval had occurred in the presidential election of 1964.[15] The upheaval hinted at by Pomper was significant and continued through the election of 1968 and, perhaps more important, the electoral change witnessed during the 1960s was unlike any prior period in America.

Our chapter's evidence reveals the continued stability of the Sixth Party System. There is little to no evidence suggesting the so-called Republican Revolution of 1994 or recent "wave" elections in 2006 and 2010, or Barack Obama's impressive electoral victory in 2008 were indicative of a new era of disruption and discontinuity. Rather, we are in a very stable era.

Whether one looks to state-by-state correlations between successive elections, the geographic coalitions of the parties, or at our various macropattern analyses of key partisan, institutional or electorate variables, the evidence clearly suggests the emergence of a distinct and stable political era since the late 1960s. The stability, evident across our analysis of 40 systemic variables, appears in the party system as well as in behavior by voters in polling booths and by officials in national institutions. Our next chapter identifies two pillars of the current era: popular discontent and professional government.

3 Popular Discontent and Professional Government

Chapters 1 and 2 surveyed a blizzard of changes to America's national political system, and the system's stasis with these traits is—no doubt—a big trend. The following chapters explain these many changes in more detail, but next we must identify two underlying phenomena that, we argue, motivated many of the changes recorded in our data. These are: (1) the decline in trust and rise in popular discontent regarding government; and (2) the expansion of professional government. The latter trend, we believe, contributes to the former. As government became more professional and expansive in the 1960s, public trust in government withered. Those twin characteristics are with us still. In this chapter, we focus on the intersection of two distinct elements of the contemporary political system—declining levels of trust among the general public and rising levels of professionalism within government.

Since the 1960s, trust in government has declined and remained at low levels. Along with declining party identification, low trust is an indicator of greater public disaffection with the political system. Many governing professionals, however, perceive little need to mobilize the public broadly the way political parties did in previous eras, further stoking mass discontent. As this occurred, changing behavior in national institutions has transformed governance. Congressional incumbents' electoral security contributed to legislative professionalism. Presidents became more subject to frequent tides of popular disapproval than were more electorally secure legislators. In addition, bureaucratic activity grew in scale and the number of federal regulations issued annually by the bureaucracy mushroomed. As shown in Table 3.1, specific indicators tell the tale. Presidents suffered from lower levels of job approval. House and Senate incumbents gained more electoral security in the 1960s and 1970s. Party unity voting increased in both chambers. The support gap for presidents between rival congressional partisans grew and trust in government fell.

The Importance of Trust

Trust in government is an essential component of a well-functioning political system, but that trait has been in short supply in the United States since the

Table 3.1 Indicators of change in national institutions and public confidence, 1960–2008

Election year	House incumbent security (%)	Senate incumbent security (%)	Party unity House (%)	Party unity Senate (%)	President partisan support gap in House (%)	President partisan support gap in Senate (%)	President average approval rating (%)	Popular discontent (%)
1960	59	45	53	37	15	23	61	25
1964	58	47	55	36	36	16	75	36
1968	71	46	35	32	13	01	42	43
1972	76	48	27	37	17	22	56	49
1976	73	44	36	37	31	23	48	51
1980	73	39	38	46	23	17	41	52
1984	77	66	47	40	26	35	55	42
1988	87	56	47	43	32	21	52	51
1992	66	48	65	53	46	41	40	52
1996	68	30	56	62	36	46	54	61
2000	78	59	43	49	46	43	61	56
2004	85	69	47	52	50	48	51	50
2008	76	57	53	52	48	36	30	60

Sources: American National Election Studies, University of Michigan, 1952–2008, and *Vital Statistics on American Politics 2009–2010*, CQ Press.

1970s. Many scholars have studied the decline in trust and have tied it to important consequences for politics and government, none of them good. A widely studied measure of trust comes from the University of Michigan's National Election Studies (NES). Since 1964, the NES has computed a "Trust Index" of responses to four questions:

1 How much of the time do you think you can trust the government in Washington to do what is right—just about always, most of the time, or only some of the time?
2 Do you think that people in government waste a lot of the money we pay in taxes, waste some of it, or don't waste very much of it?
3 Would you say that government is pretty much run by a few big interests looking out for themselves or that it is run for the benefit of all the people?
4 Do you think that quite a few of the people running the government are crooked, not very many are, or do you think hardly any of them are crooked?

Those with positive responses about government rank high in trust and those more skeptical rank low in trust. Here we include a similar measure that Aldrich and Niemi (1996) termed "popular discontent" because it alone of similar measures has appeared in surveys since 1952, allowing analysis over a longer period. The variable measures agreement or disagreement with the statement "public officials don't care what people like me think." Political scientists term this a measure of "external efficacy"—one's view of how effective one can be when politically active. Low levels of external efficacy among the public are evidence of popular discontent.

Figure 3.1 shows the general trend of the Trust Index and popular discontent indicator since each appeared in the National Elections Study survey. They vary inversely, with a Pearson correlation of -.81, indicating a strong tendency for them to trend in opposite directions.[1] As popular discontent goes up, trust goes down. The pattern of declining trust and rising discontent is pronounced from 1960 to 1980, the period when most of the changes creating the current system occurred. Despite a brief respite in the 1980s, trust fell and discontent rose again through the early 1990s, followed by a small reversal of course and another negative trend after 2004.

What caused these trends? Scholars have identified many possible explanations: economic difficulties, crime rates, child poverty, citizens' evaluations of incumbents and institutions, political scandals and negative media coverage of politics (for a summary, see Chanley, Rudolph, and Rahn 2000, 240). Marc Hetherington draws particular attention to the performance of national government from 1966 to 1980 as a cause, a turbulent period featuring the divisive Vietnam War, the civil rights revolution, the impeachment of Richard Nixon, and the severe recessions and stagflation of the 1970s. The rise of polarized politics in the 1990s, he argues, further stimulated declines in trust (2006, 22–24). A recent study by Luke Keele

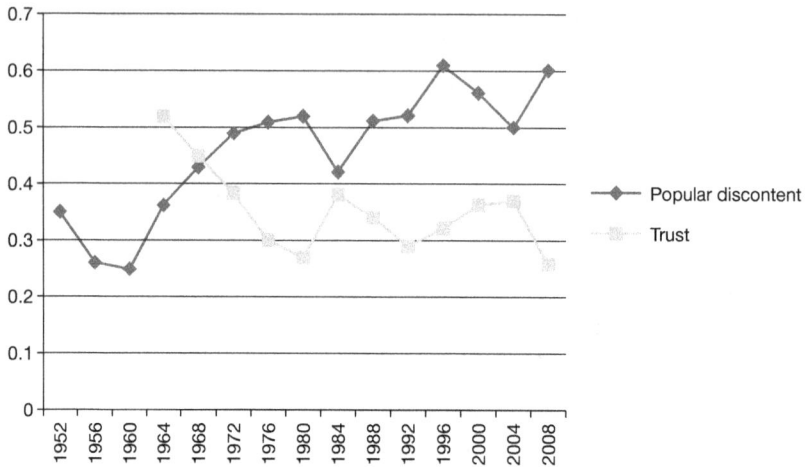

Figure 3.1 Trust and popular discontent trends

Source: American National Election Studies, University of Michigan, 1952–2008.

found that declining trust is rooted in the decay of social capital, defined as "comprised of civic participation and trusting attitudes" (Keele 2007, 40). Social capital was much higher in the 1950s and 1960s and, like trust, since then has fallen sharply. It is certainly the case that, as Virginia Chanley, Thomas Rudolph and Wendy Rahn note, "Declining trust in government is a complex phenomenon with multiple potential causes" (2000, 240).

The trust decline has big impacts on America's political system. It promoted lower confidence in governmental institutions and less satisfaction with democracy (Zmerli and Newton 2008), stimulated less confidence in Congress, the president and in federal action in domestic policy (Chanley, Rudolph, and Rahn 2000). Lower trust lowered political participation and spurred support for nonincumbent and third party candidates (Levi and Stoker 2000; Donovan, Denemark, and Bowler 2008). It discouraged citizen compliance with governmental obligations like taxpaying (Hetherington and Rudolph 2008, 499). The systemic consequences of lower trust and growing discontent are broad and important.

Among our indicators, the trust index and popular discontent variable have many strong correlates (more than +/- .67) with other measures of public disaffection with politics, testament to their wide-ranging importance (Table 3.2). Trust and discontent correlate strongly with turnout decline in presidential as well as mid-term elections and disaffection with parties, measured by percentage of whites who are independents and percentage who are neutral toward parties. They associate strongly with the incidence of direct democratic procedures employed in states to make policy by circumventing the legislature and governor: both the number of states holding initiatives and the total number of initiatives on state ballots in an election year.

Table 3.2 Systemic correlates of popular discontent, 1952–2008[1]

Element measured	Correlate
Percentage of blacks apolitical	−.83
Southern whites support for the Democratic Party	−.80
Turnout in presidential elections	−.79
Most important problem: foreign	−.77
Appeals Court nomination success	−.75
Turnout in mid-term elections	−.72
Share of Democrats in the electorate	−.63
Share of the Democratic coalition working class	−.63
Share of whites strong partisans	−.58
Presidential success in Congress	−.58
Blacks identifying as Democrats	.55
Restrictive rules in the House	.57
Presidential support party gap in House	.60
House and Senate split ticket voting	.61
Share neutral to parties	.69
Legislative and judicial branch personnel	.75
States with ballot initiatives	.81
Total ballot initiatives in states	.82
Cloture motions filed	.82
Number of professional associations	.84
Total pages in the Federal Register	.85
Share of whites identifying as independent	.86
Most important problem domestic	.87
State and local split ticket voting	.93

Note:
[1] Data sources for all of the variables included in this analysis are available in the Appendix.

Source: Available from authors upon request.

It is in the context of lower public trust in government that public hostility to specific governmental actions and policies became manifest. John Hibbing and Elizabeth Theiss-Morse, in a series of in-depth interviews with American citizens, found that they hate the actual process of politics—the "haggling and bickering" and constant disagreement (1995, 18). Rather than showing patience for the inevitable disagreements issuing from a diverse democracy, the public cannot stand it:

If open debate is seen as bickering and haggling; if bargaining and compromise is seen as selling out on principle; if all support staff and division of labor are needless baggage; if carefully working through problems is sloth; and if all interests somehow become evil special interests, it is easy to see why the public is upset with the workings of the political system.

(ibid., 20)[2]

Hostility to politics prompts a significant percentage of the public to avoid participating in politics, resulting in declining presidential turnout since 1960. Hibbing and Theiss-Morse find that many citizens—as many as two-thirds in their research—prefer a form of democracy in which decisions are made quickly and with little public input or disagreement (2002, 144). That is a fanciful view, but remarkably widespread and growing from popular distrust with political processes. Many people

> prefer a process that allows them to keep politics at arm's length. Their sourness toward government does not stem from the fact that they want to be more involved in it than they are but from the fact that they feel as though they need to be involved even though they would rather not be.
>
> (2002, 227)

The main reason many in the public stay involved, is to prevent self-interested dealing by politicians whom, as a group, they do not trust. We next introduce the object of their mistrust, the professionalized national government that burgeoned to its present size in the 1960s and 1970s and the large interest group world that surrounds it.

The Rise of Professional Advocacy

America's current political system features a large national government populated by people who are professionals in their lines of work—be it legislating, administrating, lobbying or adjudicating. Economic growth and rising education levels in the second half of the twentieth century created an abundance of professional occupations. In 1910, only 11 percent of the population had high school degrees. Now, the percentage is over 90 percent. About 30 percent of Americans have Bachelor's degrees, a record high. Since the 1950s, labor unions have declined dramatically as a proportion of the labor force while the number of professional associations has grown. People with postgraduate degrees in the professions now dominate the presidency, Congress, the courts, interest groups, the bureaucracy and political parties. Professionals develop important competences, but they are often narrow skills, closely adapted to their career paths.

Consider the meaning of the term "professional." Businessdictionary.com defines it as "an occupation, practice or vocation requiring mastery of a complex set of knowledge and skills through formal education and/or practical experience" (Businessdictionary.com 2011). Hundreds of professional associations have Washington offices. They are the result of a dramatic expansion in the number of Washington interest groups since 1960 (Baumgartner et al. 2008). Economist Mancur Olson describes group proliferation as the rise of "distributional coalitions" pursuing "struggles over the distribution of income and wealth" (1984, 44). In these battles, professional skills are very much in demand: "What we loosely call intelli-gence, or aptitude for education, will probably be favored as much as or more than before because the articulate and educated have a comparative advantage in regulation, politics and complex understandings" (ibid., 73).

The growth of interest groups since 1960 is recorded in the Encyclopedia of Associations; the number of interest groups, or associations, grew from fewer than 5000 to slightly more than 25,000 between 1955 and 2008. One reason for their growing activities in Washington was the growth of government itself. In the 1960s, the "Great Society" programs of President Lyndon Johnson expanded government in a variety of ways. Medicare and Medicaid, passed in 1965, provided government health insurance for the elderly and poor. Congress increased Social Security benefits several times between 1960 and 1980. Under Johnson's successor, Richard Nixon, new regulatory laws and new implementing agencies, such as the Environmental Protection Agency and Occupational Health and Safety Administration, further expanded the national government's reach. New cabinet departments, like Housing and Urban Development, Education and Energy, arose to implement new domestic programs. The number of annual pages in the Federal Register, the publication forum for new regulations, expanded from 14,479 in 1960 to 87,012 in 1980. Accompanying new laws, bureaucracies and regulations were groups seeking to shape the direction of governmental efforts. Professional associations—a diverse assemblage ranging from the National Science Teachers Association to the American Chiropractic Association—were at the forefront of this trend.

Educated professionals also spearheaded the formation of "new politics" or citizens' groups concerned with environmental, good government and social reform causes (Skocpol 2004). Examples of such groups founded in the 1960s and 1970s—and all still with us today—are Ralph Nader's consumer protection organizations, the "good government" lobby Common Cause and the National Resources Defense Council, leading environmental advocates. Jeffrey Berry describes the employees and supporters of these groups as postmaterial liberals. "The high standard of living, the high levels of education, and prosperous, expanding economies" created citizens who placed "a higher value on quality-of-life issues" (1999, 35–36). Berry found that postmaterial groups by the 1990s had considerable clout in Congress and received inordinately large and positive coverage in the media.

Today, a dizzying variety of advocacy organizations populates Washington, placing incessant demands upon government. Approximately 600 American corporations pursue influence there, alongside 2000 trade associations engaged in similar activities. Trade associations—ranging from the Automobile Manufacturers Association to the National Association of Theatre Owners and Association for Dressings and Sauces (the condiment-making crowd)— are groups of businesses engaged in the same area of commerce who lobby for their common interests. Dozens of unions also have a permanent Washington presence, representing crafts (such as the United Brotherhood of Carpenters), industries (United Mine Workers) and joined in broad federations (American Federation of Labor—Congress of Industrial Organizations). In addition, hundreds of organizations pursue postmaterial agendas (such as the National Gay and Lesbian Task Force, the Christian Coalition, and the Sierra Club).

These thousands of organizations hire a wide variety of professionals to further their advocacy efforts. Among the professions that have thrived in DC's interest group world are lawyers, public relations specialists, policy researchers and analysts, and lobbyists. All of these occupations have professional associations with governing boards, announced professional standards, education and training sessions and membership programs. In addition to hiring professionals, many interest groups contract the services of specialized firms of professionals. In DC, professional lobbying firms employ about 150 former Members of Congress to push clients' agendas before government. Many Washington law firms employ lawyers as lobbyists for clients. Public and governmental relations firms conduct lobbying and media campaigns on behalf of their clients.

A big, entrenched world of influence grew in response to larger national government. Its demands have further maintained and expanded the reach of that government. Mancur Olson notes the inevitable result: "The accumulation of distributional coalitions increases the incentive for distributional struggle, augments regulatory complexity, encourages the dominance of politics, stimulates bargaining, and increases the complexity of understandings" (1984, 73). John Hibbing and Elizabeth Theiss-Morse discovered that many citizens distrust government because they fear that self-dealing and corruption, rampant self-interest, dominates politics (2002, 121–128). DC's vast interest group establishment no doubt gives rise to such fears. One citizen in an interview described his views of professional government: "They're there because . . . they know what they're doing. Do I trust them? No" (Hibbing and Theiss-Morse 2002, 121). Over time, we find popular discontent to be highly and positively correlated with the total number of associations as recorded in the Encyclopedia of Associations (+.89).

Bigger, More Professional Government

Professional advocacy in DC grew in response to a larger and more professional government. The first component of the federal government to professionalize was the bureaucracy, in response to the corruption and inefficiency of an executive branch populated by political appointees with at best limited skills at their jobs. Beginning with the Pendleton Act in 1881, Congress passed a series of laws to insure more honesty and professional competence in federal administration. The principles in this reform legislation remain in place for federal administrators today. Most bureaucratic positions are protected from political hiring and firing. Hiring occurs on merit, as judged by performance in competitive examination. Dismissal of a merit-hired employee requires multiple hearings and costs hundreds of thousands of dollars, ostensibly to prevent "political" dismissals.

Bureaucratic employment practices contribute to structural stability in the federal government. Congress tends to alter the executive branch only by increments, further contributing to that stability. Presidents are too distracted by the pressing issues of the moment to devote time and effort to sweeping reorganization. Arguably, the last comprehensive reorganization of the civilian executive branch passed Congress in 1949. The structure of America's military, in contrast, altered considerably because of America's many twentieth-century wars. Management guru Peter Drucker noted the remarkable structural stability of the civilian part of the bureaucracy: "Its structure, its policies and its rules for doing governmental business and for managing people . . . were first developed under William McKinley after 1896 and were pretty much completed under Herbert Hoover from 1929 to 1933" (1995, 52).

Civilian bureaucratic stability, coupled with bigger employment and spending since 1960, has led to what Paul Light calls the "thickening" of the executive branch: "New agencies and units widened the government's base, while new management layers increased its height" (1995, 1). This led to three common performance problems: (1) diffusion of accountability; (2) hyperextended chains of command with poor communication; and (3) a crowding of staff in the bureaucracy's upper layers (1995, 73).The result has been "an onslaught of leaders but no guarantee of leadership" (ibid., 60).

A related expansion and professionalization occurred at the top of the bureaucracy in the office of the President. During the twentieth century, presidents gained additional staff and management tools from Congress in order to exert some sway over the burgeoning executive branch. The Bureau of the Budget was an early example of augmented presidential management powers. Founded in 1919 with 45 employees, it has grown into the Office of Management and Budget (OMB), currently with 528 employees and expanded duties, including bureaucratic oversight, management supervision, veto recommendations and "legislative clearance" of bureaucratic proposals for Congress. The Budget Bureau became part of the Executive Office of the President (EOP), a new organization created by Congress in 1939 to augment and expand the executive work of the president. The EOP, which includes the OMB, the White House Office, the Council of Economic Advisors, and the National Security Council and other organizations, numbers about 2000 employees. The president appoints the top staff in the EOP, with lower levels comprised of career professionals. The presidency is a much more professional operation than it was one hundred years ago.

So is Congress. Professionalism grew in the legislative branch in the 1960s and 1970s with internal reforms and the lengthening of congressional careers. Congress, in general, but the House especially, transformed from a decentralized chamber into a professionally managed institution organized around forwarding a party agenda. In the Senate, reforms enacted in the 1970s empowered individual members with increased access to staff, research capabilities, and subcommittee assignments. These reforms, combined with a rising number of professional interest groups, encouraged representatives and senators to become policy entrepreneurs (Sinclair 2011). Newly empowered members worked to expand the jurisdictions of their subcommittees to address emerging issues and forge electorally beneficial relationships with interest groups (Baumgartner and Jones 2009).

Morris Fiorina notes several reasons for the lengthening of congressional careers during this period. The number of professional staff grew to help lawmakers become electorally secure by solving constituent problems with "casework" and delivering federal funds for constituency projects—"pork barreling." In the early 1960s, Representatives were allocated nine total staff in DC and their districts and a total payroll of $20,000 (Fiorina 1977, 58). By 2011, individual Representatives were budgeted $446,009 per year for staff salaries, trips back home and mailing privileges. Senators' budgets varied according to their state's population, ranging from $3,149,536 for tiny Delaware to $4,967,505 for California (Brudnick 2011). Senators and Representatives each run their own small businesses, hiring multiple professionals to manage their offices, solve constituent problems, analyze and write legislation and communicate with the media. In addition, of course, a Congressional Staff Association exists, a professional organization of current and past staffers. Congress, like the presidency and the bureaucracy, is now a thicker organization than in 1960. The number of employees working for Congress and the federal judiciary grew rapidly, nearly doubling between the mid-1960s and 1980.

The courts are home to lawyers, one of the world's oldest professions. The federal circuit and appeals courts have not altered greatly in size and structure since 1960, but their caseload has mushroomed. Among federal district courts, pending cases grew from 199,019 in 1980 to 358,303 in 2008 (Stanley and Niemi 2010, 278). Pending appeals at the circuit court of appeals level more than doubled during that time as well. The explosion of court cases— a thickening of the federal courts' agendas—has many causes. Congress, beginning in the 1960s, broadened "standing to sue" in consumer and environmental protection legislation. Judges began to impose "structural remedies" requiring governmental officials to administer solutions in ways supervised by the judges themselves.

Structural remedies at times had big policy consequences (Fisher 1996). Judge Arthur Garrity in the 1970s single-handedly supervised the desegregation of Boston schools using this technique. Federal Judge Frank M. Johnson, Jr. in 1972 handed down rulings that established minimum standards for providing treatment and rehabilitation in state mental health and mental retardation facilities in Alabama state facilities that he deemed inadequate. From 1972 to 2003, when federal court supervision ended, implementation of these standards reshaped the mental health system in Alabama and in the nation (Ziegler 2003).

Interest groups have found the courts an attractive venue for furthering their agendas via lawsuits over congressional laws and bureaucratic regulations. In 2011, for example, the Center for Biological Diversity, the Gulf Restoration Network, the Natural Resources Defense Council and the Sierra Club filed a formal notice of intent to sue Interior Secretary Ken Salazar for ignoring marine-mammal protection laws when approving offshore oil and gas activities in the Gulf of Mexico. The suit challenged ten projects approved since Oct. 15, 2010, without permits required by the Marine Mammal Protection Act and the Endangered Species Act that are designed to protect endangered whales and other marine mammals from harmful offshore oil activities (Center for Biological Diversity 2011). Passage of major legislation into law usually prompts a rash of lawsuits. Once President Obama signed into law the Patient Protection and Affordable Care Act, the landmark 2010 health care reform, aggrieved interests filed 31 federal court suits challenging its provisions (Sack 2011). In such cases, interest groups ask the federal courts to determine law and policy. Since the 1960s, the federal courts have moved from enforcing norms in particular cases, such as convicting a person of interstate kidnapping, to broader policymaking through determining the meaning of federal laws and regulations (Mackenzie 1996). The trend increases both the amount and complexity of policy conflict in the federal government.

Federal judges themselves come from differing backgrounds than they did in the mid-twentieth century. Then the federal bench included a large number of former elected officials, skilled in negotiation, appreciative of legislators and executives and often practical in their approach to the law. From 1977 to 2009, however, fewer than one in seven federal circuit and appeals court appointees came from political or governmental career backgrounds (Carp, Stidham, and Manning 2011b, 56–57, 60–61). The Supreme Court also suffers from a dearth of justices with such backgrounds (Taylor 2005). Career lawyers, skilled in legal combat, and law professors, who approach the law with theoretical orientations, have replaced them. One result is that federal judges are more likely to challenge the authority of legislatures and executives and claim policymaking authority for themselves.

Consequences of Professional Interest Advocacy and Government

Increasingly professional government and interest advocacy have made federal policymaking a process with far more complex interactions than in 1960. This has sorely taxed the operation of a legislature, executive, and judiciary operating under our separation of powers system. Coordination and compromise are essential to the successful operation of "separate institutions sharing powers" as Richard Neustadt put it (1991, 29). Thicker government in our national institutions, coupled with a densely populated, active and professional interest group world, escalates the coordination and information costs of governing. Gone are the days of the *Iron Triangle* when a powerful congressional committee worked with one or a select few industry associations to develop policy in coordination with the executive branch agency responsible for policy administration.

The scale and complexity of information now generated in the process of governing are vastly greater than a half-century ago. A complicating element is the diversifying professional competencies among governmental players and the surrounding interest group advocates. Because of changes begun in the 1960s, few issues fall under the jurisdiction of a single congressional committee. Powerful and well-financed citizens' groups now outnumber once dominant industry associations in many issue arenas (Baumgartner and Jones 2009). The bureaucracy is caught in the struggles between these forces. Diverse competencies contribute to divergent agendas among a large group of individuals and organizations affected by government actions. What Paul Light noted regarding the bureaucracy is also true for the national political system as a whole—we now have more leaders but not more leadership.

One outcome of all this diversity and complexity is policy stasis. The multitude of actors with access to expert policy analyses now involved in policymaking requires finely crafted compromises for policy to advance. Yet with this multitude of players come numerous new veto points and obstacles to change. A recent landmark study of interest groups in Washington found that their large and diverse presence leads to durable policy stability. "The vast bulk of lobbying in Washington has to do not with the creation of new programs, but rather with the adjustment of existing programs or with the maintenance of programs just as they are" (Baumgartner et al. 2009, 240). Thus, "defenders of the status quo usually win in Washington . . . New information only rarely reorients how policy makers view the justifications for established public policies" (ibid., 39). The sole exception to stasis is when the president actively pushes for policy change: "Policy sides defending the status quo are more likely to lose when the administration is on the side of policy change" (ibid., 233). This does not happen often. Presidents have crowded domestic and foreign agendas, many distractions and limited time in office. They are far more likely to prevail when they are popular and then only with a few issues to which they devote inordinate time and energy. That means stasis rules most of the time. Even President Obama's ambitious health care reform, the Patient Protection and Affordable Care Act, relied not on substantial change but rather on modifications to two major staples of the American health care system—employer-based private insurance and Medicaid. And the private health insurance industry was a major player in crafting the legislation (Manchikanti et al. 2011).

Stephen Skowronek describes the complex, policy-centered federal government as in a mode of "permanent progressivism." Policy action determines progress and all the Washington players focus on it: "demands for government continue to grow apace . . . government itself has become one gigantic policy-generating machine . . . policy is king and performance is the standard of rule" (2011a, 190, 194). This definition signals the triumph of the professionalizers of a century ago, the Progressive Movement of early twentieth century America. Progressives championed reforms that profession-alized the bureaucracy, Congress, the presidency and the courts. Well-educated reformers sought to replace corrupt party rule in states and cities with more open accountable and professional government.

> They elevated the authority of professionalism, science, expertise and public opinion; they introduced the values of pluralism, information sharing, and publicity into the policy-making process itself; and they surrounded the presidency within dependent agencies and offices geared for cooperative management.
>
> (ibid., 192)

Constant pursuit of policy, ironically, has brought frequent stasis as so many policy players push in so many different directions.

Our national political system now abundantly possesses the qualities advocated by earlier progressive reformers. The size and complexity of national government and the multiplicity of demands brought before it require both liberals and conservatives to harness leviathan for their ends rather than dramatically restructure or downsize it. The dream of the early professionalizers, the Progressives—that national government becomes a continuing exercise in policy progress through innovation—is America's twenty-first-century reality. So why doesn't the public trust it? Why the popular discontent?

Loathing Leviathan

Professional national government has brought us complexity, diversity and stasis. Complexity makes it difficult for many in the public to understand just what national government is up to. Diversity ensures endless dispute about every public issue as groups ceaselessly jostle for advantage. Stasis signals that usually nothing much changes, that government is unresponsive in the face of many citizens' individual needs. As Hibbing and Theiss-Morse put it: "People despise pointless political conflict and they believe pointless political conflict is rampant in American politics today" (2002, 33).

Trends in our trust index and popular discontent indicator indicate that these attitudes really grew among the public in the 1960s and 1970s. In Figure 3.2, note the steady deterioration of public attitudes toward government from 1966–1980, followed by a brief respite and another decline from 1984–1994, then a brief rebound and a fall to new depth by 2008. Figure 3.2 charts similar trends in related indicators. Over the decades, gradual patterns appear: declining trust in government and turnout in presidential elections and rising

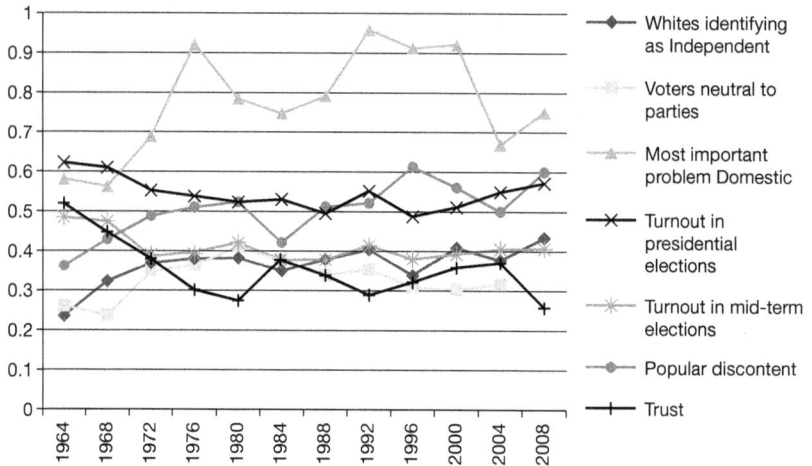

Figure 3.2 Trust Index and related indicators, 1964–2008

Sources: American National Election Studies, University of Michigan, 1952–2008, and Stanley and Niemi (2010).

percentages of independent whites, public neutrality toward parties and identification of the nation's major national problem as domestic. The Trust Index trend correlates strongly with those of the other variables in Figure 3.2 at +/- .60 to .85. In addition, the Trust Index strongly varies inversely (-.72) with the percentage of Americans identifying the country's major problem as domestic.

The rise in salience of domestic problems corresponds to both the decline in trust and rise in popular discontent (+.87). Political parties shrink in legitimacy with the rise of white independents and the percentage neutral to parties after 1965. Presidential election turnout suffers a long-term decline beginning in 1960. Despite the pointed competition in government between evenly matched parties, neither securely holds majority support from the public. In this situation, highly professionalized management of parties in government has become a more effective and necessary source of power than a reliance on parties in the electorate. Restrictive rules and cloture motions in the present era frequently are used to quash partisan and ideological rivals in Congress. Presidential success in Congress increasingly hinges on party line votes. Federal Appeals Court nominations are more likely to invoke barbed partisan controversies in the Senate. In addition, executive government continues to expand with the growth of regulations.

The growing importance of parties in government belies the seeming disarray of parties in the electorate, beset by a turbulent electoral environment of recent decades in which public support zigzagged between the parties. As noted in Chapter 2, no president has served two full consecutive elected terms from 1960 to 1980, Republicans held the Senate for the first time in 30 years from 1980–1986, the first partisan turnover of Congress in 40 years occurred in 1994 and elections from 2006 to 2010 produced shifting partisan control of the presidency and Congress. Populist uprisings are in fact an established aspect of the current American political system.

Concurrent with these shifts is a rise in the incidence of popular mechanisms to make policy without the involvement of state legislatures and executives. The trend is toward more state initiatives and more states holding initiative elections after the mid-1960s. National polls have consistently found majority support for the initiative process, ranging from 57 percent to 85 percent (Donovan 2002; Hibbing and Theiss-Morse 2002, 75). Why? The people "are eager to give more power to the people since they are convinced that current governmental arrangements give far too much power to biased governmental officials . . . people are eager to weaken the influence of political elites" (Hibbing and Theiss-Morse 2002, 105). A complex political system, dominated by professionals of governance and advocacy, has become a distant and alien phenomenon for many voters. The "bias" they see lies in the crowding of professional players at the top, pursuing their own agendas and not necessary listening to the wishes of the citizens themselves.

The central irony here is that national politics is highly organized in a way to represent more interests than ever before. Its huge scale, however, makes it all seem a confusing blur to many citizens. We find popular discontent has a strong correlation (+.85) with the increasing number of pages published each year in the Federal Register. Many in the public are afraid of the self-dealing involved in the arcane negotiations among governing professionals. Popular discontent has similarly strong correlations with the growing number of associations (+.84) and the number of congressional and judicial employees (+.75). Policy talk, after all, is not normal discourse for most citizens. Combine this with a series of governmental failures since 1960 and you have enduring public resistance to professional government.

Whenever national difficulties mount, popular anger focuses on professional governing elites. Contrary to accepted opinion with regard to the current era, these populist uprisings are in fact an established aspect of the current American political system. A system not marked by unpredictability, but rather by an era of stability in which the elections of 1974, 1980, 1994, 2006 and 2010—in which popular discontent led to major electoral shifts— are recurrent features of a larger electoral pattern. Governmental failures spur popular uprisings. In 1974, Nixon's impeachment and a deepening recession; in 1980, stagflation and American hostages in Iran; in 1994, hostility to fiscal deficits and expanding government; in 2006, concerns over the Iraq War and congressional corruption; in 2010, reaction to an expansive federal health care law and record federal spending, debt and deficits.

Popular resentments seem to have burgeoned in recent years. After six years of Republican rule in Washington, the voters swept the GOP from congressional control in 2006. The 2008 election produced a change in party control in the White House. The Tea Party movement of 2009, begun in response to the expansive spending and regulatory policies of the Obama administration, brought the GOP back into control of the House of Representatives. The Occupy Wall Street movement emerged in late 2011 and quickly spread to major cities throughout the United States and worldwide. Declining voter turnout accompanied President Obama's narrow 2012 election victory. High unemployment and low economic growth have contributed to low public esteem of government in recent years. Popular distrust and discontent has risen to new and possibly dangerous highs. In sum, our evidence accords with the view of Walter Dean Burnham, who observed of the present era: "It is an impressively stable system, many of whose parts work to reinforce each other. On the other hand [...] it suffers from endemic problems of governability and of democratic accountability and popular support" (1991, 127).

America's Dysfunctional Political System

Democrats, as the pro-statist party, often suffer more from the on-going crisis of confidence in government than do Republicans. In *Why Trust Matters*, Marc Hetherington makes a compelling case that American liberalism cannot recover without a resurgence of trust and confidence in government (Hetherington 2006). However, since the 1960s, every crisis, except 9/11, has served to erode public confidence—the savings-in-loan crisis of the late 1980s, the government shutdowns of the mid-1990s, the second Iraq War, the Troubled Asset Relief Program of 2008. Recent battles over the debt ceiling in 2011 and the "fiscal cliff" of automatic spending cuts and tax increases looming as 2012 concluded also induced public exasperation. Walter Dean Burnham (1991) argues that at some point a crisis will occur that will demand a reenergized governmental system. Thus far, however, crises have served only to reinforce the dominant narrative of ineffective governance.

Since the 1950s, American politics has featured no stable constellation of ideas, interests, and voters in a coalition rivaling that of the New Deal era. Instead, we have lived in a period of "open field politics" in which rival parties seek tactical advantage on the playing field of professional government (Barone 2010). Professionals are quite good at contesting strategies and tactics, but this narrow pursuit leaves out much of the public. With seemingly permanent professionalization and public distrust, we may have just entered the longest-lasting of all American political eras. A survey released in late 2011 reported Americans believe the federal government wastes 51 cents of every dollar it spends (Gallup 2011). Another survey, released around the same time, found the public's trust in the federal government had dropped to an all-time low, with only 15 percent of Americans indicating they trust the federal government to do what's right just about always or most of the time (CNN 2011). In the present era, American national government's two reliable traits remain rule by professionals and pervasive, persistent popular discontent. As a result, the recent cycle of turbulent elections, shifting partisan waves, and oscillating direction in national government is likely to continue.

Past party systems have resulted from mass party affiliation and mobilization. As we note in Chapter 4, however, the current state of the party system seemingly precludes the possibility of realignment and bolsters the dominance of professional government. The present era has resulted in a polarization among committed partisans, but it has also resulted in a rising number of Americans proclaiming allegiance to no party. The effects on American government and politics are far-reaching.

4 The Puzzle of Contemporary Party Politics

In their work, "The Sixth American Party System," John H. Aldrich and Richard G. Niemi (Aldrich and Niemi 1996) demonstrated the disruption of the Fifth Party System during the 1960s, and the emergence of a new and stable equilibrium by 1972. In Chapter 2, we demonstrated the continued stability of this new system. There is little if any evidence suggesting the so-called Republican Revolution of 1994 or recent "wave" elections in 2006 and 2010, or Barack Obama's impressive electoral victory in 2008 and more narrow re-election in 2012 were indicative of a new era of disruption and discontinuity. Rather, we are in a very stable era unique in its lack of any permanent partisan majority. The present stability is one characterized by party competition that translates into divided government and vacillating party control of the individual branches of government. Frequent divided government and variation in partisan control of government create the impression of instability, but they are in fact the hallmarks of the present stable era.

Yet for all the stability, there is a paradox at the heart of the contemporary political system. At a time when surveys show a rising number of independent voters, rising levels of popular discontent, and increasing two-party competition, American politics is incredibly polarized. Rather than moderating to attract more voters and gain a strategic advantage, the parties have diverged and the so-called middle ground is a barren valley between two polarized and hyper-partisan peaks. To understand the paradox and solve the polarization puzzle we must first explore how the partisan landscape has changed and then consider how the electorate responded.

The Political World Turned Upside Down

In 1964, Democrats appeared to be sitting atop the political world. The party claimed the allegiance of 55 percent of Americans. Fully 66 percent of the self-described "working class" identified as Democrats and in a rather surprising finding 74 percent of African-Americans and 71 percent of southern whites expressed allegiance to the Party. The breadth and depth of Lyndon Johnson's 1964 presidential victory over Republican Barry Goldwater cannot be overstated. Johnson carried 44 of 50 states, plus the District of Columbia and received 61 percent of the vote. It was the largest Electoral College and popular vote margin for any candidate since Franklin Roosevelt in 1936. Along with the White House, Democrats maintained and expanded their hold on Congress, winning 295 seats in the House to the Republican's 140. In the Senate, the numbers were 68 Democrats to 32 Republicans—Congress had not been so lopsided since the late 1930s.

However, beneath the surface of the Democrats' victory was evidence of a party system in transition and turmoil. Since the start of the New Deal era, the Democrats had enjoyed their greatest electoral success in the states of the southern USA. The party was weakest in the Midwest and New England. All of this was changing by 1964. Johnson lost Louisiana, Mississippi, Alabama, Georgia and South Carolina, all states once carried by Roosevelt by margins ranging from 86 percent to 99 percent. Throughout the South, Johnson's margins were below Roosevelt's by double digits, though he still carried many of the states. By contrast, however, Johnson and the Democrats were surging in New England. In Rhode Island, Massachusetts, Maine, and Vermont, the Party added roughly 25 percentage points to its vote share since the 1936 election. The national electoral map was not merely realigning, it was inverting. The once solid Democratic South was moving to the GOP and New England, once a bastion of moderate Republicanism, was moving to the Democrats. Revisiting Figure 2.1 on p. 14 tells the tale, there was a negative correlation between the Democratic share of the vote by state in 1964 with that of the average of the prior four elections. The electoral world turned upside down.

The end of the Democratic Party's hold on the South marked the collapse of the New Deal Era and the end of the Democrats' dominance of national politics. Between 1968 and 2008, Democrats would win the White House in only four of 11 elections and no Democratic presidential candidate would receive better than 50 percent of the popular vote until 2008. The Democrats' overwhelming margins in the House and Senate would begin to decline (with the exception of a mini-surge post Watergate) and America entered an extremely competitive era in which neither party could lay claim to the sustained allegiance of the American electorate.

By 1980, the share of independents in the electorate was rising. The share of Democrats had fallen from the 55 percent high in 1964 to the mid-forties and white southern support for the Democratic party had fallen to 51 percent—20 points below its level in 1964 (by 1984, it would fall even further to 43 percent). White voters were moving away from the Democrats in general; more specifically, white southerners and working-class voters were leaving the party (Figure 4.1). This created an opening for the GOP and the white flight from the Democrats is perhaps the most significant contributor to the increasing level of competition between the two parties, a level of competition that continues to define the current era.

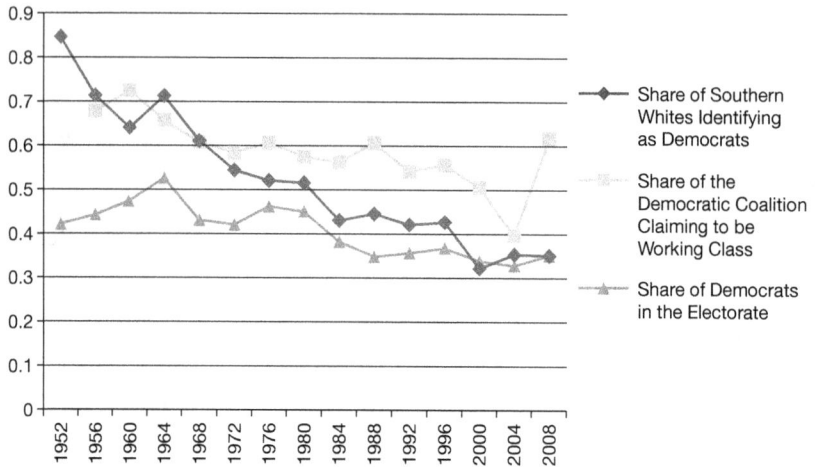

Figure 4.1 Changes in the Democratic Party coalition, 1952–2008

Source: See Appendix.

A Highly Competitive Era

The Fourth Party System that emerged in the 1890s saw the rise of the Republican Party to clear dominance in national politics. Between 1896 and 1932, Republicans held the White House for all but eight years and they held a majority of seats in the House of Representatives for all but three Congresses from 1894 until 1928. The Fifth Party System that emerged in the 1930s saw the rise of the Democratic Party and their control of the White House for all but eight years between 1932 and 1968 and the House of Representatives for all but two Congresses between 1930 and 1966. The Fifth Party System collapsed in 1964, though Democratic entrenchment in the South maintained the party's congressional dominance through the early 1990s. However, the signal factor that differentiates the current system from the Fifth and the Fourth is the lack of a dominant national party. Though Republicans won seven of the 12 presidential contests between 1968 and 2012, they enjoyed majority control in the House of Representatives in only seven of 22 Congresses between 1968 and 2012. and only experienced simultaneous control of the White House and the House of Representatives for six years.

Indeed, divided government has become the norm. If one were to compare partisan control of the White House and the House of Representatives during the Fourth, Fifth, and Sixth Party Systems, one would find unified control during 14 of 18 Congresses between 1894 and 1928 and during 13 of 18 Congresses from 1930 through 1964. During the present era, however, unified control has been present in only seven out of 23 Congresses, inclusive of the 112th Congress in 2012. For much of the 1980s and early 1990s, scholars attributed the era of divided government to split ticket voting (Fiorina 1989). It has become evident that the era of split ticket voting was an artifact of the southern realignment (Paulson 2009) and a less partisan electorate (Prior 2007). Today, divided government appears to be the result of a high degree of party competition and the fact that neither party has been able to claim the sustained allegiance of the majority of the electorate since the 1960s.

Given the gains made by Democrats between 2006 and 2008, it is easy to understand why some were quick to conclude that a new era was emerging. Nevertheless, the results of the 2010 mid-term suggest that the stability of the present system remains. Republicans gained 63 House seats and majority control in the chamber in 2010. Republicans won six Senate seats, a majority of governorships, and state legislatures. The 2010 election maintained the high level of party competitiveness that is a hallmark of the present system. In 2012, Barack Obama was re-elected and Democrats added two seats to their Senate majority. Republicans retained control of the House, saw their gubernatorial majority increase by one, and held their control of a majority of state legislatures. Much as the Republican victories in the 1950s did not signal the demise of the New Deal era, the Democratic victories in 2006 and 2008 did not represent the end of the current era.

A review of the national vote shares received by Republicans and Democrats in House elections offers more evidence of the competitive nature of the present era. Between 1932 and 1964, Democrats received a majority (or plurality) of the national vote in 15 of 17 House elections. Since 1966, Democrats have received the majority (or plurality) in seven of 23 elections. If one focuses more narrowly on elections since 1980, when the southern realignment began to trickle down to the congressional level, Democrats have won seven of 16 House elections. Republicans have won seven of nine elections since 1996 and, following a period of very close national vote shares between 1996 and 2004, the victory margins have been growing since 2006 even as party victory has continued to vary from election cycle to election cycle.

Writing in 1984, Scott and Hrebenar theorized that the post-1960s era might be a "tideless era" marked by increasing competition between the two major parties (Scott and Hrebenar 1984). Under this scenario, no party would dominate national politics and while there would be surge elections, they would come for Democrats and Republicans; there would be fluctuations in party support, close elections and landslides. This is what we have experienced in American politics since the late 1960s. The mass defection of independent voters away from Republicans in 2006 and then away from Democrats in 2010 suggests that this pattern will continue.

The Polarization Puzzle

As American politics became more competitive, the parties became ever more partisan and polarized. Daniel Coffey determined there is a direct and positive correlation between party competition and party ideology (Coffey 2011). As a state becomes more competitive between Republicans and Democrats, the respective parties become ever more conservative and liberal. V.O. Key hinted at this in 1956 when he argued that competition would force parties to offer policies that are more distinct to voters in an effort to influence their choice (Key 1956). Additionally, as competition increases, the parties come to rely more heavily, not on the mean, median, or moderate voter, but rather on the more committed and activist voter. Steven Hill writes:

> One of the defining characteristics of a winner-take-all system is that it promotes adversarial politics so that on a whole host of issues it is painfully obvious that the overriding agenda for both major parties is . . . to stake out positions vis-à-vis the other side.
>
> (2005, 14)

This means liberal activists for Democrats and conservative activists for Republicans. Parties, as result, push toward the extremes. In the 1960s, Republicans exploited several emerging schisms in the ranks of the Democratic coalition in order to become competitive—schisms revolving around national security, welfare spending, and policies with regard to race relations. The party defined itself by being what the Democratic Party was not. Over time, both parties increasingly defined themselves by being the antithesis of the other party.

As the agendas of the political parties became ever more divergent after the 1960s, Americans began to "sort" more neatly into one party or the other, a phenomenon known as *party sorting*. As the Democratic Party became more liberal and the Republican Party more conservative, liberal Republicans left the party and became Democrats or independents and conservative Democrats became Republicans or independents. Evidence of party polarization has been well documented, especially among the most active and informed voters and within elective bodies such as the U.S. Congress.[1]

However, there remains a vibrant debate within the study of American politics regarding the depth and impact of this partisan polarization. *Is the polarization limited to a small group of partisan elites, such as party activists and those in elective office, or is the polarization widespread in the larger public?* One might say that the possible answers have polarized political scientists. On one end of the polarization debate is political scientist Alan Abramowitz. Through a series of journal articles, conference presentations, and books, Abramowitz has repeatedly demonstrated the clear polarization between self-identified Republicans and Democrats and among the most engaged and informed voters. In his book, *The Disappearing Political Center*, Abramowitz demonstrated a clear contrast between voters and non-voters as well in the 2006 mid-term elections. In 2006, voters were clearly more polarized than non-voters were. Abramowitz described the difference between the two groups as "striking" (Abramowitz 2010, 54).

On the other side of the polarization divide stands another political scientist, Morris Fiorina. Fiorina and Abramowitz have waged a near decade-long war of research regarding the question of polarization. Fiorina acknowledges the polarization between Democrats and Republicans and among those in elective office, but dismisses the notion that the polarization reflects changes in the larger public. Rather, Fiorina contends that the party sorting resulting from the Democratic and Republican Parties' agenda divergence has simply made each party's voting coalition more ideologically homogenous. The Democratic Party became the home of liberals and the Republican Party the home of conservatives. According to Fiorina, the two parties polarized but the American public did not (Fiorina and Abrams 2009). In their (2009) book, *Disconnect*, Fiorina shows that the ideological distribution of the American public has changed little in the past 40 years, even as the parties in the electorate and in Congress clearly polarized.

What should a student of American politics make of this divide? Note first that Fiorina and Abramowitz are often concerned with different elements of the American electorate. Abramowitz frequently focuses his research on self-identified Republicans and Democrats and not on the general electorate. Fiorina, on the other hand, most often examines the general electorate and not self-identified Republicans and Democrats. Given the effects of party sorting since the late 1960s, one would expect to find evidence of polarization between Republicans and Democrats. In fact, on this issue Fiorina and Abramowitz agree. Abramowitz also focuses on the most active and informed voter, a much smaller subset of the electorate. Consider Abramowitz's comparison of voters and non-voters in the 2006 mid-term elections. Fully 60 percent of the electorate did not vote in that mid-term election. Therefore, Abramowitz's own research shows that polarized voters make up less than half of the electorate. Abramowitz demonstrates as well that polarization is most evident among the most active partisans—a group that Fiorina refers to as political elites, who are not reflective of the larger electorate.

Much like Fiorina, we find little evidence of polarization among the mass public. Rather the polarization has occurred among committed political activists and the interest groups they support. That is a relatively small share of the electorate. Drawing on data from the American National Election Studies (ANES), we compared the ideological distribution of the electorate with that of partisan activists. Panel A of Figure 4.2 shows the self-identified ideological orientation of the general electorate at three points, 1972, 1994, and 2008. Although the distribution has shifted over time, the distribution remains normal with most voters amassed in the center as moderates. Panel B is limited to those members of the electorate who indicated that they had worked for a campaign *and* given money to a candidate. We define these

A: Ideological Distribution of the American Electorate

B: Ideological Distribution of Party Activists

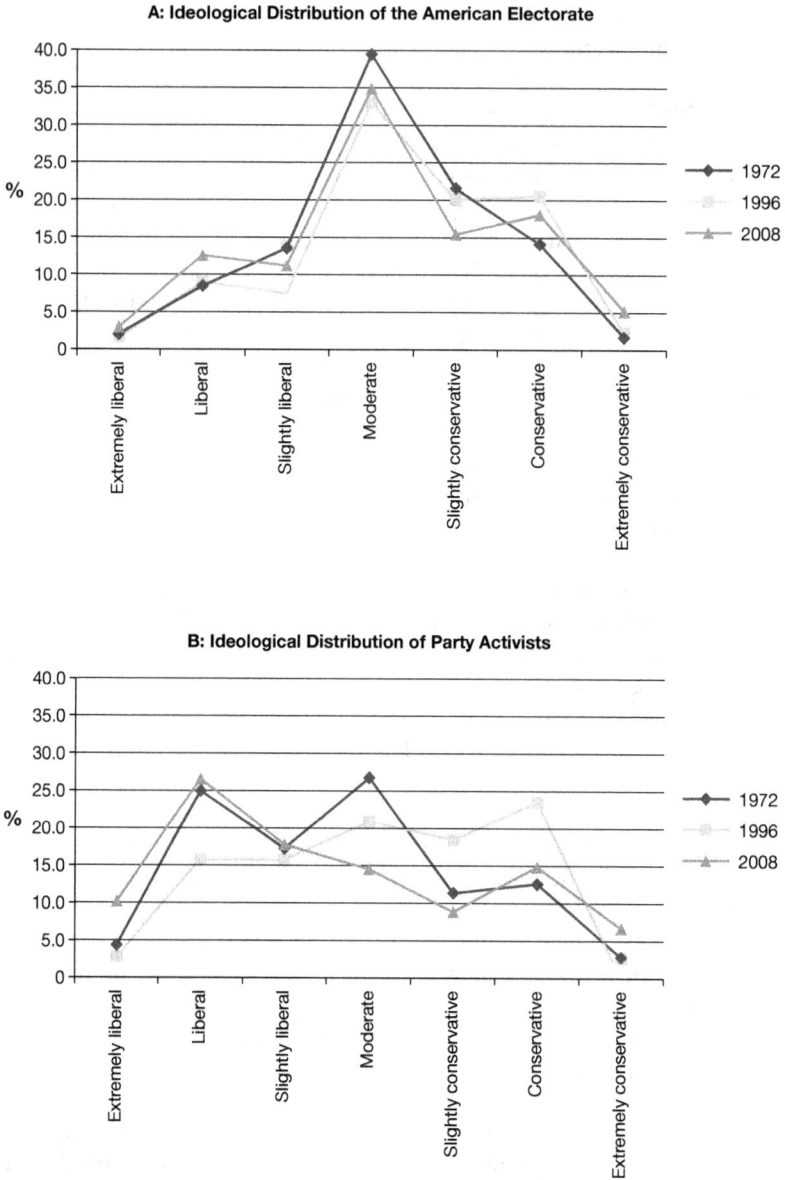

Figure 4.2 Ideological divisions among general electorate and party activists

Source: American National Election Study 2008 Cumulative Data File.

Notes: Cross-tabulations of VCF0803 (respondent self-identification on a liberal-conservative scale) with variables VCF0719 (respondent did "any other campaign work for party/candidate"), and VCF0721 (respondent "contribute to candidate") conducted by authors. Moderates include respondents who self-identified as "slightly liberal," "moderate," and "slightly conservative." Party activists were defined as those who answered "Yes" to VCF0719 and VCF0721.

voters as party activists. Among these activists, we find support for Abramowitz, in that there is a clear collapse among political moderates over time; rather, the peaks of the distribution shift to the left or the right of moderation, depending on the year considered.

So who is correct, are we polarized or not? The frustrating and unsatisfying answer is: *it depends*. Yes, party activists, and voters identifying with either the Republican or Democratic Party are quite polarized and, as we discuss in detail in Chapter 5, so are the parties in Congress. However, there is little to suggest that the broader electorate is any more polarized today than it was in 1972. Yet this is only one part of the polarization puzzle in the contemporary political system. For another important piece, we must return to a discussion of the "leaners" we mentioned earlier.

A Declaration of Independents?

Though many scholars contend that there has been a marked rise in partisanship among the mass electorate in recent years and a solidification of partisan support,[2] there is equally compelling evidence that the trek away from party allegiance that began in the 1960s continues through today.[3] According to data from the American National Election Study, in 1964, approximately 76 percent of the country identified as a "partisan" (either weak or strong); in contrast only 24 percent identified as independent or leaning independent (leaners).[4] By 1984, it was 65 percent to 35 percent and in 2008, it was 60 percent to 40 percent. Across that 42-year span, the share identifying as strong partisans (either Democrat or Republican) decreased from 38 percent in 1964 to 32 percent in 2008 and weak partisans declined from 38 percent to 28 percent. The share identifying as leaning independent, leaners, doubled from 15 percent to 29 percent. Though research has shown that many self-identified independents will express a partisan preference if pressed,[5] there has been a clear trend toward an initial preference of independent.

As shown in Figure 4.3, through 1964 fewer than a quarter of the electorate self-identified as an independent or an independent leaning Democrat or Republican. By 1968, the share of independents and leaners had risen to 30 percent, and as of 2008, was at 39 percent of the electorate. There is no indication of decline in the initial independent preference among voters. Though they may lean Democratic or Republican, Americans are clearly less willing to express allegiance to one of the two major parties than they were in the 1950s and 1960s.

Bafumi and Shapiro (2009, 4) use the same data to make the opposite argument concluding, "If voters are becoming more partisan, we would expect declines in pure independents to result in increases in independent partisans. This is evident for both Democrats and Republicans." Perhaps, but if we were seeing an increase in partisanship, then we might expect to see a rise in partisans of all stripes—strong, weak and leaning. This is not happening.

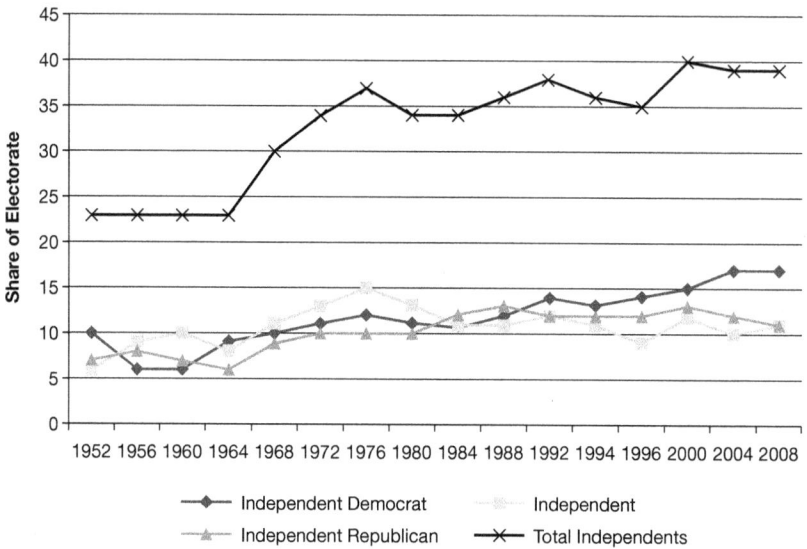

Figure 4.3 Trends in independent partisan identification, 1952–2008
Source: American National Election Studies.

A review of ANES data shows a clear decline in Democratic affiliation since 1952. From 1952 through 1968, Democratic affiliation averaged 54.9 percent of the electorate, from 1970 through 1980, the average was 52.3 percent and since 1982, the average is 49.8 percent. If one were to narrow the window to the 1990–2008 period, the average is 49.7 percent. Though the share of strong Democrats has rebounded from its lows in the 1970s, it remains well below its average from 1952 through 1968. There also has been a marked decline in the share of weak Democrats since the 1960s and it appears that a decline in weak Democrats has driven the increase in independent Democrats—not a decline in pure independents. In short, fewer people are identifying as Democrats than did so prior to 1968 and those who do identify as Democrats are increasingly identifying as independent Democrats.

The ANES data does show an increase in Republican partisanship, but this is entirely consistent with the collapse of the New Deal era and with it the prior dominance of the Democratic Party. At the end of the New Deal era and especially following the political fiasco of Watergate, which brought down Republican President Richard Nixon, the Republican Party had nowhere to go but up. Even among Republicans, however, there has been considerable growth among leaners and evidence of a rebound among strong Republicans following the lows of the 1970s—likely an artifact of the Nixon Administration and Watergate. The Republican share of the electorate averaged 33.9 percent from 1952 through 1968, then fell to 32.1 percent during the 1970s, and climbed to 38.2 percent in the decades since 1980.

However, the share of strong Republicans from 1982 through 2008 was 12.2 percent, essentially the same as the average of 12.4 percent prior to 1968—the "rise" in strong Republicans is again likely an artifact of a collapse in Republican identification during the 1970s.

The growth area in partisan (or non-partisan) politics has been among the group of Americans identifying as independent, either pure, or leaning Democrat or Republican (Figure 4.3). Though there are fewer pure independents as a share of the electorate than during the decade immediately following the collapse of the New Deal era and during the height of the Watergate era, there are more pure independents, independent leaning Democrats, and independent leaning Republicans today than during the pre-1968 era.

Polling data from Gallup released in early 2012 suggests that there has been no recent shift in partisanship (Gallup 2012). Though self-identified Democratic Party affiliation matched a 20-year peak of 36 percent in 2008, it has since fallen to its lowest levels (according to Gallup) in 22 years and the share of the electorate identifying as independent has reached 40 percent—the highest level ever recorded by Gallup. The Gallup data clearly show that neither party can claim the allegiance of a majority of the electorate and since 1990 has rarely captured a plurality. At best, the data on party affiliation, whether from ANES or Gallup, suggest that there has been some firming up of the strong partisan bases of each party, though collectively these strong partisans account for less than one-third of the electorate. A recent study by Bearnot and Schier confirmed non-ideological, persuadable voters composed more than half the electorate in 2004 and 2008 (Bearnot and Schier 2012). Writing in 1997, Ladd (Ladd 1997, 23) observed: "Regular party identifiers are now too small a proportion for anyone to win [. . .] largely on party terms." Ladd's observation was truer in 2010 than in 1996.

The question of whether partisan leaners are truly independent divides American political scientists as well. Keith et al. contend in *The Myth of the Independent Voter* (Keith, et al. 1992) that there has been little change in partisan attachment since the 1960s. The authors argue that people identifying as independents often reveal a preference for one of the two major parties when pressed to make a choice. These leaners behave much the same as their more partisan counterparts with regard to issue positions and vote choice. According to Petrocik (2009, 4), "Leaners are partisans. Characterizing them as independents underestimates the partisanship of Americans." Other studies have found that partisanship is stable over time (Lewis-Beck et al. 2008) and that true political independence is typically found among less sophisticated and less informed members of the public (Abramowitz 2010).

Studies of partisanship, however, often consider the views of leaners at a given point in time, their votes in a specific election, or examine the stability of partisan identification by merging all partisans—strong, weak, or leaning—together and measure macro-level party identification. In his book, *The*

Apartisan American, Russell Dalton argues there has been a rise in political independents in recent decades, showing they compose nearly 40 percent of the electorate. In addition, these independent voters are different from their partisan counterparts. Contrary to the findings of other researchers, Dalton demonstrates that the majority of independent voters are quite knowledgeable of politics, though they do pay less attention to the news than do their more partisan and informed counterparts (Dalton 2013). As we discuss a little later, that key distinction may prove crucial to solving the polarization puzzle.

A review of ANES data from a panel survey of the same respondents from 2000, 2002, and 2004 shows that leaners are much less attached to party than either weak or strong partisans over time (Table 4.1). Of those respondents who self-identified as an independent Democrat in 2000, 31.4 percent no longer identified with the Democratic Party in 2002, nearly as many, 29.8 percent, failed to identify with the party in 2004. For Republican leaners the results were similar, 27.2 percent no longer identified with the Republican Party in 2002, 26.1 percent in 2004.

Strong as well as weak partisans left their respective parties at far smaller rates over time. Equally worthy of note, leaners who left their 2000 party were just as likely to identify with the opposition party in 2002 and 2004, as they were to identify simply as pure independents. This is consistent with findings by Beckman (Beckman 2009) who demonstrated that party loyalty declines across broader periods than just one or two election cycles.

A review of 2004 partisan identification shows that fully one-third of independent Democrats and independent Republicans in 2004 had identified with another party or no party in 2000. Simply stated, partisan identification

Table 4.1 Party switching by partisan attachment (%)

	Year	Strong Democrat	Weak Democrat	Independent Democrat (leaner)	Independent Republican (leaner)	Weak Republican	Strong Republican
Percent no longer identifying with 2000 Party ID	2002	5.1	12.3	31.4	27.2	8.3	3.1
	2004	3.6	15.8	29.8	26.1	11.0	1.5
Percent not previously identifying with 2004 Party ID	2000	8	16.9	33	34.4	26.3	16.9
	2002	5.1	10.1	36.4	21.6	14.7	5.3

Source: American National Election Studies.

is much less stable among leaners, and research shows independent partisans are more moderate than are strong partisans.[6] Leaners may vote much like their partisan counterparts in any given election, but the ANES panel data suggest that a significant share of them may well have a different partisan stripe by the next election cycle.

Some existing research suggests that party identification is a strong predictor of voter choice, even among leaners. Keith et al. (1992) argue that leaners are partisans and present evidence that so-called leaners sometimes vote in a manner more partisan than do their weak partisan counterparts. Much of this evidence comes from the work of John Petrocik (Petrocik 1974) who first argued weak and leaning partisans are in fact quite similar with regard to vote choice, participation, and political interest. If true, then the number of actual independents in the electorate is quite small. Indeed, much subsequent scholarship, and considerable recent studies consider weak and leaning partisans collectively, lumping them together.[7] This tendency to equate leaners with weak partisans, however, may distort the true picture of leaners and the role they play in the contemporary political system.

A recent study by Drew Kurlowski (Kurlowski 2011) suggests significant flaws in Petrocik's foundational work on leaners.[8] Kurlowski corrected those perceived flaws and replicated Petrocik's study through 2008. He found no support for the contention that leaners are more partisan than are weak partisans. He concluded differences between leaners and weak partisans are not stable, but rather vary from election to election and Democratic leaners tend to be less loyal than Republican leaners.

Our review of the panel data from 2000–2004 showed leaners are more likely to change their partisan affiliation, *but what of their votes?* In *The American Voter Revisited* (2008), Lewis-Beck et al. found that 95 percent of strong partisans voted for the same party for president in both the 2000 and 2004 elections. Among weak partisans, 85 percent voted for the same party in both elections. For leaners, the rate was 84 percent and for pure independents it was 75 percent. The authors concede, however, that the 2000 and 2004 presidential elections both featured George W. Bush and the consistency in voting patterns may be a reflection of consistent attitudes toward Bush and not partisan attachment. Indeed, only two presidential elections since 1964 did not feature an incumbent president seeking re-election or an incumbent vice president seeking a promotion.

To address the possibility of a "Bush effect" on vote choice, we used the same data, but rather than focus on presidential elections, we consider partisan vote choice in congressional elections in 2000, 2002, and 2004 based on the voter's partisan identification in 2000. This offers the benefit of an additional election as well. The results of our analysis, shown in Table 4.2, suggest that leaners are less attached to party, and partisan vote choice can fluctuate significantly over relatively short periods. More than 90 percent of strong Democrats in 2000 voted the party line in House elections from 2000 through 2004. Among strong Republicans, there was a bit of a dip in 2000,

Table 4.2 Relation of strength of party identification to partisan regularity in voting for the House of Representatives (2000, 2002, and 2004)

	House election year					
Party ID in 2000	2000 (%)		2002 (%)		2004 (%)	
	Democrat (%)	Republican (%)	Democrat (%)	Republican (%)	Democrat (%)	Republican (%)
Strong Democrat	92.3	7.7	92.6	7.0	95.2	4.8
Weak Democrat	76.8	23.2	66.1	33.9	76.5	23.5
Independent Democrat (leaner)	73.2	26.8	54.1	45.9	61.8	38.2
Independent	33.3	66.7	39.3	60.7	38.7	61.3
Independent Republican (leaner)	25.5	74.5	25.5	74.5	25.4	74.6
Weak Republican	21.8	78.2	32.0	68.0	17.1	82.9
Strong Republican	16.3	83.7	8.0	92.0	8.0	92.0

Note:
[1] Partisan vote choice was determined by calculating only the two-party vote shares for each election. We excluded from the calculations respondents who indicated that they had not voted or did not know who they had voted for.

Source: Based on 2000 party identification[1] and American National Election Studies.

but in 2002 and 2004 they were as committed to party as strong Democrats. Weak Democrats and weak Republicans are less loyal to their party in each election compared to strong partisans, but with the exception of a slight decline in 2002, roughly three-quarters of weak partisans in 2000 voted the party line.

The story for leaners is quite different and conforms to Kurlowski's findings. Though voters identifying as leaners in 2000 voted in a manner nearly identical to their weak partisan counterparts in the 2000 election, they began to diverge in subsequent elections—a divergence especially pronounced among Democratic leaners. Only 54 percent of independent Democrats from 2000 voted for a Democratic House candidate in 2002, well below the 66 percent partisan loyalty of weak Democrats. Among Republicans, leaners were actually more loyal to the party in 2002 than were weak partisans. By 2004, however, both Democratic and Republican leaners demonstrated much less partisan loyalty than did weak partisans. With the exception of Republican leaners in the 2002 election, the data clearly suggest that leaners are different from their weak partisan counterparts with regard to partisan loyalty, especially among Democratic leaners.[9] We found similar trends in a review of an earlier ANES panel survey conducted in 1992, 1994, and 1996.

As with the polarization debate, our findings suggest an "it depends" answer to the debate over the role of leaners in the current era. Yes, they act very much like other partisans in a given election, but no, they are not as loyal over time. Our findings show partisan loyalty is less stable among leaners and leaners are the fastest growing segment of the American electorate. According to ANES data, fully 11 percent of the electorate are pure independents, another 30 percent are independent partisans, or leaners. Our findings suggests 25–33 percent of those leaners switch self-reported party affiliation over short periods of time and 25–45 percent change their party vote from election to election. At the very least, this suggests roughly 25 percent of the electorate is comprised of a voting bloc that is quite volatile and quite independent. That is no small number in a nation where margins of seven percentage points or less have decided our presidential elections since 2000 and the difference between the national two-party vote share in House elections averages about five percentage points since 1990.

Solving the Puzzle: Politics in an Information and Entertainment Age

There is a divide in the study of American politics between those who see our increasingly polarized politics as reflective of changes taking place within the larger electorate and those who see a disconnect between an active and polarized elite and a more moderate public. Closely linked to this disagreement is an argument over the true nature of political independents, leaners, and their impact on American elections. The disagreement is not merely an academic matter. If the American public is polarized and if leaners are really just closet partisans, then the polarization and partisanship evident in American politics are simply a reflection of the people. If this is not the case, then there is a disconnect between the electorate and our politics. In addition, it may help to explain low levels of trust and high levels of discontent. So far in this chapter, we have presented evidence that the public is not polarized and that a significant share of leaners are truly independent. So how can it be that such a polarized political environment emerged in an era of stable political moderation with a rising number of less partisan leaners? The answer may be sitting in front you, or in your backpack, or may be in displaying this very book.

In Chapter 1, we wrote of the transformation of American media in the present era. In the 1930s, radio was the only source of broadcast media and newspapers were the dominant source of information. There was little variety of programming available and it was difficult to avoid information, newsreels often preceded even movies. The advent of television introduced a dramatic and new broadcast medium, but there remained little variety. As recently as 1970, the three major networks claimed 8 in 10 viewers. A typical home had but one TV and network or local news was an evening staple (Prior 2007). This changed rapidly during the 1970s and 1980s as cable television and then satellite television became widespread. The once dominant major networks lost viewers to the hundreds of cable and satellite channels available in nearly every home. By the late 1990s, the internet had become commonplace and all manner of media exist for accessing information and entertainment. This media explosion has been transformative and may offer a solution to our puzzle.

Those with the greatest interest in politics have gained immeasurable access to news and information. Perhaps of greater import, the advent of partisan media has allowed for selective viewing. Cable news outlets such as Fox News and MSNBC have established loyal followings among political conservatives and liberals respectively. On the web, conservatives can look to the National Review Online, RedState, or American Thinker. Their liberal counterparts can seek out comforting news on the Huffington Post, The American Prospect, or Slate. In the present media environment, it is all too easy to seek and find sources of information that reinforce and rarely challenge an active partisan's worldview. Individuals with less interest in politics enjoy an array of entertainment choices as an alternative to news. Entertainment is rarely more than a web link or channel change away.

This media transformation might have had little influence on American politics if moderate and partisan individuals shared similar preferences for information and entertainment. However, it appears they do not. Moderate members of the electorate demonstrate a greater preference for entertainment over information. The proliferation of entertainment options has allowed moderates to easily fulfill their preference (Prior 2007). An established body of research shows the participation of less partisan voters is influenced by the amount of stimulus, or information, they are exposed to during a given election cycle. Markus Prior, in his book, *Post-Broadcast Democracy*, demonstrates a clear correlation between the proliferation of entertainment choices and the decrease of more moderate voices in American elections (2007). In other words, as moderate and independent members of the electorate are exposed to less and less information—given the ease with which they can meet their preference for entertainment—they have become less likely to vote. Their more partisan and information-hungry counterparts are now better able to fulfill their preference for information and they can acquire that information from sources tailored to their partisan views. Prior shows these partisan members of the electorate have come to claim a greater share of those voting on election day (2007). The result is a voting electorate more polarized than before.

Prior's findings offer the promise of solving at least part of the polarization puzzle and may provide a bridge to cross the divide between those who see greater polarization and fewer political independents and those who see no evidence of mass polarization and a greater share of truly independent members of the electorate. Simply stated, the potential electorate (comprised of all eligible voters) is no more polarized today than it was at the end of the New Deal Era, but the actual voting electorate is. Independent voters—leaners—are numerous and are different from their partisan counterparts, not only in how they vote, but also in whether or not they vote. A review of ANES data shows that turnout among strong partisans has increased since the late 1960s while turnout among leaners and pure independents has decreased. The electorate has not changed, but the mix of voters has.

However, there are periodic jumps in participation by less partisan voters. A review of ANES data shows turnout increased in the 1968 and 1992 presidential elections and in the mid-term elections in 1998, 2002, and 2006. The rise in turnout in all of those elections may have resulted from the dramatic events surrounding each of them. The presidential elections of 1968 and 1992 featured strong and conspicuous third party challengers. The mid-term election of 1998 took place in the midst of an unpopular impeachment inquiry against a popular president. The 2002 election capped a national debate over whether to invade Iraq and the 2006 mid-terms came in the midst of an unpopular war in Iraq and after the perceived failures of President Bush in response to Hurricane Katrina.

If Prior's theory on the impact of information on voting behavior is correct, it may be that during some election cycles it is more difficult to avoid information. In those years, moderate and independent members of the electorate turn out and contribute to the cycle of popular uprisings that we wrote of in Chapters 1 and 3. Such uprisings contribute to the very competitive nature of the current era. In an electoral democracy, politics will be defined less by the partisan preferences of the general electorate than by those who actually vote. There is compelling evidence that America's voting electorate has become more partisan and polarized. It should come as no surprise then that American politics has followed suit.

The declines in partisan affiliation at the dawn of the current era contributed to greater competition between the two parties and the parties responded by presenting voters with a clearer choice of agendas. The dramatic changes in media and access to information and entertainment reduced turnout by more moderate voices. A more partisan voter mix contributed to greater polarization between the two major parties. Such an environment is fertile ground for committed partisan voters and the programming designed to keep them interested, motivated, and partisan. It is an environment in which more moderate members of the electorate will continue to change the channel or find a more entertaining alternative to the rank partisanship that permeates contemporary political discourse. Within the present system, a self-perpetuating set of supports discourages political moderation and promotes partisanship and polarization among the parties and the institutions of government. We explore those institutions in the chapters that follow.

5 Congress

Professionalization, Polarization, and Competition

Writing in *Federalist 51*, James Madison observed, "In republican government, the legislative authority necessarily predominates." The framers of the American Constitution intended Congress to be the first among equals within the branches of government. In Congress were placed the powers to levy and collect taxes, declare war, raise armies, ratify treaties, and to suspend the privilege of the writ of habeas corpus. Over half of the words of the unamended Constitution are dedicated to Congress in Article I. Congress as the "first branch" hardly comports with much of the current study of the national legislature. Congressional scholars Thomas Mann and Norm Ornstein describe the contemporary Congress as "a supine, reactive body more eager to submit to presidential directives than to assert its own prerogatives" (Mann and Ornstein 2008, 16). According to the authors, many characteristics that define the contemporary Congress took shape during the period of the late 1960s. Among the changes was a shift away from the "textbook" Congress of the New Deal era characterized by a decentralized power structure, powerful committee chairs, and weak parties.

A combination of internal and external pressures dating to the late 1950s set in motion the creation of the contemporary Congress. A series of elections spanning nearly two decades changed the ideological make-up of the Democratic Party. A combination of court decisions and federal legislation changed the nature of congressional constituencies. A series of internal reforms enacted from the late 1960s through the mid-1970s empowered individual members. Concomitant with these changes was a dramatic rise in interest groups, a marked rise in two-party competition, and the frequent presence of divided partisan control of the legislative and executive branches. Collectively, they raised the stakes in the pitched battle over lawmaking. Highly professionalized members, intense partisan polarization, centralized control among party leaders, and an increased reliance on "unorthodox" procedures to secure passage of legislation mark the Congress that emerged. The cumulative effect of these changes on Congress continues to reverberate through the American political system.

The Rise of Progressive Democrats, 1958–1974

> No theoretical treatment of the United States Congress that posits parties as analytic units will go very far. So we are left with individual congressmen, 535 men and women rather than two parties, as units to be examined.
>
> (Mayhew 1974, 27)

Neither the casual political observer nor the student of the contemporary Congress would recognize the Congress of "535 men and women rather than two parties" described by David Mayhew in 1974. Indeed, any study of the contemporary Congress is likely to begin with party as the central unit of analysis and consider individual members briefly—if at all. As shown in Figure 5.1, Mayhew was describing a Congress that was already in transition. The roots of that transition extend to a series of elections in 1958, 1964 and 1974 that changed the ideological makeup of the Democratic Party. Those ideological changes prompted a series of institutional and party reforms in the mid-1970s to limit the power of conservative Southern Democrats.

Mayhew was describing a "textbook" Congress, as it had existed since the 1930s (Shepsle 1989). A Congress ruled by seniority and dominated by powerful committee chairs. A Congress rife with sectional divisions and a Democratic Party divided between northern and southern members and ideologies. The net effect of these internal party divisions was a decentralized legislative body with considerable voting overlap between its Democratic and Republican members. The Congress described by Mayhew was quite different from the Congress of the late nineteenth and early twentieth centuries when partisan polarization—the ideological distance between the parties—was more similar to current patterns. Indeed, if one were to take a House member of the 52nd Congress in 1891 and transport him through time to the 86th Congress in 1960, he would scarcely recognize the institution. Were that same member then transported to the 111th Congress in 2009, he would find a more familiar atmosphere of intense partisanship and centralized control in the House under the leadership of the Speaker.

Starting with the Speakership of Thomas Reed (R–ME) in 1889 and continuing through that of Joseph Cannon (R–IL: 1903–1910), the position of Speaker of the House grew into an incredibly powerful force in Congress. The level of centralized control exercised by Reed and Cannon is more likely in Congress, but especially the House, whenever the ideological distance between the two parties is great and the ideological diversity within each party is small. Under such circumstances, party members are more willing to surrender power to party leadership. This is called *conditional party government*. If the conditions of internal party agreement and between party distance are met, party members will empower leadership in an effort to ensure their party agenda succeeds and the opposing party's agenda does not. Strong leadership can help ensure such an outcome.

Central control becomes less acceptable to members, however, as polarization declines and the individual parties become more ideologically

**Panel A: Party Means on Liberal-Conservative Dimension –
51st–110th Congress (1789–2007)**

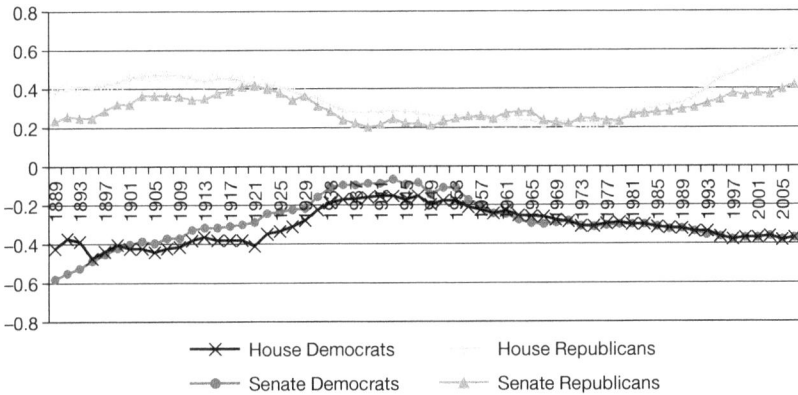

→✕— House Democrats   House Republicans
—●— Senate Democrats   —▲— Senate Republicans

Panal B: Party Polarization: 51st–110th Congress (1789–2007)

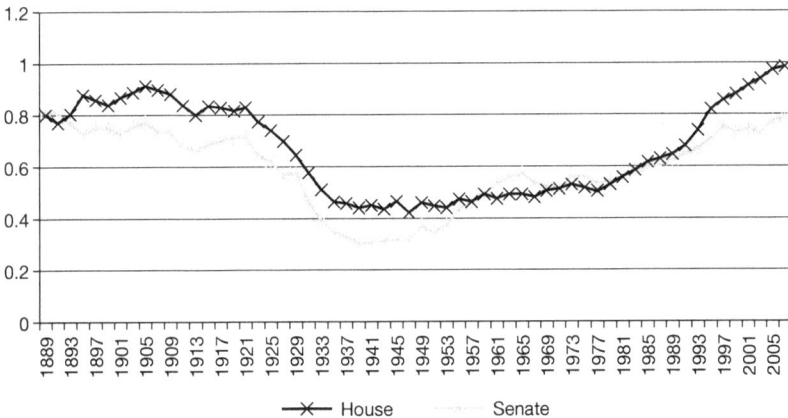

—✕— House   Senate

Figure 5.1 Polarization in Congress

diverse (Aldrich and Rohde 2009). The reasons are twofold: (1) members are unwilling to empower a leadership that may disagree with them on key policy issues; and (2) with declining distance between the parties, there is less at stake should the opposition party win control of the policy process. As partisan polarization waned in the early twentieth century, minority progressive Republicans joined minority Democrats and stripped away the power of the House Speaker. Power then was divided among committee chairs chosen by seniority.

Democrats emerged from the mid-term elections of 1930 as the majority party in American politics for the next four decades. Since the end of Reconstruction, much of the South was home to a single party, the Democrats. As a result, the safest seats and the most senior members of the party hailed from the states of the old Confederacy. During this era, coalition building and negotiations with the White House were a joint endeavor. Party leadership needed the consent and cooperation of committee chairs. It was a productive system, but it achieved efficiency and expediency at the expense of deliberation and the full participation of junior, mostly Northern liberal, members (Mackenzie 1996). Conservative Southern Democrats exercised their power as committee chairs to block or significantly amend progressive Democratic legislation. Junior members lacked institutional support and meaningful committee assignments. Progressive Democrats lacked the power of numbers needed to overcome their conservative Southern counterparts.

Though Democrats as well as Republicans in Congress occupied a middle ground for several decades, Democrats began a trek away from the political center near the end of the 1950s. Indeed, the election of 1958 brought with it an influx of new Democratic members in the House (48) and Senate (15), mostly Northern liberals (Sinclair 2006). In the election of 1964, President Lyndon Johnson crushed Republican Senator Barry Goldwater. The tidal wave of Johnson's victory brought 48 freshman Democrats to the House of Representatives and the defeat by Republicans of several Southern Democrats. As shown in Figure 5.1, Panel A, the ideological make-up of the Democratic Party was beginning to move left. The balance of power was shifting within the party as well, prompting greater pressure for internal reforms to empower individual Members of Congress. The post-Watergate mid-term election of 1974 sealed the fate of the Southern Democrats and the era of the textbook Congress referenced by Mayhew. In the election of 1974, Democrats netted 49 seats in Congress, but elected 75 freshman members. The vestiges of the textbook Congress were disappearing, as approximately 85 percent of the members in Congress in 1975 had not been in Congress prior to 1958.

Pressure from Within

The freshman class of Democrats elected in 1958 still lacked power, but they began the pursuit of institutional reforms that would distribute more evenly the powers in Congress. They formed the Democratic Study Group (DSG), a caucus of progressive members dedicated to advancing liberal causes in the House (Sinclair 2006). The efforts of these members and of the DSG met with significant resistance.

Though many issues during the late 1950s and early 1960s contributed to the frustrations of progressive Democrats, few were as crucial as the push for civil rights protections. In 1959, a civil rights bill was reported out of the House Judiciary Committee (chaired by a liberal Democrat from New York), but was then held captive by the Rules Committee when its chair Howard Smith (D-VA), a conservative civil rights opponent, refused to hold hearings. In the Senate, the measure was referred to a Judiciary Committee chaired by a Mississippi Democrat. In the end, civil rights opponents viewed the legislation that ultimately emerged in 1960 as a toothless measure watered down to ensure passage (Gueron 1995). However, the battles of 1959 and 1960 did result in important changes in Congress. The Senate changed its rules to ensure that every member received one major committee assignment, resulting in greater committee participation by junior members (Mackenzie 1996). In the House, following the election of John Kennedy in 1960, progressive Democrats convinced the Speaker to increase the size of the Rules Committee to avoid the embarrassment of having the president's agenda blocked (Sinclair 2006).This change proved crucial as the House considered the bill that would become the Civil Rights Act of 1964. Though Smith tried to block the legislation, he was compelled to send it to the floor by a majority of his committee members (Gueron 1995).

The election of Republican President Richard Nixon and the arrival of divided government made the seniority situation intolerable for progressive Democrats. Congress became the repository of the progressive Democratic agenda and the push for internal reforms accelerated after the loss of the White House. The Democratic caucus adopted a rule in 1969 requiring monthly party meetings rather than a single meeting at the start of each Congress. Another new rule provided for party ratification of committee members (Sinclair 2006). As these were changes to party rules, and not House or Senate rules, they enhanced the power of the party caucus and precluded Southern Democrats from colluding with Republicans to thwart reform efforts on the floor. A "subcommittee bill of rights" received passage in 1973 granting subcommittees and their chairs independence from their parent committee chairs and subcommittees gained budgets and support through staff. Between 1971 and 1975, a series of party rules changes subjected committee chairs to the secret ballot approval of the Democratic caucus. In 1975, as the new Congress was organizing, the Democratic caucus ousted three prominent committee chairs, among them two Southern Democrats. The seniority system that had been the source of power for the now minority Southern Democrats and a hallmark of the textbook Congress was gone (ibid.).

Under the Legislative Reorganization Act of 1970 closed door committee meetings were discouraged, committees were required to have formal written rules, committee roll-call votes were to be made public, the rights of minority members were protected, and committee hearings were opened to radio and television coverage. The Act provided for the recording of roll call votes on the floor. Until then, the only way to know how a Member of Congress had voted was to stand in the viewing gallery and watch the vote (Mackenzie 1996).

In this new era, the number of subcommittees grew rapidly, reaching 139 by 1976—twice the number as in the House just 20 years prior. The growth in number and power of subcommittees, coupled with an influx of new Democratic House members and an increasingly liberal Democratic caucus, saw power distributed among 139 subcommittees and the party's 291 members. The era following the reforms of the early 1970s received the labels of the era of the subcommittee and the era of the individual member. Regardless of the label, it was a period of decentralization and diffuse power.

Individual members long enjoyed the ability to influence the legislative process in the Senate. In a chamber where most business requires the unanimous consent of members, it was the unwritten rules of the chamber, the behavioral norms, which prevented obstruction. Among the "acceptable" behavior for Senators of the time was an expected period of apprenticeship and deference to senior Senators, courtesy and reciprocity toward fellow Senators, and a commitment to the institution over all else. This often meant exercising restraint in the use of formal powers (Baker 2010).

The Legislative Reorganization Act of 1970 signaled a move away from powerful committees and toward more power for subcommittees and individual members in the Senate. Committee members gained the ability to call for hearings, minority members received the ability to call witnesses, and individual members gained additional staff and resources. The Senate changed its rules in 1975 to reduce the power of the filibuster as a means of minority obstruction. The two-thirds (67 vote) majority required to invoke cloture—*to end debate*—was reduced to a three-fifth majority (60 votes).

The cumulative effect of these changes was a significant decentralization of power within Congress. Members in the House and Senate gained access to staff and resources, member offices received computers, and additional funds for their district offices. The Congressional Research Service—which provides policy and legal analysis to committees and members—grew in size and resources. Members of Congress professionalized. Professionalism grew in the legislative branch in the 1960s and 1970s with the lengthening of congressional careers. The number of professional staff grew to help lawmakers become electorally secure by solving constituent problems with "casework" and delivering federal funds for constituency projects—"pork barreling."

In 1960, the total individual staff for Representatives was 2,444. By 1974 that had grown to 5,109 and individual member payroll for staff had increased nearly tenfold (Fiorina 1977, 57–58). Comparable increases occurred in staff for individual Senators, chamber staff and committee staff. Committee staff in the House numbered 394 in 1960, swelled to 1843 by 1981 and remained well above 1960's total at 1241 in 2005. In the Senate, committee staff stood at 433 in 1960 before jumping to 1022 in 1981 and remained at 883 in 2005 (Ornstein, Mann, and Malbin 2008, 113–114). The total congressional workforce grew dramatically during the period between the late 1960s and 1980. We explore the implications of that growth in Chapter 7.

Pressure from Without

The constituencies of the parties were changing considerably and adding to the newly emerging distance between Democrats and Republicans in Congress. The passage of the Civil Rights Act of 1964 and the Voting Rights Act of 1965 increased voter registration by African-Americans, especially in the South, and brought African-Americans into the Democratic Party fold. African-American voter registration rates jumped from 6.7 percent before passage of the Acts to 59.8 percent by 1967 in Mississippi alone. Their increased participation in Democratic Party politics contributed to the primary defeats of conservative Southern Democrats in states such as Louisiana and Virginia (where House Rules Committee chair Howard Smith (D-VA) lost the nomination to a liberal challenger) at the hands of partisans more in line with the party's emerging progressive majority (Trende 2011). This provided an opportunity for Republican candidates in the South, as they were better able to defeat liberal Democratic nominees. Steadily, either Southern Democrats lost elections or they began to toe the party line more frequently.

The South was not the only region to experience change. In a series of court rulings during the 1960s, the manner in which states created congressional districts was greatly altered. In 1964, in *Wesberry v. Sanders,* the U.S. Supreme Court ruled that congressional districts must contain approximately the same number of people. Many states had not engaged in reapportionment or the redrawing of congressional districts to reflect population change for decades. Over the course of the next decade states engaged in a dramatic overhaul of congressional districts. Once dominant rural areas saw power and representation shift to newly emerging suburbs and urban areas achieved equitable representation. Reapportionment made Democrats more attentive to the demands of black voters in the North just as the Civil Rights Act and Voting Rights Act had in the South.

Sprawling suburban development resulted in more heterogeneous district populations and presented new challenges for representatives in the House. It was more difficult to campaign and to reach out to voters in these new suburban districts as they lacked either the community centers of urban areas or the shared history of rural areas. The varied interests, needs, and demands of these new districts required elected representatives to diversify their legislative portfolios and to reach beyond the committee-specific special-ization of the textbook Congress (Shepsle 1989). Candidates and incumbents needed a new method for securing victory. The rise of interest groups offered one such method as these advocacy organizations provided candidates and Members of Congress with a means for connecting with constituencies.

Concomitant with the rise in the number of associations in the 1960s was a rise in the numbers of congressional staff. Newly empowered Members of Congress fought to expand subcommittee jurisdictions to engage emerging policy issues. The dramatic increase in the number of bills subject to multiple committee referrals offers evidence of this expansion. Multiple referrals were once quite rare in Congress, but have become quite commonplace since the late 1960s (Sinclair 2011). Jurisdictional expansion and multiple referrals in turn attracted the attention of interest groups seeking to influence policy (Baumgartner and Jones 2009). Members derived electoral support from these groups. In return for electoral support, the groups attained access to the policy process. A self-reinforcing mechanism resulted, encouraging both more lobbying by associations and additional efforts by members to expand their sphere of policy influence. The number of congressional personnel grew at a pace similar to the rise in the number of associations between 1964 and 1980.

The congressional redistricting process was changing as well. In most states the process of redrawing district borders to reflect population changes is handled by the governor, the legislature, or both—it is a partisan process. Though the redrawing of congressional districts for the purpose of partisan gain dates to the early days of America, the advent of sophisticated computers took the process to new levels. Parties were able to easily generate district maps drawn to advantage one party and disadvantage the other. In the absence of federal guidelines sprawling or oddly shaped districts quickly emerged. The number of truly competitive congressional districts declined through-out the late 1980s and 1990s. By the 2000s, each party had a safely protected floor of roughly 180 seats. As a result, battles for the control of the House are waged on a smaller playing field and the sense of competition is heightened. Members from safe districts have more to fear from a primary challenge originating from their party base than from a general election challenge from the opposition. Such a threat encourages members to be more partisan and to reflect base voters. The base voters in primary elections are now liberal Democrats and conservative Republicans whose ideological positions are far from those of the median general election voter.

Though Democrats dominated national politics and Congress for much of the time since 1932, electoral changes were breaking that hold on power. As African-Americans moved toward the Democrats, white southerners and white working-class voters began to move away. Republicans reclaimed the White House in 1968 and retained it in 1972. Although Republicans in Congress suffered a tremendous setback in the aftermath of Watergate, the election of 1980 delivered the White House, and Republicans claimed just over 190 members in the House for only the third time since 1956. The party captured a six-seat majority in the U.S. Senate—their first majority since 1954. Of greater import, Republicans were now mirroring the Democrats' trek left and growing partisan homogeneity. Increased compe-tition, the advent of divided government, partisan redistricting, and the growth of conservative homogeneity among Republicans in Congress set the stage for the next step in the evolution of the contemporary Congress—a return to centralized party control.

The Rise of Conservative Republicans, 1976–1994

Just as Figure 5.1 shows congressional Democrats moving left, beginning in the 1950s, it also shows that Republicans began their own ideological journey right starting in the late 1970s. Though the congressional elections of 1976 and 1978 did not see significant changes in the balance of power in the House or Senate, they did witness the election of more conservative Republicans: Republicans influenced by an emerging activist and ideological conservatism (Sinclair 2006). In 1978, 35 Republican freshmen arrived in the House, including Newt Gingrich (R-GA) who became secretary of the group. In the face of what had seemed permanent minority status, these activist Republicans sought other means by which to influence the process, frequently raising questions of possible ethics violations by majority party members.

The election of 1980 changed the perspective of many Republicans and raised the possibility of reclaiming control of Congress. Republicans erased all of the losses they had suffered since 1964 and returned to pre-Watergate levels in the House. Additionally, the party continued to build on its presence in the South. Republicans netted 12 seats in the Senate, including four new seats in the South. More significantly, Republicans claimed control of the Senate for the first time since 1953. A new Republican Party was emerging. It was a more uniformly conservative party with a steadily growing Southern accent.

The arrival of recorded votes offered incentives to the minority party as well. Prior to 1971 votes on amendments were not recorded. Members of the House might vote simply by stating "aye" or "nay" or simply inform the vote teller of their position—but there would be no list of how each member voted. Only those in the chamber would know how a member voted. With the introduction of recorded and then electronic voting, every member's vote became a matter of public record. This encouraged the minority party to offer amendments to force tough or even embarrassing votes for majority party members—especially those from competitive districts. The change was dramatic. All told, there was an eightfold increase in the number of floor amendments subject to a recorded vote between the 84th Congress, convened in 1955, and the 95th Congress, adjourned in 1978 (Sinclair 2011).

Newt Gingrich saw the potential afforded by the new openness created in the 1970s. Gingrich and likeminded Republicans formed the Conservative Opportunity Society (COS) in 1983. The COS served as the conservative Republican counterpart to the progressives' Democratic Study Group established in the 1950s. The COS took advantage of House rules and used floor amendments to force Democrats to make politically challenging votes. This was an effective way to embarrass Democrats from vulnerable districts in an era of televised floor proceedings and recorded votes. The minority party lacks the power to overcome majority party advantages in the House, so the COS instead used the House floor as a platform to undermine confidence in the Democratic majority.

Republicans used ethics reforms adopted in the 1970s to target Democratic leaders. In quick succession, ethics inquiries and investigations led to the resignations of Democratic Speaker of the House Jim Wright and Majority Whip Tony Coelho in 1989—that same year Gingrich gained election as Minority Whip, the second highest-ranking Republican leadership position in the House. A scandal involving the House bank in 1991 and the House Post Office in 1993 followed the resignations of Wright and Coelho. Though Democrats and Republicans alike were found to have overdrawn their accounts in the House bank, the scandal contributed to a COS narrative of a corrupt Congress controlled by Democrats. Nearly 80 House members either retired or were defeated in 1992 because of the bank scandal. The election of 47 freshman Republicans to the House accompanied the election of Democrat Bill Clinton as president in 1992. Figure 5.1 clearly shows the growing conservatism of House Republicans during that time. Senate Republicans steadily followed suit. Conservative House members, first elected after 1978 and subsequently elected to the Senate (Theriault and Rohde 2011), helped to produce the growing polarization within the Senate.

The House Post Office scandal erupted in 1993 and effectively ended the career of Democratic Representative Dan Rostenkowski (D-IL), the very powerful Chair of the House Ways and Means Committee. The cumulative effect of the scandals and public dissatisfaction with President Clinton was the Republican sweep of the 1994 mid-term elections. In the 1994 election, Republicans realized a net gain of 54 seats in the House and 8 seats in the Senate and assumed full control of the U.S. Congress for the first time since 1954. Gingrich gained election as Speaker of the new Republican-controlled House. Republicans would hold the majority in the House and Senate until 2007, with the exception of a brief period in the Senate from 2001–2003.

The Contemporary Congress: Polarization, Professionalization, and Competition

Rising levels of professionalization, and growing polarization coincided with new levels of electoral competition in Congress as the 1970s ended. How did the combination of polarization, professionalization, and electoral competition alter the institution of Congress? Several of the variables included in our macropattern analysis examine institutional changes that differentiate the Sixth Party System from the Fifth. Among those changes is a rise in party unity in House and Senate voting, House and Senate incumbent security, and the use of procedural tactics in each chamber as measured by the use of closed or restrictive rules in the House and cloture motions filed to end debate in the Senate.

Others have documented additional changes in Congress during the critical era of the late 1960s and early 1970s, including a decreased reliance on the traditional role of committees in shaping legislation. Barbara Sinclair notes a marked rise in the number of changes made to major legislation after it was reported by committee as well as an increase in the tendency to bypass committees with jurisdiction (Sinclair 2011). When committees do their work, substantial post-committee adjustment is now common in both chambers. Legislation often undergoes substantive changes after a committee reports it but before consideration on the floor. The party leadership typically makes these changes and opportunities for full member consideration and debate are then restricted on the floor.

As shown in Figure 5.2, post-committee adjustments and the bypassing of a committee, as well as the use of restrictive rules to limit debate in the House, were once quite rare. The first signs of change are evident in the early 1970s, just as the House and Senate are adopting internal reforms, and then accelerate markedly after the mid-1980s. Fully 40 percent of major legislation has been subject to post-committee adjustments in the House and Senate in recent years (Sinclair 2011). The time for debate and deliberation has been cut short as well. Since the 1960s and 1970s, the average number of days that Congress is in session has fallen from roughly 320 per Congress to approximately 250. During that same period, the average number of committee and subcommittee meetings per Congress fell from nearly 5400 to just over 2100. In the nation's premiere deliberative body, deliberation was increasingly not possible—by design.

What explains the change? To understand what was happening, we must return to the internal reforms of the 1970s. Concomitant with House and Senate members' press for greater power was a dramatic rise in the number of special interest associations in Washington. This was especially meaningful

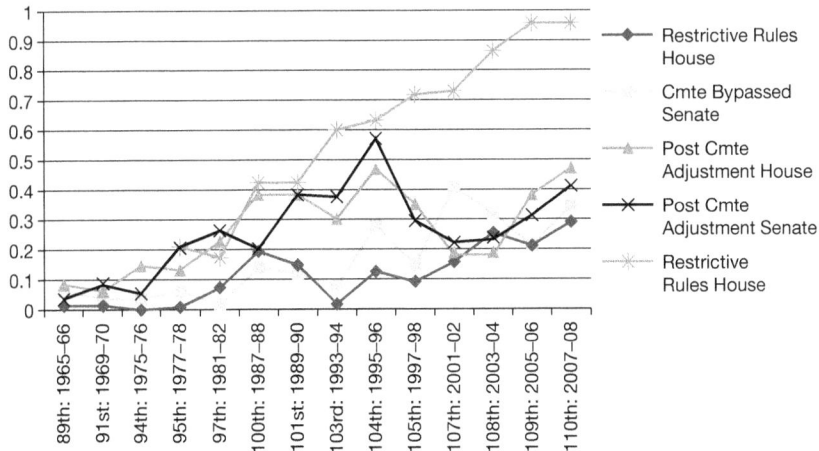

Figure 5.2 Process changes for major legislation in Congress

Source: Data collected from Sinclair (2011), Table 6.3, p. 147.

to those progressive Senators elected in 1958, 1964 and 1974. According to Barbara Sinclair, the rise in the number of interest groups motivated Senators to "exploit fully the powers that Senate rules confer on the individual" so as to maximize media exposure and interest group support (2011, 135). The folkways of the past that promoted deference to the institution and a respect for seniority gave way to an emerging class of Senators eager to effect change. The reforms enacted in the 1970s provided committee assignments, staff, and resources sufficient to support individual senators as policy entrepreneurs. The new motivation was to gain the attention of interest groups, to gain notice, to impact legislation.

A "free-wheeling individualism" characterized the Senate of the 1970s as the number of amendments receiving a roll call (recorded) vote doubled in less than a decade (Lee 2012, 112). Additionally, filibusters increased and, as shown in Figure 5.3, there is a related, and more dramatic, rise in the number of cloture motions (Sinclair 2006). The increase began in the early 1970s, and then declined, only to begin a new rise in the 1980s.

In the House, individual members were similarly liberated. The reforms stripped power from committee chairs and gave all members a piece of the action via committee or subcommittee assignments as well as subcommittee and individual office staff support and resources. Just as members were gaining the resources necessary to professionalize their offices and committee work, sunshine rules opened the doors of Congress to public scrutiny via open

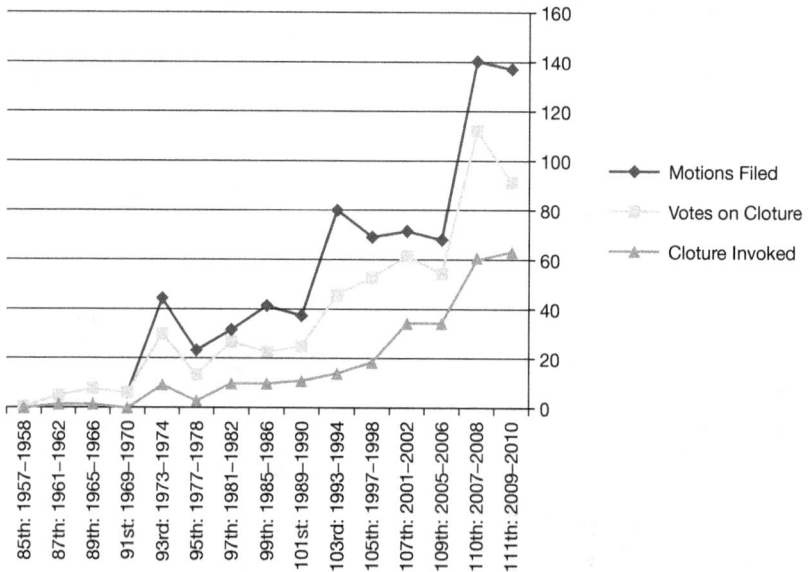

Figure 5.3 Senate action on cloture motions

Source: Official website of the U.S. Senate. Retrieved on May 17, 2012, from: http://www.senate.gov/pagelayout/reference/cloture_motions/clotureCounts.htm.

committee hearings and the televising of floor action. As in the Senate, there was now every motivation for House members to become active, even activist, participants in the legislative process. Much was to be gained from taking ownership of an issue and taking positions of high profile legislation that might garner media coverage or gain the attention of interest groups.

The result of the reforms of the late 1960s and early 1970s, however, was a Congress made more difficult to manage. As described by Mackenzie, "Congress at work came to resemble a confederation of independent, self-interested entities" (1996, 77). Though Southern Democrats lost control of the party agenda, they could work with newly empowered and emboldened minority party Republicans to take advantage of arcane rules of debate and amendment to influence legislation. The legislative process was no longer closed to all but a select few. As discussed in Chapter 7, the days of the iron triangles or "policymaking by subgovernments—congressional committees, interest groups, and governmental agencies" were over (Shepsle 1989, 247). Members had the resources and the motivation to influence the process either in committee or on the floor.

The cumulative effect of the changes taking place in the early 1970s was a significant increase in the time and resources necessary to pass legislation. Hard-fought compromises hammered out in committee were subject to serious alteration on the floor and fragile voting coalitions were difficult to maintain. The passage of significant legislation peaked around 1970 and then a significant decline ensued (Howell et al. 2000).

The rise of divided government post 1968 heightened partisan differences, prompting Democratic members to seek ways to improve congressional productivity and to maintain agenda control. Toward these ends, Democratic House members instituted additional reforms in the mid and late 1970s that strengthened party leadership in general and the Speaker of the House specifically. The Speaker received the power to determine the majority party makeup of the House Rules Committee. The Rules Committee determines the rules of debate and amendment for nearly every piece of legislation brought to the floor. The power to appoint committee members went to a new committee mostly consisting of party leadership. The Speaker also gained the power to refer legislation to more than one committee. Though the House became more centralized, Senate rules continued to emphasize the power of individual members. One of the few limitations placed on individual members in the Senate was reduction from two-thirds to three-fifths of the votes needed to invoke cloture and end a filibuster.

The new level of competition after the 1980 election caused minority Republicans to change tactics in the House, resulting in tactical changes by Democrats as well. There was little need for Republicans to obstruct the process prior to 1980 because they had become a permanent minority in Congress. When one party thoroughly dominates, the minority party gains little from obstruction, so it is better to participate in the process and win any level of concession. In a highly competitive era, however, party control may last no longer than the next election cycle. This produced new motivations and tactics exploiting the minority's ability to obstruct, delay, and wait to reclaim power. Then, once in power, the newly ascendant majority party could restrict debate, bypass committees and conferences, and do whatever is necessary to pass an agenda before again losing power. All of these elements appear and accelerate as the battle for control of Congress becomes more competitive after 1980.

In response to GOP tactics, Democrats accelerated the use of restrictive rules and limitations on the minority's ability to influence the outcome of legislative debates (Figure 5.2). It was under the leadership of House Speaker Jim Wright in the 100th Congress in 1987 and 1988 that the reforms of the 1970s merged with the partisan politics of the contemporary era. As Speaker, Wright was willing to use all available means to protect the agenda of a majority of the majority party (Rohde 1991). As recounted by Thomas Mann and Norm Ornstein:

> With its complete control of the Rules Committee, the majority leadership may write special rules to control debate and amendments on the House floor [. . .] During the last decade of their forty-year control of the House, Democrats made increasing use of this power to deny the minority Republicans opportunity to participate in any meaningful fashion in the legislative process.
>
> (2008, 171)

The use of restrictive rules went from being uncommon to quite the norm in the House of Representatives under the leadership of Speaker Wright. Between 1977 and 1982, roughly 20 percent of major legislation proceeded under restrictive rules. In the first Congress under Wright's leadership that figure doubled to 41 percent. Post-committee adjustments increased by a similar margin. To protect the majority party's agenda and marginalize the minority, Wright made extensive use of the Rules Committee to limit floor activity, limit amendments, and structure the terms of debate. Wright's leadership style, now typical of the contemporary Congress, was on full display in 1987 when the House considered the fiscal year 1988 budget bill. Wright insisted that any budget bill passed by the House include tax increases in order to address the growing federal deficit. Though the Reagan White House and many in his own party objected, Wright would not yield. Wright had the Rules Committee add a provision stipulating that if the rule passed on the House floor, a controversial welfare reform bill also would be deemed approved by the House. Under this approach, a contentious bill would win passage without any member ever having to cast a vote for it. Much to Wright's displeasure, a coalition of Democrats and Republicans narrowly defeated the rule. The Speaker then immediately sought consideration of an amended rule minus the welfare reform measure. The rules of the House, however, precluded consideration of a revised rule on the same day that it was defeated. Undeterred, Wright used his power as Speaker to adjourn the House, thereby concluding the day's business. He then reconvened the chamber mere minutes later—constituting a new "day" of business.

Though the revised rule passed, the budget bill itself faced stiff headwinds and at the end of the 15 minutes allotted for the vote, it was on the losing end of the vote. Down by only one vote, Wright kept the vote open beyond the 15 minutes allowed and finally found a wavering member and convinced him to change his vote. The vote switcher later received the reward of a choice committee assignment (Rohde 1991; Palazzolo 1992). Wright secured passage of the bill. Another tactic employed by Wright was the use of rules to limit the ability of minority Republicans to offer piecemeal amendments to legislation. Securing sufficient support from within his party often required post-committee adjustments and delicately constructed compromises on legislation. Even minor changes to a bill could cause enough members to withdraw their support and kill a bill. To prevent this, Wright would structure rules allowing minority Republicans to offer only comprehensive substitutes rather than minor changes to bills. This denied the minority the opportunity to offer politically popular amendments and cut the minority party out of the process of shaping legislation.

When Gingrich and the Conservative Opportunity Society brought Wright down on ethics charges in 1989, the move was as much personal as it was political. Many Republicans despised Wright's treatment of the minority party. Gingrich believed that Republicans had too long accepted their role as a permanent minority. For Gingrich, Republican compliance created the appearance of a functioning and productive Congress. This gave voters little reason to elect new leadership or a new majority. Wright was the perfect foil for Gingrich because the Speaker responded to Republican obstructionism by taking full advantage of the rules of the House to stymie minority rights. Wright's actions then served to further and justify the Republicans' obstruction. Majority party abuses coupled with minority party obstruction served to unify the parties further and to undermine public confidence in the institution—note in Figure 5.1 the increase in polarization between the two parties throughout the late 1980s.

Wright's majoritarian tactics continued beyond his tenure. When the House considered the Civil Rights Act of 1991, the process was much different than it had been in 1964. Unlike the 1964 bill, which languished in the House for much of 1963, the various committees of jurisdiction quickly reported the 1991 bill. The House Rules Committee reconciled the differences between the various committee versions. In 1964, the independent Rules Committee attempted to kill the Civil Rights Act. In 1991, the Rules Committee was simply another tool available to party leadership and dedicated to the passage of legislation by limiting minority party obstruction. The restrictive rule issued for the 1991 legislation limited debate to 3 hours, allowed only three amendments, and limited the motion to recommit (a House motion to send the bill back to committee) such that the minority party could not recommit with instructions—making any vote to recommit a vote to kill the measure. An additional rule stipulated the order for considering of the three amendments and applied a "king of the hill" procedure for their consideration. Under the king of the hill rubric, only the last amendment to pass gains adoption regardless of whether previous amendments had received majority support. Minority party Republicans decried the restrictive rule and reminded the House that the Civil Rights Act of 1964 had passed under an open rule with no restrictions on amendments and 10 hours allotted for debate.

Republicans nationalized the 1994 mid-term elections as a referendum on a corrupt Congress and a counter to the Clinton White House. The GOP promised a restoration of minority rights in the House. Yet the new and narrow Republican majority quickly realized that replicating, not reforming, practices established by Wright best protected the GOP agenda. The newly elected Speaker Gingrich declared votes no longer would remain open beyond the customary 15 minutes—as Wright had done with the 1988 budget bill. But in 2003 as the GOP majority was trying to pass the Medicare Modernization Act, a major piece of legislation adding a long-sought prescription drug benefit to Medicare, Republican Majority Leader Tom DeLay held the vote open for nearly three hours until he secured majority support. Future Democratic Majority Leader Steny Hoyer objected, citing Gingrich's earlier pledge.

Democrats reclaimed control of Congress in the 2006 election. They made similar promises about minority rights and amended the rules of the House to prevent holding a vote open after its time had expired. During House consideration of an appropriations bill in 2007 Republicans appeared to win a vote to defeat the bill. Under the guidance of Majority Leader Steny Hoyer, the vote was declared a tie. Voting continued past the time allotted and three Democrats switched their votes, securing passage over Republican objections. Upon claiming the House in the 2010 elections, Republicans again proclaimed an adherence to more bipartisanship, but as with previous pledges, it was short-lived.

Partisan tactics in the Senate changed as well. The freewheeling individualism of the 1970s Senate came to an end after the 1980 election and the Democrats' loss of control of the chamber. Democrats used to take their majority status for granted, so individual Democratic Senators had seen no need to exercise restraint with regard to floor amendments. The GOP electoral gains in 1980 challenged Democratic complacency. As it became clear neither party could count on majority control and as the ideological distance between the parties increased, the pursuit of individual objectives— as opposed to party objectives—became too costly. Prior to 1980, the majority party was more likely to be responsible for most of the amendments proposed on the Senate floor. The majority party virtually stopped offering amendments on the floor after 1980. Floor amending activity declined overall and became distinctly partisan. Increasingly, floor amendments offered by the minority furthered party objectives, not member objectives. Likewise, the majority party practiced restraint in an effort to forward party objectives. Introduction of amendments declined precipitously throughout the 1980s. As recently as the 110th Congress in 2007 and 2008, amending activity fell to the levels of the late 1960s (Lee 2012).

Though the Senate does not provide the party leadership powers of the House, only strong "within party" leadership could explain the discipline that has resulted in majority party Senators toeing the line and minority party Senators pursuing "party amendments" on the floor. Additional signs of a more centralized Senate became evident in other areas. Unique Senate responsibilities such as judicial nominee approval became more partisan, for reasons we explain further in Chapter 8. The success rate of presidential nominations to the U.S. Court of Appeals fell by half between 1956 and 2008 and the length of time required to secure approval in the Senate increased dramatically. As in the House, the president's support gap between members of his party and members of the opposition party grew significantly. The Senate also came to rely on very complex unanimous consent agreements (UCAs) before beginning floor consideration.

Any Senator can raise an objection to, or filibuster, most floor proceedings. The process for obtaining cloture is time-consuming even when the majority has the 60 votes required. Therefore, there is every motivation for party leaders to avoid such objections. Majority and minority party leaders negotiate unanimous consent agreements to ensure consensus on the terms for bill consideration. These UCAs have become increasingly complex and often include details on the amendments allowed and the time allotted for debate—resembling the work of the House Rules Committee. It is now common for UCAs to establish a 60-vote majority threshold for any vote held under the UCA. In a Senate with unified parties, this 60 vote super-majority requirement addresses the reality of united partisan opposition to a bill more than the opposition of a single rogue member.

Disputes over the use of the filibuster came to a head in 2005, as the Republican majority grew increasingly frustrated by Democratic filibusters of President Bush's judicial nominees. Senate Majority Leader Bill Frist circulated a plan to end the practice of filibustering judicial nominees. Though Senate rules call for 60 votes to end debate, changes to Senate rules require 67 votes. The rule makes it nearly impossible for a majority party to secure the votes necessary to reform the filibuster procedure. Frist's solution was to object to the Democrats' filibuster of a judicial nominee because the Constitution calls for a simple up or down vote on judicial nominations. Under Frist's plan, Republicans first would call for a vote on a blocked judicial nomination and if then unable to overcome a Democratic filibuster, Republicans would look to the presiding officer of the Senate—

then Vice President Dick Cheney—to rule on the constitutionality of filibustering judicial nominees. The presiding officer would then declare it unconstitutional. Objections raised by minority Democrats then could be tabled via a simple majority vote (Palmer 2005). Democrats threatened to shut down the Senate in retaliation. Frist's tactic gained the label of "the nuclear option."

Republicans never implemented the nuclear option. After Democrats reclaimed the Senate majority in 2007, they grew increasingly frustrated by Republican filibusters. A coalition of Democratic Senators unsuccessfully lobbied for reforms to the filibuster in early 2009. Yet in late 2011, Democrats used the nuclear option procedure to deny minority Republicans the long-established right to offer motions to suspend the rules of debate allowing for the consideration of additional amendments to a bill even after overcoming a filibuster. Senate Majority Leader Harry Reid argued that motions to suspend the rules effectively served as a "post-filibuster filibuster" forcing countless additional votes (Bolton 2011). Republicans of course objected. Majority Leader Reid endorsed the call for filibuster reform in the summer of 2012. Democrats added two seats to their party's Senate majority in 2012, but remained well shy of the 60 votes needed to end a filibuster. Reid restated his support for reform, but the filibuster survived with only minor changes.

The Senate has come to rely on a once obscure process known as "reconciliation" to enact legislation without the threat of a filibuster. Changes to the congressional budget process enacted in 1974 contained a provision allowing the Senate to consider particular "reconciliation" types of budget bills under rules that limited debate to only 20 hours and limiting the types of amendments offered to the bill. As a result, budget reconciliation measures require only a bare majority to pass. Though originally intended as a means for streamlined consideration of budget matters, reconciliation has become a means by which to enact sweeping policy changes—so long as tax and spending policy is involved in the legislation. Since 1980, Congress has used reconciliation to enact significant tax reform under Presidents Reagan and George W. Bush, to restructure federal welfare policy under President Clinton, and to ensure passage of health care reform under President Obama. The Republican minority objects to Democratic use of reconciliation as an abuse of process. Democrats, when in the minority, level that same accusation against Republicans.

The Broken Branch?

Congressional scholars Thomas Mann and Norm Ornstein view the contemporary Congress as a broken branch of government. The deepening partisan divide, the increased reliance on closed and restrictive rules in the House, the obstructive use of the filibuster in the Senate, and the seeming disregard of the traditions and norms of the two chambers represent a seemingly irreparable breach. The authors contend, "Only a president can alter the political climate in a way sufficient" to mend the problems evident in the contemporary Congress (Mann and Ornstein 2008, 262–263). Readers of our Chapter 6 on the presidency may well be skeptical of that conclusion. Not all share Mann and Ornstein's perception of a broken branch. Barbara Sinclair argues the very elements of dysfunction cited by Ornstein and Mann have empowered the majority in the House and the minority in the Senate to function and to perform the task of legislating during an era of great division (2011, 275–276).

Our evidence supports neither side of this argument. We found no correlation between the increasingly restrictive rules used in the House and the passage of major laws (note the variable's absence from Table 5.1). If Sinclair were correct, a positive correlation would be evident. We also discovered no correlation between cloture motions and the passage of major laws. If Mann and Ornstein were correct, one would have found a negative correlation. Rather than uncovering any impact of increasing ideological polarization and partisanship on the enactment of major laws, our findings simply reveal an institution in which the mechanisms of ideology reinforce one another.

We find both restrictive rules and cloture motions to be highly correlated with our measures of the Democratic Party's electoral strength—southern whites' support for the Democratic Party and share of Democrats in the electorate. This suggests these procedures reflect a response to increased electoral competition. A strong positive association of restrictive rules and cloture motions also exists with the number of associations. Both correlate highly and negatively with another aspect of the polarized Congress—the success of federal Appeals Court nominations. Restrictive rules in the House appear to have no impact on a president's success in Congress, but cloture motions in the Senate impede that success. Notable positive correlations exist between a president's partisan support gap in the House and Senate and both restrictive rules and cloture motions. Though we found no correlation between restrictive rules and cloture motions and the number of major laws passed by Congress, we found a strong positive correlation between both and the total number of pages in the Federal Register. These unorthodox measures thus may enhance lawmaking in general, but not the passage of major laws specifically.

Division and polarization in Congress may not be so bad if those divisions represent cleavages within the American electorate. Recent research, however, found that Members of Congress are out of step with the citizens they represent. Joseph Bafumi and Michael Herron discovered a "distinct lack of congruence between federal legislators and their constituencies." Further, "this lack of congruence is due to the fact that both senators and House members are politically extreme compared to the voters who put them in office" (Bafumi and Herron 2010, 519). With few exceptions, the ideological makeup of Congress does not represent either the median voter or the

Table 5.1 Systemic correlates of congressional polarization

	Turnout mid-term elections	Restrictive rules in the House	Senate cloture motions filed
Public interaction with the system			
Popular discontent	−.72	+.57	+.82
Turnout presidential elections	+.87	−.62	−.58
States with ballot initiatives	−.75	+.75	+.79
Total ballot initiatives in states	−.72	+.79	+.85
System thickening variables			
Total associations	−.71	+.86	+.85
Total pages Federal Register	−.66	+.79	+.80
Legislative and judicial branch personnel	−.71	+.86	+.78
Party coalition variables			
Share of whites any independent	−.74	+.60	+.77
Southern whites support for the Democratic Party	+.69	−.83	−.83
Share of the democratic coalition working class	+.58	−.84	
Share of Democrats in the electorate	+.70	−.82	−.73
Share neutral to parties	−.70		+.59
Congressional polarization variables			
House incumbent security	−.69		
Presidential support party gap in House		+.83	+.76
Presidential support party gap in Senate	−.55	+.79	+.61
Restrictive rules in the house			+.84
Cloture motions filed	−.62	+.84	
Presidential leadership/ capital variables			
Appeals Court nomination success	+.58	−.91	−.89
Duration successful confirmation process (% of a year)		+.73	+.67
Presidential partisan approval gap	−.61	+.79	+.67
Presidential success in Congress	+.60		−.70

Sources: See Appendix.

median partisan voter. When partisan control of Congress shifts from one party to the other—a rather common election outcome in the present era—the partisan make-up of the body shifts significantly and voters in the middle are "leapfrogged" as representation shifts from one ideological extreme to the other (ibid.). The authors noted the ideology of Members of Congress was more reflective of donors than of voters. That finding is consistent with evidence in Chapter 4 comparing the ideological distribution of non-activist voters with their more activist partisan counterparts.

In 2012, Mann and Ornstein examined the dysfunction of the current Congress and concluded, "The Republican party has become the insurgent outlier [. . .] and as such contributes disproportionately to its dysfunction" (Mann and Ornstein 2012, 185). We believe, however, the evidence supports a clear case for joint partisan responsibility. One must look to the years of precedent and practice that have brought Congress to its present state. Practices once considered unprecedented became more common and then simply accepted. In the 1980s, rules-based limitations on debate in the House began as an effort to stifle the Republican minority. Minority party obstruction then became a viable path for delay. Scandals and ethics inquiries gained use in place of electoral politics, whether by minority Republicans against Speaker Jim Wright in 1989 or by minority Democrats to unseat Majority Leader Tom DeLay in 2006. In the Senate, Figure 5.3 clearly reveals that the filibuster has become an ever more frequent tool of the minority since the late 1970s. Both Republican and Democratic minorities frequently have filibustered, and both when in the majority have sought to revoke the minority's filibuster power. We found a strong negative correlation between cloture motions and both presidential legislative success and Appeals Court nomination success. The filibuster has become a reliable and effective tool used by the minority party to thwart the agenda of a president of the rival party.

Mann and Ornstein base much of their verdict against congressional Republicans on the summer 2011 debate over extending the U.S. debt limit in order to avoid a possible credit default and a politically costly downgrade in the nation's credit-worthiness. The authors recount the intense negotiations between President Barack Obama and House Speaker John Boehner as they tried to hammer out a "grand bargain." Boehner was willing to accept tax increases and the President was willing to accept cuts to expensive entitlement programs. The grand bargain collapsed when it became clear that Boehner could not deliver Republican support for a deal that included tax increases (Mann and Ornstein 2012). Overlooked by Mann and Ornstein, however, were statements by Minority Leader Nancy Pelosi and Minority Whip Steny Hoyer that Democrats would not accept any deal that included cuts to entitlement benefits (Beutler 2011). President Obama and Speaker Boehner had been willing to reach a compromise; both a Republican unwillingness to vote for tax increases and a Democratic unwillingness to allow for cuts to entitlement programs torpedoed the possible deal.

Congress instead passed legislation to create a "deficit reduction super-committee" tasked with identifying $1.2 trillion in budget savings over ten years. Any proposal endorsed by a supercommittee majority was guaranteed an up or down vote on the House and the Senate floors. The Democratic and Republican leadership in each chamber selected an equal number of committee members. The failure of the supercommittee to agree on any plan was not surprising. In a Congress where the House is controlled by Republicans and Senate by Democrats, no supercommittee was going to succeed where majority party leadership had failed in designing legislation amenable to opposing partisan majorities in each chamber. In the end, the only true area of bipartisanship in the contemporary Congress is the assignment of blame for its present dysfunction.

Conclusion

Two deeply polarized political parties engaged in a close-fought and bitter struggle for electoral victory and legislative control mark the contemporary Congress. Though the even level of electoral competition has been especially evident in recent years, it first emerged in the late 1970s when Republicans gained a congressional foothold in the South. Increased electoral competition coupled with the advent of divided government gave rise to reforms in the Congress that first empowered individual members to become highly pro-fessional representatives but then gave way to further changes that effectively centralized control around the organizing principle of party. In the House and Senate, members realized that the best way to ensure success of the party agenda and to obstruct the minority party was through greater centralization of power in party leadership. This was more readily achieved in the House, but even in the Senate changes in the minority/majority approach to floor activity and amendments show that centralization around party—if not necessarily party leadership—has occurred.

In today's Congress, lawmakers pursue initiatives important to their constituents, to key interest groups, and to their party in a professional environment of ideologically uniform parties with sharp agenda differences. Washington's professional and partisan legislature often supports a president in the same party as a congressional majority and obstructs an opposition party president. As measured by the number of pages in the Federal Register, the contemporary Congress appears capable of legislating, though not when addressing issues of major concern. Why? The congressional parties diverge sharply on major issues, leading to attempts at legislative domination by partisan majorities and obstruction by partisan minorities.

There are now so many voices at play in policy-making, described fully in Chapter 7, that it has become more difficult to legislate and easier to obstruct. Multiple congressional committees and subcommittees enjoy some degree of jurisdiction over major issues. These committees in turn have established mutually beneficial relationships with interest groups. Multiple committee referrals are quite common as a result. Party leadership uses restrictive rules and post-committee adjustment to ensure buy-in by the multitude of interested voices. Such buy-in requires difficult and finely crafted compromises. In a closely divided and polarized environment, every incentive exists for a minority party to derail or prevent such compromises. The result is often congressional inaction and policy stasis.

The great challenges of the present era will often require congressional action. By acting, Congress frequently defines the scope and powers of the executive bureaucracy—Washington's "permanent government"—and the scope and jurisdiction of the judiciary. Since the 1960s and 1970s, Congress has become increasingly divided by party and unable to perform its duties with decorum and dispatch. Dysfunction within Congress reverberates throughout the entirety of the American political system. Evidence of this reverberation receives attention in the following chapters.

6 The Presidency
Uncertain Leadership

In the post-1965 American political system, presidents have found the exercise of effective leadership a difficult task. To lead well, a president needs support or at least permission from federal courts and Congress, steady allegiance from public opinion and fellow partisans in the electorate, backing from powerful, entrenched interest groups, and accordance with contemporary public opinion about the proper size and scope of government. This is a long list of requirements. If presidents fail to satisfy these requirements, they face the prospect of inadequate political support or, as we define it here, political capital, to back their power assertions. In recent years, presidents' political capital has shrunk while their power assertions have grown, making the president a volatile player in the national political system.

The concept of political capital captures many of the requirements for effective leadership. Paul Light defines several components of political capital: party support of the president in Congress, public approval of the president's conduct of his job, the president's electoral margin, and patronage appointments (Light 1999, 15). Light derived this list from the observations of 126 White House staff members he interviewed (ibid., 14). Light's research reveals that these factors are central to the "players' perspective" in Washington. That is, those "in the game" view these items as crucial for presidential effectiveness. On a practical level, the components of political capital are central to the fate of presidencies. Since 1965, presidents have suffered from a trend of declining levels of political capital, a trend that is at the heart of their frequent leadership problems.[1]

Many scholars have examined particular aspects of presidential political capital, from congressional support (for example, Bond and Fleisher 1992, 2000; Peterson 1993; Mayhew 2005) to job approval (Kernell 1978; Brace and Hinckley 1991; Nicholson Segura and Woods 2002). From these, we know that presidential job approval is influenced by economic performance, tends to drop over time, and that divided government can boost job approval. Also, job approval and control of Congress by fellow partisans raise presidential success in floor votes but do not produce more important legislation than do periods of divided government. These "micro" findings, however, comport with a "macro trend" of declining presidential political capital over time.

Presidential Political Capital: Gathering the Evidence

In the following sections, we chart the trajectory of presidential political capital since 1937—the year Gallup began polling on presidential job approval—using data from a variety of sources. The measures involve three central "governance" elements: presidential job approval, support for the president's party and congressional support for the president. Problems of political capital should appear in public opinion regarding the president and his party, congressional elections, and votes on the House and Senate floor.

Three variables involve the Gallup job approval ratings. One is average annual job approval, measured by the Gallup poll of presidential job approval ratings. The second is the standard deviation of annual job approval for the Gallup presidential job approval polls of that year.[2] A third is net annual job approval, the annual average difference between presidential job approval and disapproval scores each year, which reflects the public polarization around presidential job performance.

Our analysis also presents measures of presidential party identification using Gallup data from 1937 to 2009. These include annual percentage identifying with the president's party and annual standard deviation of the president's party percentage. Also included is presidential net party advantage, which measures the difference between the average percentage identifying with the president's party and the percentage identifying with the opposition party.

Additional measures of political capital concern congressional support for presidents. One such measure is the percentage of fellow partisans holding House and Senate seats from 1937 to 2009. Another measure is voting support as evident in Congressional Quarterly support scores for votes on which the president has announced a position. Examined here are annual scores for each chamber from 1953 to 2008.

Also employed is James Stimson's (2009) annual "public mood" indicator based on thousands of survey questions on national issues from 1952 to 2008 and tabulated on a liberal–conservative continuum. A higher number indicates a more liberal score. Stimson's measure is "a time series of public liberalism/conservatism," resulting in "a continuous time series of citizen preferences for each year" (Wood 2009, 58). Stimson describes the variable as his "best effort at measuring the public's movement regarding support for government programs or movement on the liberal–conservative continuum" (Erickson, MacKuen, and Stimson 2002, 193).

One "Stimson" variable employed here is the annual public mood score itself, ranging from 0 to 100 with a higher number indicating a more liberal issue position, tabulated from 1952 to 2008. Democratic presidents are coded in this score as liberals and Republican presidents as conservatives. A second is annual mood shift, the difference in annual mean public mood score from that of the previous year, with a negative value indicating a shift away from the president's ideological position and a positive score a movement toward a president's ideological position.

Trends across Time

Given that political capital variables interrelate, do they evidence decline and increasing volatility across time? We explore the evidence across eras, presidencies, and presidential terms. Eras are divided into three: 1937–1965, 1966–1992, and 1993–2008. The results for these eras are not the product of arbitrary temporal definitions. When classified in different fashion, with cut points of 1968–1969/1988–1989 or 1968–1969/1992–1993, results for the temporal patterns are identical.

Why these temporal boundaries? As Chapter 2 demonstrated, they occur at moments of important transformation in America's politics. The 1960s brought several major systemic changes, we noted in Chapter 1. The year 1966 signaled the beginning of a big decline in public confidence in government and the fragmenting of the New Deal coalition (Nye, Zelikow, and King 1997). John Aldrich and Richard Niemi discovered a "new party system" arising around this time in which

> elections center on the individual candidates and the "party in the electorate" has greatly deteriorated as an unnecessary and often irrelevant loyalty. The critical era of the 1960s was, therefore, critical for the party as well as the polity as a whole.
>
> (1996, 101)

Candidate-centered elections contributed to the rise of divided government and to less partisan verdicts by the public and both trends probably contributed to lower congressional voting support for presidents during this period.

The mid-1960s also witnessed a realignment of party coalitions, as we noted in Chapter 4, notably a departure of southern white voters from the Democratic electoral coalition (Petrocik 1987). The issues prompting this exit were both racial and economic (Carmines and Stimson 1989; Lublin 2004). By the late 1980s, political scientist Harold Stanley declared, "the decline in Democratic identification, the surge of independence in the 1960s, and the more recent increase in Republican identification have ended the previous Democratic domination" of the region (1988, 86). The trend of southern whites toward the GOP was gradual, culminating in a breakthrough in the 1994 elections, when majorities of them cast their votes for Republican candidates and helped elect the first GOP Congress in 40 years (Campbell 2006). This regional realignment abolished a major component of the New Deal electoral coalition that had kept political capital strong and stable for pre-1965 Democratic presidents. Since the 1960s, presidents of neither party could count on a persistent majority party coalition to bolster their political capital.

The early 1990s also coincided with the rise of polarization between self-identified Democrats and Republicans in the electorate and more competitive battles for partisan control of Congress (Abramowitz and Saunders 1998). Chapter 5 noted how this period involved higher levels of congressional partisan unity and either divided government or congressional rule by one party (Poole and Rosenthal 2007). It also produced more important legislation annually than previous periods, a phenomenon discussed later in this chapter (Mayhew 2009). The legislative productivity may help to explain why presidential political capital recovered a bit after 1993 but not to near pre-1966 levels.

Evidence across Eras

A pattern of declining political capital appears for presidents across several measures in the post-1965 era in Table 6.1. In the evidence, the 1960s are a turning point producing a lasting decline in presidents' political capital. The 1966–1992 period witnessed a marked drop-off in the level and rise in volatility for average and net job approval by the public. After 1992, average and net job approval levels recovered a bit but remained much lower and more volatile than they were prior to 1966. Similar patterns appear regarding presidential party identification. It was much higher before 1966—41.8 percent compared to 32 and 33.1 percent in the latter two periods—in large part due to the persistence of the New Deal coalition under Franklin Delano Roosevelt (FDR) and Harry Truman. It dropped to lower but less volatile levels after 1966. In this case, lower volatility augured poorly for a president's political capital when it accompanied shrunken levels of allegiance to a president's party.

The congressional measures also show substantial drops in political capital after 1965. The percentage of Representatives and Senators of the president's party dropped considerably, from 55 in the House and 56.4 in the Senate before 1966 to 46.5 and 50.4 from 1966 to 1992, and 50.7 and 49.4 from 1993 to 2008. The proportion of Senators of the president's party reached its lowest level in the most recent era. The most recent era also had lower volatility in congressional membership, reflecting the stable and closely competitive electoral balance between the congressional parties since 1993. Fewer fellow partisans and lower membership volatility are not good news for a president's political capital. The membership numbers may be stable, but the partisan balance does not consistently facilitate effective presidential leadership.

Congressional support for the president's position also dropped considerably after 1965 and stayed low. House support fell on average to a level 17 percentage points below 1952–1965 levels, from 76.4 to 59.6 and 59.4 in the later eras. Senate support dropped by about 7 percentage points, from 78.1 to 70.7 and 71.5. House support volatility skyrocketed after 1993, from standard deviations of about 12 percent in the previous two eras to 25.8 percent. Senate volatility increased somewhat in this latest era, a standard deviation of 13.8 percent compared to 11.1and 10.9 percent in the earlier eras.

Table 6.1 Presidential political capital indicator averages by era

	Avg. public approval (std. dev.)	Net public approval (std. dev.)	Public mood (std. dev.)	Mood shift	Pres. party ID (std. dev.) %	House membership (std. dev.) %	Senate membership (std. dev.) %	House support (std. dev.) %	Senate support (std. dev.) %
1937–1965	61.5 (4.3)	34.9 (8.0)	60.1 (6.0)	−1.1	41.8 (3.0)	55.0 (9.9)	56.4 (11.3)	76.4 (12.6)	78.1 (11.1)
1966–1992	50.8 (5.2)	14.5 (10.3)	58.5 (4.3)	−.29	32.0 (2.1)	46.5 (10.8)	50.4 (8.7)	59.6 (12.1)	70.7 (10.9)
1993–2008	53.9 (4.8)	13.9 (9.2)	57.6 (2.0)	−.80	33.1 (2.9)	50.7 (4.2)	49.9 (4.3)	59.4 (25.8)	71.5 (13.8)

Sources: See variable coding addendum.

Public mood over time demonstrated a distinctive pattern. In absolute terms, it moved a bit in a conservative direction across eras and demonstrated lower volatility. Across eras, as Dan Wood (2009) discovered, public mood tended to move against presidents. The biggest mood shifts against presidential issue stances, however, occur in the early and late periods, shifting -1.1 before 1966, -.29 from 1967 to 1992 and -.80 after 1993. Persistently negative public mood trends bode ill for presidential political capital. It is difficult to maintain public job approval, public support for one's party, and congressional support when the public issue mood is moving consistently against a president.

Presidents from 1952 to 1965 faced this problem as well, but were buoyed by greater congressional support and higher job approval than their successors. In sum, 1965–1966 seems a turning point in presidential political capital. After that, volatility in job approval and congressional voting support increased, and presidential backing decreased in public job approval, in terms of partisan identification, and in congressional membership and voting support. The national political system altered in ways inimical to effective presidential leadership.

Evidence across Presidencies

Similar trends appear in political capital when we examine them across presidencies since 1937 in Table 6.2. Average public approval of presidents dropped considerably after John F. Kennedy (JFK). Only George H. W. Bush averaged over 60 percent since then but highly volatile public opinion denied him reelection. Approval volatility varied greatly across presidencies, with the "war presidents" Truman, Lyndon Baines Johnson (LBJ), and the Bushes encountering greater volatility as their popularity dropped greatly because of military conflicts or their aftermaths. Richard Nixon's impeachment troubles also produced high volatility in job approval across his presidency. Net approval again showed its highest levels before 1965, with FDR, Dwight Eisenhower and JFK registering the most elevated levels. Since 1965, average approval levels have dropped, and volatility in net approval has grown. Net approval before 1966 stood at +34.9, but tumbled to +14.9 from 1966 to 1992 and +13.9 after 1993.

The large advantage in presidential party identification for Democratic presidents from the 1930s to the 1970s—due to the persistence of the New Deal coalition—vanishes after 1980. Presidential party identification stood at 43.8 percent for FDR, 42.2 percent for Truman, 49.9 percent for JFK, 47.7 percent for LBJ, and 46.2 percent for Jimmy Carter, with net party identification advantages ranging from +7.2 percent for FDR to +24.1 percent for Carter. Since then, net party identification has turned negative for all GOP presidents and only modestly positive for Bill Clinton (+5.7). Presidents of both parties since 1980 also encountered relatively low levels of presidential party identification, ranging from +29.4 to +34.7 percent. That ranks considerably below the presidential party identification of the

Table 6.2 Presidential political capital averages and standard deviations by presidencies

	Average public approval (std. dev.)	Net public approval (std. dev.)	Public mood (std. dev.)	Mood shift	Pres. party ID (std. dev.) %	Net pres. party ID %	House membership (std. dev.) %	Senate membership (std. dev.) %	House support (std. dev.) %	Senate support (std. dev.) %
FDR	62.4 (9.5)	30.9 (18.5)			43.8 (3.6)	7.5	62.3 (9.8)	66.8 (6.9)		
Truman	42.0 (15.0)	-1.2 (29.8)			42.2 (4.4)	8.3	53.3 (6.8)	51.0 (5.1)		
Eisenhower	64.9 (6.9)	43.5 (12.6)	59.6 (5.1)	-1.9	32.4 (3.6)	-14.0	44.8 (6.1)	44.0 (6.2)	70.0 (11.8)	73.6 (12.1)
Kennedy	70.8 (7.1)	54.2 (14.2)	66.5 (1.4)	0.3	49.9 (2.7)	22.1	60.1 (.7)	65.0 (1.7)	83.7 (1.1)	85.3 (4.5)
Johnson	56.1 (13.3)	25.6 (27.0)	64.4 (1.2)	-.1	47.7 (4.8)	21.1	61.8 (5.6)	66.2 (2.0)	80.1 (5.4)	67.9 (9.5)
Nixon	48.0 (13.8)	10.2 (29.5)	60.2 (1.7)	.9	25.9 (2.6)	-8.6	43.0 (1.4)	43.3 (1.4)	72.7 (13.7)	63.0 (10.6)

Ford	46.5 (7.1)	9.9 (15.7)	56.0 (0.9)	1.6	22.2 (1.4)	−22.9	33.1 (0)	38.0 (0)	51.0 (8.1)	64.2 (6.8)
Carter	46.6 (12.2)	8.3 (26.0)	52.3 (1.3)	−1.1	46.2 (2.2)	24.1	65.4 (3.5)	53.5 (0.6)	73.3 (3.1)	78.9 (5.2)
Reagan	52.1 (7.7)	14.6 (15.7)	56.8 (3.3)	−1.3	29.4 (3.4)	−8.8	41.2 (2.3)	51.3 (3.9)	46.5 (13.8)	77.1 (11.6)
Bush I	61.9 (14.4)	34.3 (28.8)	62.2 (0.3)	−0.1	31.5 (3.1)	−2.8	39.2 (0.9)	44.5 (0.6)	40.7 (7.6)	64.4 (8.4)
Clinton	55.9 (7.8)	18.7 (13.6)	56.7 (1.4)	−0.6	34.7 (3.3)	5.7	50.6 (5.4)	48.5 (5.3)	51.8 (17.9)	65.4 (16.0)
Bush II	53.7 (14.7)	12.2 (29.9)	58.5 (2.3)	−0.5	31.7 (3.7)	−1.2	50.8 (2.9)	51.3 (2.4)	67.0 (27.2)	77.6 (8.8)

Sources: See variable coding addendum. Evidence Across Presidential Terms.

pre-1966 Democratic presidents, which stood in the mid to upper +40 percent level.

Congressionally, the average number of seats held by the president's party declined over time, but trends were more volatile earlier when strong party identification and lower incumbent security in congressional elections produced greater partisan waves and thus more turnover. We also discovered a statistically significant linear relationship of declining House and Senate seats for the president's party from 1937 to 2008. House and Senate voting support reached its apex in the LBJ presidency, but recent presidents have encountered the less favorable condition of lower and more volatile support.

Examined by presidential terms, the variables further reveal the problems of political capital for presidents in recent decades.[3] Average public approval is lower for post-1965 presidents. The decay of presidential political capital is particularly evident in the low scores of most second-term presidents' measures of party identification and net party identification. Only Clinton since 1937 has achieved both a higher average and a higher net popular job approval score in his second term. Only Reagan during that time presided over an increase in his party's identification with the public during his second term. House and Senate voting support also proved consistently lower for presidents in their second terms. When confronted with a Congress controlled by the opposing party, presidential success on floor votes is understandably lower, as was the case for Republicans Eisenhower, Nixon, Gerald Ford, Reagan, the first Bush, and Democrat Clinton.

Public mood also shifts across presidential terms. Several presidents experienced shifts in the public mood in their ideological direction despite suffering lower job approval, declining party identification for their party, or falling congressional membership or support. The public mood swung slightly in the president's ideological direction under JFK (+0.3), during LBJ's second term (+0.3), during Nixon's two terms (+0.8 and +1.3), and under Ford (+1.6). More common, however, was movement away from the president's ideology. The positive ideological moves during the Johnson and Clinton presidencies were eclipsed by greater countermoves. The move against liberalism during LBJ's first term (-2.6) far exceeded the countermove during his second term (+0.3). Clinton's presidency featured a net negative shift in the public mood (-1.2) despite his second term improvement.

Trends in the National Political System

A broader perspective on presidents' political capital appears in its relationship to several systemic indicators. Our evidence includes two central measures of White House political capital: annual average presidential job approval, and annual presidential support in congressional floor votes. Since 1937, they evidence a slight positive correlation (+.15). In contrast, the partisan gap in public job approval varies inversely with the two political capital measures

(-.20 with average public job approval and -.47 with success in Congress), indicating that partisan polarization among the public is inimical to the health levels of political capital for presidents. As political party membership has sorted more neatly along ideological lines in recent years, presidential political clout has suffered.

The political capital measures have very similar patterns of association with several important systemic variables, as depicted in Table 6.3. Popular discontent correlates with lower public job approval and congressional success. As the national political system has thickened with more interest group associations and regulations, as proxied by the number of pages in the Federal Register, presidential political capital has shrunk. The rise of a "no majority party" era is also associated with lower political capital for presidents. Several measures of Democratic Party identification—among whites, the working class and the electorate as a whole—correlate positively with the political capital variables. As Democratic identification has declined, so has the political capital of presidents over time. Democratic presidents once governed with large amounts of political capital, but with the collapse of the New Deal coalition, their political capital has withered. So it is no surprise

Table 6.3 Systemic correlates of presidential leadership

	Average Presidential approval rating	*Presidential partisan approval gap*	*Presidential success in Congress*
Popular discontent	−.43	+.43	−.58
System thickening variables			
Number of associations	−.54	+.72	−.61
Total Federal Register pages	−.32	+.49	−.53
Party coalition variables			
Percentage Democrats	+.35	−.84	+.59
Percentage Democrats among working class	+.30	−.59	+.13
Percentage Democrats among southern whites	+.14	−.67	+.72
Percentage independent among whites	−.41	+.44	−.69
Congressional polarization variables			
Presidential party support gap in House	−.26	+.54	−.42
Presidential party support gap in Senate	.00	+.77	−.45
Restrictive floor rules in House	−.04	+.79	−.44
Senate cloture motions filed	−.37	+.67	−.70

Sources: See Appendix.

that the rise of independent identification among whites correlates negatively with both measures of presidential political capital. Many measures of partisan polarization in Congress also correlate negatively with the political capital variables, particularly with presidential success in Congress. As partisan divisions in floor voting have grown and the use of restrictive rules for House floor debate and cloture motions to fight numerous Senate filibusters has become more frequent, presidential success in Congress has declined.

The growing gap in job approval among partisans in the public, negatively associated with public job approval and congressional success, correlates with systemic variables in a pattern opposite of the two political capital measures in Table 6.3. The approval gap correlates positively with popular discontent, rising numbers of interest groups and increasing regulations. It correlates negatively with Democratic strength in the electorate but positively with growing numbers of independent whites. A growing partisan gap in the public accompanies partisan polarization in Congress as well. Again this illustrates how partisan polarization is inimical to presidential political capital. As discussed in Chapter 4, the public appears to be no more polarized today than in the 1970s. However, as membership in the two parties more neatly sorted between liberals and conservatives, the parties did polarize. This fact, coupled with a greater partisan mix among the voting electorate, certainly contributed to the growing partisan approval gap.

A transformed party system and thicker system of Washington governance have reconfigured the landscape of presidential governance. Presidents have found that after the "no party" realignment of the 1960s, their ability to maintain formidable levels of political capital had vanished. Congressional support shrank, partisan polarization in Congress and in the public regarding the president's program increased. Greater partisan divisions effectively put a lower ceiling on presidential job approval and congressional success. Washington itself, meanwhile, became a more complicated arena for presidential leadership due to growing number of interest groups and federal regulation. We explore many of these challenges in Chapter 7. The new American political system produced lowered levels of political capital for presidents and added to the frustrations of executive leadership.

Implications of the Evidence

This chapter's evidence consistently depicts a decline in presidential political capital after 1965. Since that time, presidents have had lower job approval, fewer fellow partisans and less voting support in Congress, less approval of their party, and have usually encountered an increasingly adverse public policy mood as they governed.

Specifically, average job approval dropped. Net job approval plummeted, reflecting greater polarization about presidential performance. The proportion of fellow partisans in the public dropped and became less volatile. Congressional voting support became lower and varied more. The number of fellow partisans in the House and Senate fell and became less volatile. Public issue mood usually moved against presidents as they governed. All of these measures, with the exception of public mood, correlate positively with each other, suggesting they are part of a systemic phenomenon.

The decline in political capital has produced great difficulties for presidential leadership in recent decades. It is difficult to claim warrants for leadership in an era when job approval, congressional support, and partisan affiliation provide less backing for a president than in times past. Because of the uncertainties of political capital, recent presidents have adopted a governing style that is personalized, preemptive, and, at times, isolated. Given the entrenched autonomy of other elite actors and the impermanence of public opinion, presidents have had to "sell themselves" in order to sell their governance. Samuel Kernell (1997) first highlighted the presidential proclivity to "go public" in the 1980s as a response to these conditions. Through leveraging public support, presidents have at times been able to overcome institutional resistance to their policy agendas. Brandice Canes-Wrone (2001) discovered that presidents tend to help themselves with public opinion by highlighting issues the public supports and that boost their congressional success—an effective strategy when political capital is questionable.

Despite shrinking political capital, presidents at times have effectively pursued such strategies, particularly since 1995. Bill Clinton's centrist "triangulation" and George W. Bush's careful issue selection early in his presidency allowed them to secure important policy changes—in Clinton's case, welfare reform and budget balance, in Bush's case tax cuts and education reform—that at the time received popular approval. This may explain the slight recovery in some presidential political capital measures since 1993. Clinton accomplished much with a GOP Congress, and Bush's first term included strong support from a Congress ruled by friendly Republican majorities. David Mayhew finds that from 1995 to 2004, both "highly important" and "important" policy changes were passed by Congress into law at higher rates than during the 1947–1994 period.[4]

A trend of declining political capital thus does not preclude significant policy change, but a record of major policy accomplishment has not reversed the decline in presidential political capital in recent years, either. Short-term legislative strategies can win policy success for a president but do not serve as an antidote to declining political capital over time, as the difficult final years of both the Bill Clinton and George W. Bush presidencies demonstrate.

Political scientists have long identified economic performance as an important influence on job approval (Kernell 1978; Brace and Hinckley 1991; Nicholson, Segura, and Woods 2002). The economic difficulties of the 1970s and early 1990s pushed job approval down, but the evidence here indicates lower approval after 1965 regardless of the economic performance of presidencies (Frendreis and Tatalovitch 2009). Isolation can result when both economic and political circumstances become adverse, as fellow partisans object to presidential leadership and Congress offers stiff resistance, once a president becomes unpopular. The evidence here finds this a more frequent occurrence for presidents since 1965.

The frustrations of popular and Washington leadership encourage presidents to exercise their formal powers to get results. As Sidney Milkis and Jesse Rhodes put it, this leads a president "to impose his will through the bureaucracy in pursuit of politics that substantially outstrip congressional and public support" (2009, 3). Presidential appointments remain a resource for such assertions (see note 2). As we explore in Chapter 7, recent presidents —including President Obama—have also employed executive orders as a way around important policy difficulties. The president issues executive orders to guide the executive branch of the government. They have the force of law, but can be overturned by Congress, a future president or by the federal courts. Though the total number of executive orders per year has not increased greatly since the 1940s, the number of important executive orders has risen since 1960 and particularly since 1985 (Howell 2003, 81–82) as has, over the past 20 years, presidential use of signing statements, issued at the moment a president signs legislation, to shape policy (Congressional Research Service 2007; Savage 2009).

The frustrations of maintaining political capital thus encourage presidents to rely on their formal powers. Nixon attempted this when surrounded by Democrats in Washington, as did Clinton when surrounded by Republicans. Neither attempt ultimately did their parties any good. Nixon's efforts led to constitutional violations. For both Nixon and Clinton, the use of formal powers when political authority was deficient led to charges of illegitimacy and impeachment proceedings.

Because of the "presidential leadership problem," the Congress and bureaucracy are less workable for presidents. Mandates and perceptions are now evanescent, much less enforceable. Maintaining leadership is hard and frustrating work, and in seeking to maintain it, presidents encounter widespread constraints.

While attempting to manage the executive branch, presidents encounter many obstacles. The "thickening" of the federal government since 1960, in Stephen Skowronek's phrase, impedes effective presidential leadership. Permanent Washington—comprised of dozens of "issue networks" of bureaucrats, congressional committees and interest groups clustered around particular policies—is an impediment to presidential leadership in ways that can sap a president's political capital. The proliferation of issue networks accompanied the increase in federal regulation writing, expansion of interest groups and general growth in federal spending since 1960—important structural changes again originating from 1960 to 1980. The negative correlation of presidential political capital variables with the number of Washington associations and executive branch regulations in Table 6.3 illustrate the problems of governmental thickening. Following the rise of divided government in 1969, Congress expanded its ability to influence the bureaucracy, policy, and interest groups and attempted to curtail presidential influence. As discussed in Chapter 7, the size of the executive bureaucracy peaked in 1969 and has since fallen. Meanwhile, the number of congressional staff, interest groups, and pages of regulations has grown dramatically.

One consequence of growing executive branch complexity since 1960 is bureaucratic fragmentation that saps the management ability of the White House. For example, 96 agencies are involved with issues of nuclear proliferation and ten different departments and agencies administer more than 100 human services programs (Edwards and Wayne 2006, 316). Bureaucrats can impede presidential management through adherence to "standard operating procedures" that can stifle White House-sponsored management innovations. Further, Congress "has become less and less willing to give the president discretion of any kind over the executive establishment" (Light 1995, 115). This is a reflection of institutional power struggles as well as an artifact of an era of divided government. Presidential scholar Peri Arnold notes: "The plain fact is that no modern president has fully managed the executive branch . . . [The task] places impossible obligations on presidents" (1998, 361–362).

Yet the modern presidency grants an incumbent several formal powers over executive branch administration, foreign, and national security policy. And if persuasion doesn't work with bureaucrats and Congress because political capital is meager, why not just assert power? Power exertion via unilateral decisions, signing statements and executive orders is tempting for presidents in such circumstances. Such exertions, however, often receive much media attention due to the conflict they create—and conflict can be politically costly to presidents. The risk is that by using such powers, a president effectively can further erode his political capital. That is the political power trap.

Richard Nixon's presidency—with its constitutional violations that ended his presidency—is the signal example of this, but one can find evidence of the political capital problem and power trap among other recent presidencies. Jimmy Carter took his political capital for granted, ignoring the maintenance of its elite and mass aspects, and paid the price. Ronald Reagan gradually relied more on executive power as his political capital declined, leading to the Iran–Contra imbroglio. George H. W. Bush exerted war powers but never found a stable basis of political capital. Bill Clinton usually suffered a political capital shortage and found his use of powers under steady political attack. George W. Bush's political capital was weakened in the aftermath of the federal response to Hurricane Katrina in 2005 and his use of war powers destroyed what political capital remained by the end of his second term.

Presidential efforts to expand the office's unilateral powers have steadily grown in recent decades. As William Howell noted, regarding these efforts, "almost all the trend lines point upward" (2005, 417). A recent manifestation of increasing power claims is the theory of the unitary executive introduced during the Reagan presidency and repeatedly asserted by George W. Bush. Exponents Steve Calabresi and John Yoo argue the Constitution "gives presidents the power to control their subordinates by vesting all of the executive power in one, and only one, person: the president of the United States" (2008, 4). Thus, Congress's power to interfere with executive branch decisions is quite limited, and the president has total control of all executive agencies within limits set by Congress.

Several legal and presidential scholars have argued this theory gives too much rein to unilateral presidential action in a way that threatens the constitutional separation of powers and individual liberty (for example, Rudalevige 2006; Matheson 2009; Fisher 2010). Accompanying the unitary executive theory in the second Bush administration was an aggressive use of signing statements, presidential memoranda, and executive orders. Ambitious claims of unilateral presidential power have ominous implications: "The assertion by the executive that it alone has the authority to interpret the law and that it will enforce the law at its own discretion threatens the constitutional balance set up by the Constitution" (Pfiffner 2008, 227).

Barack Obama and the Power Trap

It is in the context of such controversies that Barack Obama served as president and continued to use unilateral tools when they proved convenient. Though he publicly disavowed the theory of the unitary executive, like his recent predecessors, he made unilateral policy via executive order, presidential memoranda, and signing statements (Schier 2011). Upon taking office in 2009, Obama's executive orders reversed his predecessor's policies on U.S. government support for international family planning organizations, union organizing, and terrorist interrogation techniques. Another executive order secured passage of his landmark health care reform in early 2010. The order, banning the use of federal funds for abortion, secured the vital support of a group of antiabortion House Democrats. Obama employed presidential memoranda to order his Energy Secretary to formulate higher fuel efficiency standards for automobiles and energy efficiency standards for appliances (ibid.). Several of these actions receive more attention in Chapter 7.

In 2012, President Obama relied on executive discretion and legal ambiguity to allow home owners to more easily refinance federally backed mortgages, to help veterans find employment, and to make it easier for college graduates to consolidate federal student loan debt and place caps on federal student loan payments (Savage 2012). President Obama even used an executive order to authorize the Department of Education to grant states waivers from the requirements of the No Child Left Behind Act—though the enacting legislation makes no accommodation for such waivers. However, Congress' failure to reauthorize the Act, owing to partisan politics, placed the program in a state of administrative limbo. That is hardly an unusual scenario for contemporary policy. President Obama also sought to expand his powers by appointing "czars" to carry out special tasks for the president. We explore the "czar" phenomenon more closely in Chapter 7.

In 2009, two of Obama's signing statements drew strong protests from a Congress dominated by fellow Democrats. In the statements, the president indicated he would not enforce certain provisions of the law with which he disagreed (Associated Press 2009; Weisman 2009). This stance echoed the approach of his predecessor, George W. Bush (Schier 2008). The ensuing uproar caused the administration to declare it would no longer issue such policy declarations in signing statements but would instead quietly disregard enforcement of laws it found unconstitutional (Savage 2010). In May 2011, Obama ignored the requirements of the War Powers Resolution regarding his military incursion into Libya. The use of force occurred without prior consultation of Congress as required by the resolution. The administration also ignored the resolution's provision that Congress approve the use of the military within 60 days of their initial engagement in conflict until after the deadline had passed (Ackerman and Hathaway 2011).

Obama initially enjoyed strong public approval but his job approval gradually sank, in part because of continuing slow economic growth and high unemployment. His impressive successes with Congress in 2009 and 2010 also accompanied a shift in the public mood against him, evident in the rise of the Tea Party movement and the large GOP gains in the 2010 elections. During 2009, James Stimson (2011) calculated the public mood shifted -.88 against Obama's policies, a dramatic change. In comparison, the public's notable move against Obama's policy position was greater than that registered during the JFK, LBJ, and the first Bush presidencies. It also exceeded mood shifts during Clinton's second term and during either of the second Bush's two terms.

By mid-2011, Obama's job approval had slipped well below its initial levels, and Congress was proving increasingly intransigent. In the face of declining public support and rising congressional opposition, Obama, like his predecessors when faced with similar circumstances, continued to resort to the energetic use of executive power. Declining political capital and accompanying assertions of executive power—we have seen this movie before. Like many recent presidents, Obama responded to Senate obstruction of appointees by making recess appointments. Article II of the Constitution empowers presidents to fill executive department vacancies that occur while the Senate is in recess. Such appointments are temporary and expire at the conclusion of the next congressional session. In lieu of recesses, the Senate has met in short "pro forma" sessions in recent years during extended breaks. The practice was begun under Democrats in the waning years of the George W. Bush administration and Republicans have continued the practice. President Obama caused a bit of controversy in 2012 when he refused to acknowledge the pro forma sessions and made several appointments during relatively short breaks. The National Federation of Independent Business, a trade association, and a group of Republican members of Congress filed suit in federal court challenging the legality of the recess appointments (Agence France-Presse, 2012).

Conclusion

Obama, like all post-1965 presidents, faced a political capital problem and a power trap. Only by solving the former is a president likely to avoid the latter. Presidents in recent years have been unable to prevent their authority—evident in their political capital—from eroding. When it did, their power assertions often got them into further political trouble. None of Obama's post-1965 predecessors solved the political capital problem. It is the central political challenge confronted by modern presidents.

The post-1965 political system features a party system that includes no majority party. This has burdened presidents with lower public and congressional support that limits their leadership ability. Partisan polarization, a consequence of the development of two highly ideological minority parties in recent decades, impedes presidents' attempts to strike bipartisan deals in furtherance of their agenda. A thicker Washington political system, featuring issue networks accompanied by growth in interest groups and federal regulations, further complicates presidential leadership. As a consequence, politically risky and controversial assertions of unilateral presidential power are recurrent features of the new American political system. The resultant conflicts from presidential power assertions often garner media attention and arouse resistance in "thick" Washington. This power trap is a core feature of post-1965 politics and governance, born of the political weakness of recent incumbents. Barack Obama's narrow 2012 reelection victory, coupled with the reelection of a Republican majority House and Democratic majority Senate, hardly signals a grand resurgence of his political capital.

7 Public Policy and the Bureaucracy
Delegated Authority and Divided Priorities

According to Elaine Kamarck, a public policy lecturer at Harvard's John F. Kennedy School of Government, "the policymaking process goes through two major stages" first, deciding what to do and then, deciding how to do it" (Kamarck 2007, 15). In traditional teaching of policymaking, students learn a policy process model that proceeds through multiple stages—agenda setting—policy formulation—policy legitimation—policy implementation—policy evaluation—policy change (Kraft and Furlong 2007). Agenda setting, policy formulation and legitimation may best be understood as the deciding "what to do" stage. They receive attention in the following section on policymaking. Policy implementation, evaluation and change represent the second phase and are addressed in a later section about the bureaucracy—the collection of folks who often decide "how to do it."

The initial section of this chapter addresses the issue of "what to do," that is to say, policymaking. Since the late 1960s, the challenges of polarization, partisanship, interest group participation, the proliferation of policy experts, and frequent divided government have produced significant barriers to sound policy decisions. The solutions adopted by elected officials to overcome those barriers, however, may actually reduce public trust more than either the policies ultimately adopted or the impacts those policies have. As we show, there is a strong and negative correlation between the issuance of ever more federal regulations (as measured by pages in the Federal Register) and popular discontent. A relationship that suggests more is not always better. The Patient Protection and Affordable Care Act, the comprehensive health care reform adopted by Congress and signed into law by President Obama in the Spring of 2010 serves as an apt example.

Later, we address "how to do it," the process of implementing policy once it has been enacted into law. The federal bureaucracy enjoys a tremendous amount of power with regard to the interpretation and implementation of policy. Though Congress could minimize bureaucratic discretion via the enactment of highly detailed laws, its tendency is to pass laws that outline goals and objectives, but delegate responsibility for specifying how to meet those goals to the implementing agency. Since the late 1960s, the average length of each piece of legislation has increased, reflecting both the complexities of contemporary problems and the multitude of voices involved in the process (Baumgartner et al. 2009). Polarization, partisanship, interest group participation, and frequent divided government have introduced significant obstructions to implementation as well, making the bureaucracy a frequent partisan battleground and the subject of much public disdain. Because much of the Patient Protection and Affordable Care Act has yet to be implemented, we rely on other examples to demonstrate the challenges of American bureaucracy.

Scholars once described the close and interdependent policy relationships that existed between federal agencies, congressional committees with oversight responsibility, and the regulated industry as an *iron triangle*—a seemingly impenetrable subgovernment managed by the mutual self-interest and interdependence of the participants involved. In recent years the advent of more interest groups, of a more professionalized congressional membership, and of increased media scrutiny has produced an expanded number of players. A multitude of players forms a broader issue network or "policy community" in which additional participants—including the press and public interest groups—have increasingly infiltrated the old iron triangles (Rourke 1991; Baumgartner and Jones 2009). Multiple, porous issue networks place policy-making and the federal bureaucracy in the midst of heated political battles.

A Confidence Game

The current era's high levels of party competition and tenuous partisan control of Congress and the presidency have important impacts on political elites. Parties must motivate their faithful followers and convince unaffiliated voters to support their cause. They can do this by undermining support for and confidence in the opposing party's policies and competency. Benjamin Ginsberg and Martin Shefter document Republican efforts to undercut confidence in the American welfare state and Democratic efforts to weaken confidence in American national security policy—the areas of political and policy entrenchment for each targeted party (Ginsberg and Shefter 2002).

Recent years provide many examples of such partisan assaults. Though efforts at undermining confidence in the other party may offer short-term political gain, they also erode public confidence in government. The Democrats criticized President George W. Bush's handling of the War in Iraq, called for a 9/11 Commission to study breakdowns in America's intelligence and security apparatus, and inquired into the government's response to Hurricane Katrina in 2005. More recently, Republican criticisms of President Obama's handling of the Deepwater Horizon explosion and subsequent spewing of oil into the Gulf of Mexico, and challenges to the constitutionality of the Patient Protection and Affordable Care Act have chipped away at confidence in government, particularly bureaucratic capability. Solutions to big problems, such as budget deficits, often seem too risky for either side to pursue in this "confidence game." The recently enacted health reform law represented only a limited change to American health policy because it relied mostly on private insurance and the expansion of existing public programs. Democrats, though in control of the Congress and the White House, narrowed what they could propose, owing to a pervasive lack of trust in government.

Alongside this "confidence game" is a growing use of bureaucratic regulation to address policy problems. The number of pages in the Federal Register annually continues to expand. Policy complexity is the fruit of professionalism. As shown in Figure 7.1, the mid-1960s witnessed significant growth in the number of pages printed annually in the Federal Register as well as increases in the total number of associations (home to a new class of policy professionals) and the congressional/judicial workforce (mostly congressional). Professional lobbyists present detailed briefs in support of regulation, professional congressional staffs oversee bureaucratic regulatory activity, congressional policy experts in the Congressional Research Office offer analyses, and bureaucrats create, as a professional duty, rules that are ever more complex.

In the mid-1960s, Congress became less accepting of broad executive authority over the bureaucracy. The rise of divided government after the election of 1968 accelerated the level of congressional intolerance. As shown in Figure 7.1, 1968/69 was the high watermark of executive branch civilian employment—the bureaucracy—followed by two decades of stasis and decline. The national bureaucracy stopped growing, and Congress denied presidents the authority to reorganize the executive branch, even as the growth of other elements of professional government accelerated between 1968 and 1980. An ever "thicker" executive branch resulted.

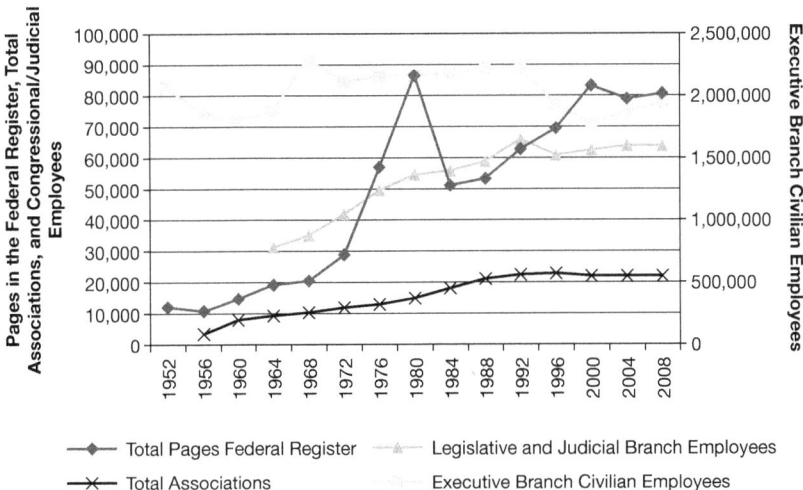

Figure 7.1 Growth of the federal bureaucracy

Comprehensive reorganization becomes impossible given the entrenched interests motivated by a complex status quo. With this thickening came more opportunities to intervene and attempt to influence and even undercut the process of implementation. One result is more public distrust, as majorities of the public now see the federal government as too big, too wasteful, and too disconnected from the concerns of voters.

Making Policy in a Hyper-Partisan Era

Tremendous competition exists for a spot on the decision-making agenda. Getting an issue on the agenda—or successfully keeping it from the agenda— is a significant achievement. Agenda influence and policy formulation involve multiple actors discussed in prior chapters. Candidates, presidents, Members of Congress, party operatives, interest groups, and even individual voters try to influence the decision-making agenda and the formulation of policy. Prior to the interest group explosion of the 1960s, policymaking was often a much more closed affair consisting of a powerful congressional committee or committee chair, a single (or a select few) industry association(s) and the implementing agency in the executive branch. Today, most issues involve multiple congressional committees and attract the interest of myriad industry and citizen, or public interest, groups. The political stakes for these players are often large.

Republicans and some business groups worked for years to keep comprehensive health care reform from the decision-making agenda—just as Democrats, labor unions and liberal citizen groups worked to place it on the agenda. Once President Obama placed it on the agenda in 2009, opposing interests fought over the appropriate policy response to the problems of rising costs and of the growing number of uninsured. Republicans argued for policies that relied less on the government and more on the private market. Democrats sought a more active government role including the creation of a publicly managed health insurance option. Contrasting perspectives on the nature of the problem and the appropriate governmental response fueled this fight. Balancing the demands of the interest groups was crucial to securing the legislation's success. The Democratic leadership in Congress needed to craft a bill that would be acceptable to the private health insurance industry, to the pharmaceutical industry, to labor unions, and even the United States Conference of Catholic Bishops—if possible. Failing to represent the interests of a crucial interest group could mean the loss of the group's support, or worse, the group could organize to oppose the measure. Balancing the needs and demands of so many actors produces an ever-increasing length of legislation. Average bill length increased by roughly 300 percent between 1968 and 1988 (Baumgartner and Jones 2009). The health reform legislation surpassed 2500 pages.

Legislating is especially difficult and contentious in a Congress of polarized parties. The multitude of voices to be pleased increases avenues for opponents to obstruct the process and undermine delicate compromises. Because of such battles, Congress often resorts to enacting laws through unorthodox methods, such as those discussed in Chapter 5—bypassing committees, multiple committee referrals, post-committee adjustments, and the use of restrictive rules to limit debate and amendment. Unorthodox lawmaking, however, has a direct impact on policy legitimation and public confidence in government. Legitimation refers to the process by which policy options are considered and then adopted or rejected. Legitimation requires more than a majority vote. "Policy legitimacy . . . flows from several conditions" such as "demonstrable public support . . . and a full and open airing of the issues and controversies" (Kraft and Furlong 2007, 81). Calling into question the legitimacy of a policy is a potent political tool, one used against Obama's health reform.

For much of 2009, Democrats enjoyed a comfortable majority in the House and a filibuster-proof 60-seat majority in the Senate. Late that year, the House and Senate passed differing versions of health reform along party-line votes. Before the two chambers could reconcile their differences, Republicans won a special election in Massachusetts to fill the seat vacated by the death of Democratic Senator Edward Kennedy. With their filibuster-proof majority gone, Democrats sought a new way to pass health care reform legislation. To avoid Republican delays, negotiations between the House and Senate bypassed the traditional conference committee and instead involved bargaining by the two chambers' majority party leaders. The House and Senate bills differed enough that a majority of House members were unwilling to adopt the Senate version of the bill—the easiest solution. Any House amendments to the Senate bill would necessitate a new vote in the Senate, which would be subject to a Republican filibuster. In the end, a procedural tactic secured passage, but it provided the bill's opponents an opportunity to question the bill's legitimacy. Democratic leaders had chosen to use the budget reconciliation process, which provides for a streamlined debate procedure in the Senate. Reconciliation measures are not subject to a filibuster and therefore need only 51 votes to secure passage. For this process to work, the House would first need to approve the Senate version of the health care reform bill and then pass a reconciliation measure containing the negotiated changes.

To provide political cover for House Democrats' unease with the Senate bill, the House Rules Committee initially considered a highly restrictive rule for consideration of the reconciliation measure. The rule, remarkably, would have "deemed" the Senate version of the bill to have passed the House upon that chamber's adoption of the rule. Thus, a House member could deny having ever voted for the Senate version of the bill, arguing instead that they voted only for the rule providing for consideration of the more politically attractive reconciliation measure (Sinclair 2011). *Confused?* So were many observers. In the end, Speaker of the House Nancy Pelosi (D-CA) abandoned the plan when it became clear that it was damaging the legitimacy of the process.

Though the "deeming" language disappeared, the reconciliation measure proceeded under a closed rule that allowed for no amendments, other than via a motion to recommit the whole bill, because any amendment would undermine the use of reconciliation. Concerns about whether the legislation would allow for public financing of abortion—something opposed by many moderate and conservative Democrats—were assuaged not via amendment but rather by the promise of a presidential executive order declaring no funds would be used for such a purpose. The executive order was necessary because without it Republicans would have used the motion to recommit to force a vote on an amendment banning public coverage of abortion (Sinclair 2011). The defeat of the amendment would inflict political damage upon many Democrats from competitive districts, but its adoption would have meant the death of the legislation in the Senate. In the end the reconciliation measure passed by a party line vote. The Senate passed the reconciliation measure a few days later.

As the House was considering the use of "deeming" to adopt the Senate bill, then House Majority Leader Steny Hoyer (D-MD) defended the approach: "We talk a lot about process in this town. We are seized of the process issue. 'So what?' says the American public. They are not focused on process. They are focused on substance" (Pear 2010).

Hoyer's conclusion is debatable. Consider this contrasting view:

> People separate the process by which a decision was made from the outcomes of the decision itself. Belief that a fair process was used increases satisfaction with the . . . decision . . . Procedural fairness increases the likelihood that the outcome will be accepted regardless of whether that outcome was preferred.
>
> (Funk 2001, 194)

Closed rules, "deeming," reconciliation, executive orders—all were used to limit debate and ensure passage of a controversial and highly significant piece of legislation. This is common in the contemporary Congress. The public, however, cares most about process regarding divisive or controversial issues. In such situations, the "actions of politicians that can be interpreted as furthering divisions, acrimony, partisanship, ideological extremism, and, generally, the self-interest of politicians all diminish government in the eyes of the people" (Hibbing and Theiss-Morse 2001, 249–250). Partisanship, polarization, intense party competition, and issue activism encourage this style of policymaking. The manner in which policy is formulated, debated, and adopted has changed in ways that undermine public confidence in those who make the laws, those charged with implementing the laws, and, ultimately the laws themselves. "Policies . . . face serious hurdles. They may well fail to command public support, affected interest groups may . . . challenge them in court, and their implementation could be adversely affected" (Kraft and Furlong 2007, 81). If the public doubts the legitimacy of a legislative act, if there are reasons to question the decision-making process, a legally enacted bill, no matter how needed or well intentioned, can ultimately produce policy failure. Health care reform divided the public and in the years since its enactment, public support has further eroded. The media highlighted enduring conflicts over the law prominently in its coverage of the topic. As unorthodox lawmaking has increased, popular discontent has risen, and public confidence in Congress has collapsed.

Republicans and interest groups opposed to the health reform law continue to question the legitimacy of the policy. A collection of states and interest groups challenged its constitutionality. Prior to the bureaucracy having an opportunity to implement much of the Patient Protection and Affordable Care Act, the courts have been engaged in the policy process. Conflicting rulings from federal courts regarding the constitutionality of various aspects of the law resulted in a hearing before the U.S. Supreme Court. In late June 2012, a narrowly divided Supreme Court upheld most of the law. With the exception of Chief Justice John Roberts, a George W. Bush appointee, justices broke mostly along partisan lines—much as many of the lower court rulings varied based on the party affiliation of the president who appointed the judges considering the case. With the major provisions of the law upheld, future battles over bureaucratic implementation of the law remain to be fought.

The Federal Bureaucracy

Few topics are more likely to elicit yawns from students of American politics than the federal bureaucracy. Translated quite literally from their French and Greek roots *bureau* and *cracy* the term bureaucracy means to rule or govern from an office or desk. The definition no doubt comports well with the impression many have of the federal bureaucracy. Bureaucrats tend to garner the most notice in the midst of events that reinforce the public perception of a vast, inefficient and ineffective government. Examples include the Federal Emergency Management Agency's (FEMA) response to Hurricane Katrina in 2005, the failures of the Minerals Management Service to adequately inspect BP's Deepwater Horizon oil rig that spilled 5 million barrels of oil into the Gulf of Mexico in 2010, or the revelation that the General Services Administration (GSA)—created to promote efficiency in the federal government—spent over $800,000 on a morale-building staff party on the Las Vegas strip in late 2010.

Though bureaucratic failings merit criticism, they also present an incomplete picture of federal administration. In reality, the federal bureaucracy is essential to governance. Though ostensibly placed under the president in the executive branch, the bureaucracy can exercise only those powers delegated to it by Congress. The heads of most federal agencies serve at the pleasure of the president, but they are subject to oversight by a Congress that determines agency budgets and powers. In many respects, the bureaucracy operates in service to two masters—the president and Congress—all the while being increasingly subject to the judgment of a third—the judiciary. The overlapping power and influence of the three branches create special challenges for a federal bureaucracy that is ultimately responsible for translating various decisions of the president and Congress into actual policies.

Efforts to enact the Clean Air Act of 1990 illustrate the challenges of bureaucratic responsibility. Regarding this Act, Gary Bryner notes, "The coalition building and compromise that are central to the legislative process often result in bills that are imprecise and leave much room for interpretation by administrative officials" (1995, 19). Power then shifts from Congress to the executive branch where—at least in the realm of environmental policy— few administrations have "sought to implement the laws in ways that would actually achieve the goals they contain" (ibid., 19).

The delegation of responsibility to either the judiciary or an administrative agency under the executive branch has become quite common in the contemporary Congress. Delegation reflects a conscious legislative decision: "When Congress is faced with a controversial choice [. . .] Congress announces some lofty goal, but skirts the difficulties of attaining it" and then "orders a government agency to achieve the goal and thus to take the heat for the difficult steps needed to do so" (Schoenbrod 2006, 36). Congress delegates because legislators can take credit for acting on public concerns while avoiding a possible backlash against the specific measures adopted by the agency with delegated authority. Others see a less nefarious cause for the delegation of responsibility. Given the division of Congress into two houses with distinct constituencies and electoral demands, achieving consensus on specific policy can be difficult to achieve. That is particularly the case in a Congress with narrow partisan majorities and two parties increasingly separated by ideology. Resulting laws consequently are often vague and leave to the implementing agency the responsibility for policy specifics. Lawmakers also frequently assume that a bureaucracy staffed by policy professionals may be better able to make specific, technical, implementation decisions regarding environmental, health, transportation, housing and other such policies.

It is not only the congressional majority party that can achieve advantages by deferring policy specifics to the implementing agency. Such an approach offers four avenues by which either the majority or minority may influence the final direction of policy. First, the majority party could rely on control of Congress and its oversight authority to influence the implementing agency. Second, the minority party may play the odds of obtaining control of Congress and exercising similar influence. Third, the parties may look to the presidency as a means by which to influence the implementing agency through the power of appointments or executive orders. Fourth, another option for parties, and interest groups, is to use the courts to challenge an agency's interpretation or enforcement of laws. Regardless of the motivations or the path chosen, congressional delegation brings the bureaucracy directly into the political process.

The implementing agency, under the influence of the executive, develops rules interpreting the goals and objectives of the policies. Its regulatory interpretations often reflect the varying pressures of congressional intent, presidential preference, public opinion, and interest group demands. Most regulations appear in the Federal Register under a notice of proposed rulemaking, subject to a public comment process dominated by interest groups. Prior to or after implementation "most major regulatory initiatives are challenged in court," either by those who believe the regulations exceed the delegated authority of the implementing agency or by those who believe the regulations fail to adequately fulfill the law's intent (Bryner 1995, 7). The "business necessity" aspect of the Civil Rights Act and the power of the Environmental Protection Agency to regulate greenhouse gases under the Clean Air Act, both discussed in Chapter 8, are but two examples.

The bureaucracy occupies a precarious position during the current era. Though staffed by a more educated and more independent class of civil servants than at any time in American history, it is burdened now with ever more implementation and policy development responsibilities. Concurrent with this expansion in its duties, it is subject to a wide variety of pressures that can undermine its effectiveness. In addition, the bureaucracy no longer claims any dominance of policy expertise. Congress and interest groups are now home to policy experts capable of offering independent evaluation and analyses. As the responsibilities of the federal bureaucracy increase and the pages of the Federal Register proliferate, public confidence in the professional bureaucracy declines.

American Bureaucracy Phase One: The Fourth Branch

Though the federal bureaucracy began to grow well before the start of the New Deal Era in the 1930s, the introduction of the alphabet soup of agencies and programs associated with the administration of Franklin D. Roosevelt constituted the arrival point of the modern administrative state. The litany of programs established to combat the Great Depression—the National Industrial Recovery Act, the Agricultural Adjustment Act, the National Labor Relations Act, the Social Security Act—required an expanded and staffed bureaucracy to carry out implementation and deliver services—the National Labor Relations Board, the Securities and Exchange Commission, the Public Works Association, the Agriculture Adjustment Administration, the Social Security Board (later Administration). The New Deal programs' success depended upon a competent bureaucracy. Roosevelt thus sought to bypass the "spoils system" that often appointed politically connected, but not necessarily policy-competent, individuals.

Between 1936 and 1939, Roosevelt sought legislation to expand executive control over the bureaucracy. Roosevelt's goal was to maximize executive authority and reduce the oversight and influence of Congress. Roosevelt wished to diminish the power of Southern Democrats who often opposed his New Deal policies. The president instead sought a bureaucracy that would operate as a "federal work force dedicated to advancing the cause of the New Deal" (Milkis 1993). Many in Congress objected, and ultimately Roosevelt failed to obtain the executive-centered control that he desired. He did succeed, however, in establishing an entrenched administrative state—a larger bureaucracy subject to the executive and legislative branches.

Throughout the 1930s and 1940s, Congress debated the power of the federal bureaucracy and the question of who controlled this emerging "fourth branch" of government. Congress granted the president authority to reorganize the bureaucracy in the waning days of the Hoover administration in 1932. During much of the late 1930s, many Members of Congress objected to a bureaucracy under the control of the executive and resisted the growing calls to delegate power to bureaucratic agencies. By the mid-1940s, most in Congress accepted delegation to the bureaucracy as inevitable and sought to enhance congressional oversight. The Administrative Procedures Act of 1946 (APA) required that administrative policymaking, or rulemaking, be published in the Federal Register. Disclosure involved the substance of the rule, key agency contacts, instructions for submitting comments on the proposed rule, and information about public meetings concerning the rule. The APA also outlined the standards allowing for judicial review of agency rulemaking and defined the terms under which individuals could challenge the rules in court. The APA established the bureaucracy as an extension of Congress and as such subjected it to similar levels of public scrutiny and judicial oversight (Rosenbloom 2000).

Congress passed the Legislative Reorganization Act of 1946 (LRA) to empower itself to enforce the APA. The LRA reformed the congressional committee structure, enhanced committee staff, created parallel committees in the House and Senate, assigned members to fewer committees to promote expertise and focus on the issues within their committees' jurisdictions, and instructed Congress to maintain oversight of the bureaucracy (ibid.). The Reorganization Act of 1949 institutionalized the president's authority to reorganize the bureaucracy, subject to congressional approval. The LRA began the process of professionalizing Congress, a process not completed until after 1968. The rise of divided government and polarized parties would add greater significance to the APA and the LRA as would multiple subsequent amendments to the Acts and the enactment of other measures affecting oversight of the bureaucracy. Congress began curtailing presidential power to reorganize the bureaucracy in the mid-1960s and the authority lapsed in 1973 under President Nixon (Moe 2001).

American Bureaucracy Phase Two: The Arrival of Divided Government

A second wave of bureaucratic expansion took place in the 1960s, resulting from President Lyndon Johnson's Great Society initiatives. LBJ's "War on Poverty" expanded the social welfare activities of the federal government, the creation of Medicare and Medicaid—medical insurance for the aged and poor, respectively—expanded the Social Security Administration. A new Economic Opportunity Act directed community-based anti-poverty programs and the Food Stamp Act greatly expanded the federal food assistance for low-income individuals. Though many New Deal and some Great Society programs were partnerships between the federal and state governments, Johnson sought to consolidate administrative power under the federal bureaucracy to bypass state resistance. Following his landslide election in 1964, Johnson enjoyed lopsided majorities in Congress and had many Great Society programs enacted and delegated to the federal bureaucracy. The size of the federal civilian workforce peaked at three million employees in 1968, the final year of Johnson's presidency.

A divided Democratic Party in Congress at times frustrated Democratic presidents from Franklin Roosevelt to Lyndon Johnson. Under unified partisan control, the emergence of polarized, clearly delineated parties might have helped to bridge the separation of powers inherent in the Madisonian design, yielding greater uniformity in the direction of the bureaucracy. At the very time when the lines between the parties were starting to become more clear—when internal party homogeneity was beginning to emerge—divided government became the new norm in American politics. Republican Richard Nixon won the presidency in 1968, having campaigned against many of the Great Society programs that had expanded the bureaucracy. During the 1970s, a great tug of war began between Nixon and congressional Democrats over control of the federal bureaucracy. As Nixon sought greater executive control, Democrats sought to minimize executive influence and expand congressional authority. The increasing presence of delineated parties widened the gap between branches. An administrative presidency emerged in which Nixon, and subsequent presidents, frequently attempted to bypass Congress in directing the bureaucracy. Nixon went so far as to impound—refuse to spend—funds that Congress had appropriated for programs that he opposed. Increasingly the bureaucracy was caught between an executive with one set of objectives and a Congress with another. Ultimately, the federal courts and Congress intervened.

In a series of rulings, federal courts determined that the executive lacked the authority to impound funds appropriated by law. Democrats in Congress built upon the APA and LRA by passing the Legislative Reorganization Act of 1970 (LRA 70), the Congressional Budget Impoundment and Control Act of 1974 (Budget Act), and the Inspector General Act of 1978 (IGA). As discussed in Chapter 5, the LRA 70 added to Congress's research capacity through staffing and technology. The legislature also created the Congressional Research Service to serve as a policy resource for Congress. The Budget Act instituted a Congressional Budget Office, enhanced Congress' role in budget making, and effectively ended the practice of executive impoundment. The IGA created independent investigatory offices in designated agencies and departments to monitor activity and report to Congress and agency heads. Congressional committees, subcommittees, and members acquired additional staff support. In addition, newly empowered subcommittees exercised greater oversight.

Figure 7.1 reveals that the congressional and judicial workforce grew significantly during this time, increasing by nearly 80 percent between 1964 and 1980. In 1973, Congress allowed the president's authority to reorganize the bureaucracy—subject to congressional veto—to expire. Collectively, these acts reinforced Congress's position of influence over the bureaucracy at the expense of presidential authority and completed the legislative professionalization process begun in the 1940s. They also allowed for greater interaction between Congress and the ever-rising number of interest groups.

The seeds of America's current bureaucratic state also were sown in pitched and partisan battles between the emerging American Left, increasingly evident among congressional Democrats beginning in the 1950s, and the new American Right that became ever more evident in the GOP by the late 1970s. It was the election of 1968 and the arrival of divided government that allowed those seeds to take root and grow. Nixon's attempts to control the bureaucracy led progressives to pursue bureaucratic controls that relied on Congress, the federal courts, and public interest groups. Unlike the industry-specific associations of the past, the associations and groups that began to emerge in the 1960s were disproportionately citizens' and consumers' groups. These newly emergent groups are dedicated to causes—the environment, civil rights, and consumer protection (Cook 1996; Baumgartner and Jones 2009; Fiorina and Abrams 2009). "Cause" groups joined bureaucratic battles with zest and entrepreneurial Members of Congress worked to expand committee jurisdictions to attract the interest, and electoral support, of these new groups (Baumgartner and Jones 2009). This contributed to the increase in the number of multiple committee referrals discussed in Chapter 5.

Progressives of the 1960s and 1970s aimed to limit the discretion and independence of the bureaucracy, holding that those who administered the nation's policies were "delivery vehicles for the will of the people" as represented by "group activists, judges, and members of Congress and their staffs" (Cook 1996, 126). It was a vision of the bureaucracy desired by Franklin Roosevelt, but this new iteration sought to circumvent the president, insulating programs from the predations of future conservative chief executives. Note in Figure 7.1 the halt in bureaucratic expansion post 1968. The executive bureaucracy ceased to grow even as the number of interest groups and personnel serving Congress and the judiciary grew significantly.

Increasingly, Democrats and interest groups representing those affected by targeted programs turned to the federal courts to compel federal agencies to act in accordance with congressional intent and not executive direction (Rourke 1991; Ginsberg and Shefter 2002).

In response, the presidency became the means by which the newly emerging American Right fought the liberal vision of the American bureaucracy. Congressional battles with President Nixon were but a precursor of what was to come after the 1980 election of Ronald Reagan. Under Reagan, conservatives launched an effort to defund, devolve, and deregulate. The bureaucracy and the programs it administered were subject to funding cuts and efforts to devolve social programs to the states. Conservatives rolled back regulations on business, the economy, and the environment. The goal was to de-bureaucratize the bureaucracy (Cook 1996). Using the power of appointment, Reagan named agency heads loyal to his agenda and often openly opposed to the mission and purpose of the agencies they were to head (Rourke 1991).

During the final year of the Carter administration, Congress passed the Paperwork Reduction Act in an attempt to reduce the burden placed on society by bureaucratic "red tape." The Act required federal agencies to seek approval from the Office of Information and Regulatory Affairs (OIRA)— housed within the Office of Management and Budget—before imposing information collection burdens on those subject to their regulatory authority. The OIRA then had to approve the information collection before the agency could proceed (Rosenbloom 2000). This delegation of authority to the executive branch via the OMB passed in 1980 when Democrats enjoyed unified control of the government. Once inaugurated, Reagan issued an executive order directing OIRA to conduct a cost-benefit analysis and centralized review for all executive branch regulations. OIRA was empowered to suggest changes to proposed regulations—a suggestion issued by a review authority housed within OMB, the executive agency responsible for reviewing and approving all agency budget requests, making it a very powerful suggestion. Figure 7.1 offers some indication of Reagan's impact. After years of dramatic increases, the number of pages published annually in the Federal Register fell by nearly half between 1980 and 1984.

So aggressive was the Reagan administration's use of the OIRA that congressional Democrats threatened to defund the agency in 1986 and ultimately passed legislation requiring OIRA to clear all agency requests within 60 days. Request denials by OIRA became subject to judicial review. Reagan's executive order remained in effect throughout his and the first Bush administrations with OIRA reviewing an average of 2,300 draft and final rules each year. Nearly 10 percent of regulations came from a single agency— the Environmental Protection Agency. Even at that rate of review, only about one-third of all proposed and final rules received inspection each year. OIRA had the discretion to exempt rules from review and tended to reserve its authority for major rules and regulations—those with estimated costs or benefits in excess of $100 million (Arbuckle 2008). Major rules were more likely to receive OIRA review and the reviews tended to take nearly twice as long as for non-major rules. Agencies therefore had every incentive to avoid major rulemaking, to divide major rules into multiple non-major rules, and to underestimate costs and benefits.

In 1993, President Clinton issued a new executive order that reduced the number of rules subject to review. The annual average fell to roughly 600 per year, with the EPA still heavily represented. Agencies gained the authority to designate whether their rules were major or not—subject to OIRA agreement. The review discretion enjoyed by OIRA under Reagan and the first Bush administrations had ended. Total annual pages published in the Federal Register increased by better than 30 percent during Clinton's tenure. Clinton did not dismantle the process of OIRA review. Rather, his executive order made explicit what the Reagan order had implied—the review process was intended to advance the president's policy agenda (West 2004).

In 1995, Republicans found themselves in charge of Congress with a Democratic president at the head of the executive branch. No longer able to rely on the administrative presidency, Republicans sought new ways to debureaucratize the government. In 1996, congressional Republicans passed the Congressional Review Act, which made all new regulations subject to congressional disapproval, though the resolutions of disapproval were subject to presidential veto. The Congressional Review Act created the threat of strict congressional oversight of the bureaucracy, but other actions taken by the new Republican majority reduced congressional influence. They reduced committee staffs, the Congressional Research Service and the General Accounting Office endured budget cuts, the institutional memory and policy expertise of Congress shrank. Republicans proposed new reforms requiring cost-benefit analyses for all new regulations and tried to devolve many federal programs to the states, thereby reducing the need for many federal agencies and congressional oversight (Ginsberg and Shefter 2002).

Republican attempts to pare the federal bureaucracy did not arise solely from an ideological opposition to activist government. Many on the right viewed the bureaucracy as an extension of Democratic voter mobilization efforts. To conservatives, the array of social welfare and regulatory programs created during the decades of Democratic dominance resulted in con-stituencies reliant on those programs. The programs represented "policies with publics"—which is to say policies whose communities work to sustain them (May 1991). According to this argument, the explosion of citizen and consumer interest groups starting in the 1960s and 1970s constituted the newly created policy communities impacted by the programs created during that era. In such a system the bureaucracy is more than a collection of program administrators, it becomes the new equivalent of old political machines—delivering services in return for party loyalty. In addition to delivering constituent services, federal bureaucrats are heavily unionized and the labor unions representing the workers have a stake in defending their Democratic benefactors (Ginsberg and Shefter 2002).

As shown in Table 7.1, strong correlations exist between policy and bureaucratic professionalization variables and measures of Democratic strength in the electorate. As Democratic Party strength began to wane in the mid and late 1960s, congressional and interest group professionalization began to rise. Though those correlations offer support of the theory of bureaucratic mobilization of the electorate, strong correlations of bureaucratic professionalization with lower voter turnout undermine the theory. Additionally, measures of policy and bureaucratic professionalization share a strong positive correlation with measures of direct democracy via state ballot measures. If the goal of policy professionalization was the motivation of the electorate, there is little to suggest success. Rather, both turnout and public satisfaction with the government have declined.

For Republicans, breaking up that bureaucracy/constituent relationship, breaking down newer policy communities, and reducing the size of the bureaucracy made electoral sense. In the 1980s and 1990s, GOP efforts began to reduce regulations and to take federal welfare programs and decentralize them by devolving them to states. Proposals arose to end the federal administration of most public assistance programs and Medicaid, medical assistance to the poor, programs serving millions of Americans. The GOP aimed to privatize service delivery where possible, to sever the bureaucratic link between Democrats and those served by Democratic policies. Republicans, however, enjoyed only partial success. Perhaps the most significant GOP achievement involved welfare reform in 1996. The Personal Responsibility and Work Opportunity Reconciliation Act of 1996 effectively ended the federal entitlement to welfare, created as part of Johnson's Great Society. Federal administration of much of welfare policy ended and control went to the states. A 60-month limit replaced the lifetime eligibility for cash assistance once afforded to low-income families with children. Private charities entered in the process of service delivery. The message was clear; the federal bureaucracy was shrinking and it was no longer in the business of administering the services (Ginsberg and Shefter 2002).

Such battles did not end in the 1990s. Subsequent to the events of September 11, 2001, Congress and the White House engaged in a struggle over the creation of a new cabinet-level Department of Homeland Security (DHS). Much of the political maneuvering occurred in 2002 under divided government, with a narrow Democratic majority in the Senate often at odds with the GOP House and the White House. Creation of the new DHS would represent one of the most significant bureaucratic reorganizations in decades and would affect an estimated 175,000 federal employees. The DHS would coordinate and manage efforts to protect the security of the United States. The biggest battle stemmed from Republican demands that those employed by the DHS be exempt from many civil service protections and

Table 7.1 Systemic correlates of policy professionalization

	Total associations	Total pages Federal Register	Legislative and judicial branch employees
Public interaction with the system			
Popular discontent	+.84	+.85	+.75
Most important problem foreign	−.69	−.73	−.60
Most important problem domestic	+.74	+.79	+.70
Turnout presidential elections	−.74	−.76	−.68
Turnout House elections	−.71	−.66	−.71
State and local split ticket	+.78	+.75	
States with ballot initiatives	+.86	+.90	+.92
Total ballot initiatives in States	+.88	+.81	+.83
System thickening variables			
Total associations		+.85	+.95
Total pages Federal Register	+.85		+.87
Legislative and judicial branch personnel	+.95	+.87	
Party coalition variables			
Percentage of blacks apolitical	−.74	−.71	
Blacks identifying as Democrats			−.68
Share of whites any independent	+.76	+.84	+.77
Southern whites support for the Democratic Party	−.95	−.87	−.94
Share of the Democratic coalition working class	−.71	−.71	−.59
Share of Democrats in the electorate	−.85	−.64	−.85
Share neutral to parties	+.56	+.73	
Congressional polarization variables			
Presidential support party gap in House	+.77	+.70	+.68
Presidential support party gap in Senate	+.62	+.55	+.82
Restrictive rules in the House	+.86	+.79	+.86
Cloture motions filed	+.85	+.80	+.78
Party unity Senate	+.55		+.82
Presidential leadership/capital			
Presidential success in Congress	−.61	−.53	−.71
Appeals Court nomination success	−.92	−.80	−.85
Duration successful confirmation process	+.57	+.60	+.74
Presidential partisan approval gap	+.72		+.76

Sources: See Appendix.

collective bargaining rights of unionized federal employees. President Bush also was proposing to privatize nearly half a million other positions within the federal bureaucracy. The GOP proposal for DHS would remove another 175,000 employees from the traditional bureaucratic framework. This was a battle over control of the bureaucracy (Light 2002).

An agreement ultimately exempted the DHS employees from traditional collective bargaining rights and empowered the executive branch to devise new rules for DHS employees. Employees of the new Transportation Security Administration (TSA) received the right to unionize, but not to negotiate the terms of their employment. A coalition of federal labor unions filed suit in federal court to protect the collective bargaining rights of existing federal employees reassigned to the DHS. The court upheld many of their collective bargaining rights in 2006. Battles have been ongoing over the bargaining rights of TSA employees. Under the Bush Administration, the Secretary of DHS argued for the need to exempt TSA employees from traditional bargaining rights. President Obama's DHS secretary has sought ways to expand those rights.

The budget battles of 2011 and 2012 constitute another example of conflicts over efforts to de-bureaucratize national government. Representative (and subsequent Vice Presidential nominee) Paul Ryan (R–WI) proposed reforming the Medicaid program by turning control of the program over to states as was done with welfare in 1996. Presently, the federal government determines who is eligible for Medicaid and sets minimum standards for the services covered. The Ryan proposal would turn such decisions over to the states and the policy community once focused on federal level policy would face 50 separate state programs (Pecquet 2012). The Republican plan would restrict the federal role in Medicaid and likely result in millions fewer covered by the program. The Democratic alternative, contained in the Patient Protection and Affordable Care Act, expands the Medicaid program to millions more recipients and reduces state discretion. In ruling to uphold the major provisions of the Patient Protection and Affordable Care Act, the Supreme Court did determine states could opt out of the Medicaid expansion free of the threat of lost federal dollars. This introduces a new wrinkle in the partisan battle.

Bringing the Pieces Together: The Intersection of Policy and Bureaucracy

America's national bureaucracy relies on an assumption of routine and incremental change. Now, however, sudden and frequent changes in partisan control of the executive and legislative branches result in very dramatic alterations in policy, increasing demands upon administrators. The bureaucracy also now no longer has exclusive claim to the level of professionalization and specialized skills that it once enjoyed. Congressional staff and interest groups and associations have enhanced their own policy capacities. The result is often policy stasis as these forces and the multitude of voices involved in policymaking bring added complexity and very diverse perspectives to policy implementation.

For example, in the waning days of the first Bush administration, the Occupational Safety and Health Administration (OSHA) issued a proposal to draft new rules for workplace safety. Though controversial, draft regulations were published in 1994 under President Clinton. The rules called for more ergonomic workplaces and required employers to reduce musculoskeletal disorders caused by repetitive motion or other occupational motions and movements. The draft rule received immediate resistance from interest groups representing employers and resulted in the formation of a new interest group alliance—the National Coalition on Ergonomics—dedicated solely to opposing the new rule. The new Republican Congress also opposed the new rule and used the power of the purse to deny OSHA the authority to propose ergonomic rules. Congress further required OSHA to produce studies proving a link between workplace functions and the disorders the rule sought to prevent. In 2000, the congressional prohibition lapsed and OSHA issued final rules intended to take effect in early January 2001.

The rules were immediately challenged in federal court, but the election of 2000 ultimately determined their fate. A unified Republican government, employing the Congressional Review Act, passed a joint resolution disapproving the new rule and President George W. Bush signed the disapproval into law in late March of 2001 (Rosenberg 2008). Almost ten years of administrative, congressional, judicial, and interest group wrangling had delayed the issuance of final rules. Yet the rules, once issued, were in effect for less than two months due to the arrival of the Republican Bush administration. The rare occurrence of unified partisan control of government made the Congressional Review Act a potent weapon. The saga of the ergonomics regulations illustrates why the public often questions the efficiency and the effectiveness of the federal bureaucracy.

In practice, Congress and the president rarely have employed the Congressional Review Act to override agency rules. They have voided less than one-tenth of 1 percent of rules since 1996. That statistic obscures the fact that Congress, or even a single lawmaker or a small group of members, have been able to use the threat of disapproval as a bargaining chip with administrative agencies in order to secure substantive changes to, or even outright suspension of, issued rules. Republicans successfully employed the strategy during the Clinton administration (Rosenberg 2008).

Regulation of greenhouse gases under the Clean Air Act (CAA) provides another example of policies and bureaucracies caught in the battle between polarized parties. The CAA directs the Administrator of the Environmental Protection Agency to set emissions standards for any air pollutant that the Administrator judges to cause or contribute to air pollution that endangers public health or welfare. The CAA therefore offers clear direction—*set standards for any air pollutant*—but also clear discretion—*the Administrator judges to cause or contribute to air pollution that endangers public health or welfare* (Bryner 1995).

In 2003, interest groups petitioned the EPA to use their regulatory authority under the CAA to regulate greenhouse gas (GHGs) emissions. The petitioners agued the broad definition of air pollutant contained in the CAA would naturally include GHGs, viewed by many as being the primary contributors to global climate change. In response, the EPA Administrator denied the petitioners' request, arguing the CAA did not authorize the regulation of GHGs' emissions. The administrator further stated that even if the EPA did have the authority to regulate such emissions, it would not, as the EPA and the Bush Administration already had other emissions reductions programs in effect.

An association of cities, states, and interest groups filed suit against the EPA in federal court, challenging the Administrator's decision. In September of 2005, a divided U.S. Appeals Court upheld the Administrator's decision. In June of 2006, the U.S. Supreme Court agreed to review the case and in a 5–4 decision, issued during the final months of the Bush Administration, the Supreme Court determined that GHGs met the definition of air pollutants contained in the CAA and the EPA had the authority to regulate them. Further, the Court determined that the Administrator of the EPA had the discretion not to regulate GHG emissions, but only based on scientific evidence demonstrating such emissions do not present a danger to the public health or welfare. The EPA was directed to develop a more sound rationale for denying regulation (*Massachusetts v. Environmental Protection Agency* 549 U.S. 497, S. Ct. 1438 (2007)).

In early 2009, under President Obama, the EPA determined carbon dioxide and five other GHGs are a danger to public health and welfare and therefore such emissions from all major sources—be they motor vehicles or power plants—are subject to regulation under the CAA. At the time of the EPA decision, Democrats enjoyed unified control of government and various legislative proposals under their consideration would limit GHG emissions in lieu of relying on EPA regulations (Eilperin 2009). The administration used the threat of possible EPA action to motivate congressional action. The House ultimately passed the American Clean Energy and Security Act by a narrow party-line vote in July of 2009. The measure called for an 83 percent reduction in GHG emissions by mid-century and would have stripped from the EPA the authority to regulate GHGs under the CAA. The legislation died in the Senate in July of 2010 when Democrats were unable to muster the 60 votes needed to overcome an expected Republican filibuster (Chaddock and Parti 2010). The mid-term elections of 2010 ended the brief period of unified Democratic government and policy momentum shifted back to the EPA.

In late 2009, the EPA used the power afforded under the CAA to issue new emissions standards for automobiles and in early 2010 implemented a new GHG reporting program for large emitters. In January of 2011, the EPA implemented new emissions standards for new and upgraded power plants. The new Republican majority in the House of Representatives threatened legislation stripping the EPA's authority to regulate GHG emissions (Walsh 2011). In April 2011, the House did vote to strip the EPA of such authority, even though the measure had no chance of passing the Democratic Senate. The vote was as a warning to the EPA to be less aggressive. Minority Republicans in the Senate readied similar legislation. In late 2011, the EPA appeared to be slowing its pace in the face of these actions (Gardner 2011) and it is likely the 2012 election will have a significant impact on the agency. A unified Republican government would have stripped from the EPA its authority to regulate GHGs. Such an action would effectively void the regulations issued by the EPA since early 2009. Should Democrats block such legislative changes, a Republican president could have appointed an EPA Administrator less committed to GHG regulation.

These examples illustrate that one cannot separate policymaking from policy implementation. Nor can we conclude that the work of policymaking ends with a policy's adoption by Congress and the president or with its interpretation and implementation by the bureaucracy. Those initially engaged in the battle of agenda setting and policy formulation continue to clash over implementation and policy evaluation. The sheer number of voices engaged in such battles has increased considerably since the 1960s. The bureaucracy's accountability to the executive, the legislative, and judiciary and therefore its indirect accountability to those who influence the three branches of government creates a situation in which ever more is asked of the bureaucracy at the very time its capacity to carry out its delegated duties is severely constrained.

Presidential Czars and the Bureaucracy

A president facing an opposition Congress may seek to circumvent the legislative branch altogether through the mechanisms of the administrative presidency. As discussed in Chapter 6, presidents have come to rely on recess appointments to major offices as a means to bypass congressional obstruction. Presidents have increasingly appointed "czars" to take responsibility for significant areas of public policy. Though the specific definition of czar varies, we rely on the definition offered by Mitchel Sollenberger and Mark Rozell in *The President's Czars* (2012). A "czar" refers to an executive branch official who was never confirmed by the Senate yet enjoys "final decision-making authority that often entails controlling budgetary programs, administering/coordinating a policy area, or otherwise promulgating rules, regulations, and orders that bind either government officials and/or the private sector" (ibid., 7).

The authors acknowledge that their definition of czar may be more exclusive than that of other people and as a result may undercount the number of czars cited in popular media. Though examples of czars stretch to the beginnings of the nation, they have become common under recent presidents. With the exception of a two-month window during President Reagan's first term, Congress has been unwilling, especially during divided government, to grant presidents the bureaucratic reorganization authority most enjoyed between 1932 and 1974 (Moe 2001). Lacking such authority, presidents have relied on the unilateral appointment of czars. President Clinton named a czar to deal with the arrival of the year 2000 and the possibility of computer compatibility problems (Y2K Czar). Following the events of 9/11, President Bush named a Homeland Security Czar—who later became the first Secretary of Homeland Security. Among the many czars named by President Obama were several responsible for aspects of the federal bailout of the U.S. auto industry and a czar to make determinations regarding benefit receipt from a $20 billion victim's fund established by British Petroleum following the Deepwater Horizon oil spill (Sollenberger and Rozell 2012). Based on Sollenberger and Rozell's definition, there were five czars during Lyndon Johnson's presidency, 13 under Nixon, none under Ford or Carter, three under Reagan, two under the first President Bush, and four under Clinton. In recent years, the number has grown to 10 under the second President Bush and 27 under President Obama.

The proliferation of czars raises significant constitutional questions because presidents lack the authority to create offices unless specifically empowered by Congress. Though the Subdelegation Act of 1950 allows presidents to delegate power to officials confirmed by the Senate, many czars receive power via presidential decree—powers not authorized by Congress (ibid.). The bureaucracy's position between the executive and legislature makes it a location of battles between presidents and Congress for control over administrative actions. Presidential "czars" are one tactic for bureaucratic control in this ongoing struggle.

Conclusion

If one party could secure a prolonged hold on the mechanisms of governance, the current party system would enable the executive and legislative branches to coordinate and execute significant policy action through the bureaucracy. Party homogeneity would promote better cooperation between the two branches and minimize the institutional gamesmanship used to delay or derail bureaucratic action. However, the party system that emerged between 1968 and 1980 is precisely what is preventing either party from securing such a prolonged hold on governance. Two highly polarized and ideologically homogenous parties dominate current American politics. But those parties govern a public that is neither polarized by party nor ideologically homogenous. These public and party traits have produced a highly competitive period where divided government and rapid vacillation of partisan control of government or both have become the norm. Therefore, the bureaucracy and policy implementation continue to be caught in the partisan struggle and subject to the oscillations of party control.

For reasons explored in this chapter and others, Congress frequently looks to the bureaucracy not only for the implementation of policy but also for the formal interpretation of policy goals and objectives. For all of the talk of ending the era of big government or the efforts by Republicans to debureaucratize, Figure 7.1 shows the number of pages published in the Federal Register offering new rules and regulations continues to grow. Even as Republican presidents have sought to reduce regulations, the pages published in the Federal Register in 2008 had increased by nearly 60 percent compared to 1984. Paradoxically, as the scope of the bureaucracy expands, its capacity to administer is greatly restrained. The obstacles to bureaucratic administration are many—OIRA, divided government, congressional review, judicial review, interest group pressures—and the number of personnel has not kept pace with regulatory growth. Meanwhile the ranks of other players, from professional associations to those who work for Congress, continue to grow. The two parties use the bureaucracy as a battlefield in a form of institutional combat (Ginsberg and Shefter 2002), often covered with relish by the media. Programs created by legislation enacted by one Congress may face defunding by a subsequent Congress or be challenged in the courts.

In order to make policy, Congress and the executive resort to methods that circumvent public debate and foster a perception of policy made to serve narrow special interests or political self-interest. Policy-making in the present era includes far more voices than in the days of the iron triangles. Yet with the explosion of citizens' and consumers' groups and the increase in the number of congressional committees exercising jurisdiction over policy issues, the public appears to feel less represented than ever. Citizens appear less invested in the process and less confident in the policies made.

We are left with ongoing political wars waged on the battlefields of the bureaucracy. Dispassionate career civil servants who were supposed to engender public confidence via their expertise and freedom from partisan influence are instead embroiled in partisan warfare. Policy experts are now found everywhere and their diversity of perspectives and judgments undermines the ability to make clear policy decisions. Public confidence in government continues to decline. At some point a crisis may well emerge that will challenge the limitations of the current governing era and motivate citizen demands for change. To date, however, economic, environmental and national security crises alike have reinforced existing pathologies and further undermined public confidence in the nation's policymaking and policy executing capacities.

8   The Federal Courts

The Rise of Judicial Policymaking

Check an American government textbook nowadays, and you will find policymaking described as a central function of America's courts. A recent edition of *American Government: Power and Purpose* by four leading political scientists describes the federal judiciary as composed of "legislators in robes" (Lowi et al., 2010, 348). Such court behavior is not a new phenomenon, but one created by a revolution in the federal judiciary's role beginning in 1954 and consummated during the 1960s and 1970s. In 1984, political scientist Herbert Jacob defined the then-new trend away from traditional norm enforcement and toward judicial policymaking: "The difference lies in the intended impact of the decision. Policy decisions are intended to be guideposts for future actions; norm enforcement decisions are aimed at the particular case at hand" (Jacob 1984, 37).

The impetus for expanded policymaking came from the Supreme Court, specifically the Court headed by Chief Justice Earl Warren from 1954 to 1968. In a series of sweeping decisions—most during the 1960s—the Warren Court created national policy regarding racial integration, state and local criminal justice, conditions in state and local prisons, school prayer, the personal right to privacy, and state and federal legislative apportionment. In these decisions the Warren Court indeed set guideposts for a large variety of federal, state and local government actions. Accompanying the audacious policymaking of the Supreme Court were changes in legal rules and federal court practices during the 1960s and 1970s that made policymaking much more common by federal judges—institutionalizing the practice.

Congress, for its part, abetted judicial policymaking by passing many new domestic laws in the 1960s and 1970s that permitted adjudication as a means of enforcement (Farhang 2010). As demonstrated in Chapter 7, the number of judicial branch personnel grew considerably as well. Presidents, consumed by their duties, conceded the importance of judicial policymaking by emphasizing ideological considerations in federal judicial appointments. Judicial appointment politics gradually became beset by partisan polarization in the Senate. New judicial policymaking avenues spurred the creation and activity of many interest groups. In the 1960s, a "liberal legal network" formed to vigorously pursue policy change through the courts.

This produced a countermobilization of think tanks and interest groups promoting a conservative judicial agenda (Teles 2008, 22–90). Note in Figure 7.1 on p. 103 the similar trajectories of the growth of interest groups, congressional and judicial personnel, and pages of federal regulations. The impact upon America's national political system was great, creating a complex, elite arena of policymaking dominated by legal professionals and interest groups.

The major result was

> the judicialization of politics—the reliance of courts and judicial means for addressing core moral predicaments, public policy questions, and political controversies . . . arguably one of the most significant phenomena of late twentieth and early twenty first century government.
>
> (Hirschl 2008, 119)

This chapter explains the rise of judicial policymaking as a cardinal feature of the new American political system born during the 1960s and 1970s. Judicial politics involve complex battles by political elites. Its guiding force is federal judges appointed for life. Popular accountability is largely lacking from this new policymaking arena, except through the indirect mechanism of presidential and senatorial elections. The public never voted to make judges "legislators in robes," and until the 1960s and 1970s, federal courts rarely operated as such.

The Origins of Judicial Policymaking

The national political system is interconnected in surprising ways. It may not seem obvious that changes in the national party system helped to create federal judicial policymaking, but that is the case. As the New Deal party system crumbled in the 1960s—documented in Chapter 4—parties themselves became dominated by issue activists sharing a common ideological agenda. Unlike the old-style pragmatic party leaders they replaced, these activists sought to put their ideological stamp on the federal judiciary and formed liberal and conservative interest groups to pursue that end. In the late 1960s, political scientist Nancy Scherer notes, the demands of ideologically driven party activists and interest groups led to judicial appointments on ideological grounds, partisan polarization in the appointment process, and big differences in judicial behavior by judges depending upon which party dominated the appointment process at the time of their appointment (Scherer 2005, 38–45). Political scientist Robert Kagan notes that as parties weakened, it made sense for "interest groups and momentarily strong political coalitions to demand enactment of highly detailed laws, enforceable in court" to help "insulate today's policy victories from reversal following tomorrow's electoral loss" (2001, 49). Congress in the 1960s and 1970s obliged.

For most of American Constitutional history before the 1960s, the federal courts functioned differently and so did the judicial appointment process.

Courts before then were "small in number and, with only occasional exceptions, small in their impact on public policy" (Mackenzie 1996, 135). Federal judicial appointments operated on the basis of patronage, not ideology:

> Because the old party system left judicial selection in the hands of local party leaders and home state senators who placed their patrons on the bench, the appointees of a given president—Democrat or Republican— were ideologically heterogeneous, just as local party leaders and home state senators were ideologically heterogeneous.
>
> (Scherer 2005, 28–29)

Because courts seldom made policy but confined themselves to norm enforcement in particular controversies, few national interest groups paid attention to judicial selection. Most lawyers were sole practitioners, in contrast to the many "mega law firms" of today. Congress took less initiative in domestic policy, producing fewer legal controversies for the federal courts to address.

During this period, a form of judicial activism arose in the Supreme Court, but one quite different from that pioneered later by the Warren Court. From about 1890 to the late 1930s, the Court struck down 43 federal and 390 state laws, holding that progressive social and economic reforms were inconsistent with the language of the Constitution (Stanley and Niemi 2010, 281). In this earlier form of activism, the Court made policy by blocking actions of legislators and restricting the actions of the national and state governments. Contemporary judicial activism, however, operates far more expansively in policymaking. Now, federal courts are far more likely to approve legislative expansions of government policy, and where federal courts have deemed legislative action was insufficient, courts have made policy themselves: "setting standards, issuing detailed rules, establishing goals—generally performing a broad array of what had once been conceived of solely as legislative or administrative responsibilities" (Mackenzie 1996, 134). Beginning with the Warren Court, such policymaking gradually became institutionalized as a normal practice of the federal judiciary.

Institutionalizing Judicial Policymaking

The institutionalization of federal judicial policymaking occurred gradually, in several steps from the 1950s to the 1980s. The Supreme Court inaugurated the process with its landmark decisions *Brown vs. Board of Education of Topeka* 347 U.S. 483 (1954) and 349 U.S. 294 (1955). In the first *Brown* decision, the Court ruled that segregation of public schools by law (de jure segregation) was a violation of the Fourteenth Amendment's requirement that no state may deny its citizens "equal protection of the laws." In justifying its decision, the Court relied on the findings of recent social science, arguing that segregation marks the "colored race" with a "badge of inferiority." The policy action produced a sweeping and laudable restructuring of race relations. It is arguably one of the most important policy decisions of the twentieth century. The second *Brown* decision began a new process of "structural remedies" to enforce policies announced by the Court, in this case in the original 1954 decision. In *Brown* II, the Court required affected districts to desegregate with "all deliberate speed" and ordered federal district courts to oversee the desegregation process. With the cooperation of the Department of Justice, this administrative regime slowly rolled back legal segregation in state and local school districts.

Judicial scholar Gordon Silverstein explains how the *Brown* decisions boosted judicial policymaking:

> [W]hen the Warren Court first signaled the possibility that, in addition to its traditional function of saying what government *could* and what it could *not* do, the courts might now also be available to say what government *must* do as well, the Justices opened a new path to policy goals.

(2009, 29)

So it proved. Since the *Brown* decisions, structural changes have been ordered by federal courts in several policy areas. The Supreme Court in *Swann v. Charlotte Mecklenburg Board of Education* 42 U.S. 1 (1971) issued an extensive list of structural remedies, including mandatory busing, to eliminate legally segregated schools. Judge Arthur Garrity in the 1970s single-handedly supervised the desegregation of Boston schools by requiring busing and supervising the implementation of busing plans. Federal courts applied the Eighth Amendment's ban on "cruel and unusual punishments" in regulating state prison systems and requiring several state legislatures to fund prison improvements (Feeley and Rubin, 2000). Federal Judge Frank M. Johnson, Jr. in 1972 handed down rulings that established minimum standards for providing treatment in state mental health facilities in Alabama that he deemed inadequate. From 1972 to 2003, when federal court supervision concluded, implementation of these standards reshaped the mental health system in Alabama and in the nation (Ziegler 2003).

Lawsuits became a prime vehicle for making policy through federal courts. The Supreme Court in 1966 amended the Federal Rule of Civil Procedure 24a, relaxing the rules for interveners to have "standing to sue" in federal cases, opening the way for an avalanche of lawsuits in federal courts in ensuing decades. From 1950 to 1969, the number of civil lawsuits involving the U.S. government as a plaintiff or defendant stood at about 22,500 per year. In the 1970s, that civil caseload doubled and by 1985 it had doubled again (Dungworth and Pace 1990, 8). During that time, federal courts began to respond favorably to "class action" lawsuits filed on behalf of large groups of people—not individual litigants—regarding product liability, medical

Table 8.1 Comparison of traditional and contemporary lawsuits

Components	Traditional	Emerging new style
Actor	Identifiable individual	Abstract collection of people or nonidentifiable person, possibly predecessor of defendant
Time of act	Immediate past	Distant past, continuing, or potentially in future
Nature of act	Specific	Nonspecific or a variety of acts
Unlawful by virtue of	Specific statute or clear court precedent	No clear statutory provision or judicial precedent
Harm	Palpably injurious	Intangible
Who hurt	Identifiable individual directly harmed by actor	Many persons, not necessarily identifiable and not necessarily directly affected by actor
Relief	Narrow, directly related to injury	Broad, not necessarily deducible from the nature of the harm
Will bind	Parties only	Nonparties, potentially millions
Court's involvement	Ceases on entry of judgment	Continues indefinitely

Source: Lieberman (1981), p. 31, based on Chayes (1976).

malpractice, environmental protection and the government's use of "eminent domain" to seize privately-owned lands (Lieberman 1981, 41, 67, 103, 149). Courts in the 1960s and 1970s gained the ability to make rules regarding large groups of citizens through lawsuits. Table 8.1 details broader grounds for lawsuits, still largely in place today, as are much larger numbers of civil suits involving the national government than before 1970 (Administrative Office of the U.S. Courts 2012, Table C-2A).

Congress abetted the institutionalization of judicial policymaking by passing many social and environmental laws. Between 1964 and 1977, Congress passed 25 major civil rights and environmental acts, plus new legal regulations regarding workplace safety, consumer lending, product safety, private pension funds, and local public education. Included among these were the Civil Rights Act (1964), the National Traffic and Motor Safety Act (1966), the National Environmental Protection Act (1972), the Clean Air Act (1970), the Occupational Safety and Health Act (1970), the Clean Water Act (1972) and the Equal Employment Opportunity Act (1972). The laws expanded bureaucratic regulations, which were then adjudicated in the courts.

Robert Kagan explains how many of these laws greatly increased litigation and spawned more judicial policymaking:

> Congress assigned primary enforcement responsibility to state and local government officials. Then how could reformers and their congressional allies be sure that the new federal norms would be faithfully implemented? . . . individual victims of injustice and energetic reform lawyers could act as "private attorneys general," bringing lawsuits against state and local governments for half-hearted implementation of federal laws, or they could sue regulated businesses directly.
>
> (2001, 47)

Congress, in other words, came "to rely on private litigation in statutory implementation" (Farhang 2010, 3). As we note in Chapter 5 on Congress and Chapter 7 on the bureaucracy as well, legislators avoided the at times messy politics of implementation and left them to the courts. That gave the courts the ability to define implementation, that is, to make policy.

The Education for All Handicapped Children Act, passed by Congress in 1975, provides an example of how lawmakers handed policymaking authority to federal courts (Lieberman 1981, 29–30). The law required the states to provide "free, appropriate" education to disabled children. One provision required special programs for children demonstrating a "severe discrepancy" between actual and expected achievement on learning disability tests. The law, however, did not define a standard of "severe discrepancy." Similarly vague standards appeared in civil rights statues passed during this era. A federal court in New York eventually defined the "severe discrepancy" standard in 1980, when it ruled the state's 50 percent discrepancy standard was too high (Carroll 1980).

While the federal courts were increasingly deciding policy about state and local implementation of federal laws, their authority over federal bureaucratic agencies also expanded. Richard Stewart in 1975 summarized the many new powers federal courts had assumed over bureaucratic regulation due to congressional delegation and related federal court decisions. The presumption of judicial review of agency actions increased and a larger class of interests became entitled to participate in agency hearings, decisions and judicial review of agency actions. Because "administrative authorities have assumed an increasing measure of power over the wealth, income, education and other advantageous opportunities enjoyed by individuals," federal court authority was expanded "to control this increased governmental power" (Stewart 1975, 1716). Increased court control over the bureaucracy thus boosted court policymaking. A prime example of court power over bureaucratic regulation writing is *Massachusetts v. Environmental Protection Agency* 549 U.S. 497, S. Ct. 1438 (2007) discussed later in this chapter.

The Supreme Court, for its part, after 1954 became less deferential toward Congress and the president. Federal judges are far less likely to have had legislative or executive experience. None of the present members of the Supreme Court, for example, have such backgrounds. With less experience with other realms of governance, the Supreme Court in recent decades has more vigorously stamped its interpretation upon Congress and presidential actions. From 1789 to 1960, the Supreme Court declared 72 federal laws and 689 state and local laws unconstitutional. Since 1960, the court had ruled 89 federal laws and 612 state and local laws unconstitutional, a much brisker pace. Constitutional interpretation is a fundamental form of national policy-making, a major duty the Supreme Court in recent decades aggressively has pursued.

All this adds up to a federal judiciary in which "litigation is more like problem solving than grievance-answering" (Horowitz 1977, 7). Judicial scholar Robert Kagan described federal judicial policymaking as an enduring regime of "adversarial legalism" whose basic structures are:

> the fragmentation of governmental and regulatory authority among levels of government and many agencies; a dense web of highly prescriptive, analytically and procedurally demanding statutes; and ready access by affected interests to a politically selected, self-confident and rather unpredictable judiciary.
>
> (2001, 232)

Such a regime is "very easy to maintain and very difficult to dislodge" (Teles 2008, 14). A reconfigured legal profession, riven by ideological divisions yet commonly committed to pursuing policy solutions in court, provides a vital support structure for contemporary judicial policymaking.

Congressional Delegation and Judicial Policymaking

As discussed in Chapter 5, the Civil Rights Act of 1991 demonstrated how lawmaking in Congress had changed. It serves as well to illustrate the growing policy-making role of the judiciary. In 1964, a southern bloc of conservative Democrats filibustered the Civil Rights Act. The 1991 Act was not subject to a North/South division but rather a Democrat/Republican division based on party constituencies—minority voters and Democrats versus the business community and Republicans. Ultimately, both sides deferred to the courts to settle the dispute. At issue was a provision in the bill referred to as the "business necessity" standard that stipulated employers may legitimately use employment practices that disproportionately impact minority employees so long as there is a demonstrable business necessity for the practice.

The Supreme Court had interpreted Title VII of the Civil Rights Act of 1964 as prohibiting not only intentional discrimination or "disparate treatment," but also unintentional discrimination that has a "disparate impact" on protected class members (see, e.g., *Griggs v. Duke Power Co.*, 401 U.S. 424 (1971)). Disparate impact exists if ostensibly neutral selection or promotion criteria exclude or reduce the opportunities of minorities disproportionate to non-minorities. Employers may argue as a defense to a disparate impact charge that the challenged criteria are a "business necessity." Much disagreement existed between Democrats and Republicans over what to do about "business necessity" and whether the 1991 Act should define it (Gueron 1995).

In the end, the Senate and the House punted on the issue of defining business necessity. Instead, the Senate published an interpretive memorandum in the Congressional Record to accompany the 1991 Act. The three-paragraph memorandum indicated judicial interpretation of "business necessity" should be governed by concepts enunciated by the Supreme Court in prior rulings. Legal experts agreed, however, that existing court rulings offered little in the way of a clear definition of business necessity. In an effort to pass a law, the Senate in effect had to make a deal—any meaningful effort to settle one of the key points of contention would have likely derailed the legislation. So the Senate, and ultimately the Congress, opted for ambiguity and delegation of responsibility to the judiciary (Runkel 1994).

In the case of the Civil Rights Act, Congress chose to defer to the courts with regard to defining "business necessity," but, as discussed in Chapter 7, Congress typically delegates the specifics of policy design to the bureaucracy. Such delegation can frequently result in judicial intervention as well. In the case of the Clean Air Act (CAA), the Court was called upon to determine whether the Environmental Protection Agency was properly interpreting the CAA with regard to defining and regulating greenhouse gas (GHG) emissions as air pollutants. In *Massachusetts v. Environmental Protection Agency*, 549 U.S. 497 (2007), the Supreme Court ultimately determined that GHG emissions did meet the definition of an air pollutant and directed the Administrator of the EPA to act in accordance with the CAA. A key question before the Court in that case concerned standing and whether or not the coalition of cities, states, and interest groups had the legal standing to sue the EPA. The Supreme Court had relaxed the requirements for standing in 1966, but had begun to retighten them in recent years. Standing is based on a plaintiff meeting each of three criteria: that it had suffered a "concrete and particularized injury," that the injury was "fairly traceable to the defendant," and that a favorable decision would be likely to "redress that injury" (Greenhouse, 2007).

A majority of justices determined that the coastal states and cities that had filed suit, especially the state of Massachusetts, met all three conditions given that rising sea levels along the coast presented the risk of catastrophic harm that could be reduced by government regulation of GHG emissions. In his dissent, Chief Justice John Roberts argued the Court's decision on standing "has caused us to transgress the proper—and properly limited—role of the courts in a democratic society [...] redress of grievances of the sort at issue here is the function of Congress and the chief executive, not the federal courts" (Greenhouse, 2007). Time will tell whether this decision with its expanded concept of standing increases further the role of the judiciary in policymaking.

Ideology among Lawyers and Federal Courts

Accompanying the rise in federal cases and lawsuits was a huge growth in the number of American lawyers and of liberal legal activism. The total number of American lawyers swelled from 180,000 in 1940 to almost 800,000 by 1988 (Mackenzie 1996, 136). Many law schools, busy producing a burgeoning population of lawyers, gave birth to a new "Liberal Legal Network" (Teles 2008, 22–58). Following the Warren Court's path-breaking decision *Gideon v. Wainwright* 372 U.S. 365 in 1963, which established a "due process" civil right for indigent criminal defendants to be guaranteed a lawyer in criminal trials, many law schools developed programs in "public interest law." Law in the public interest directed legal efforts broadly toward social change, through such means as representation of criminal defendants and class action suits to achieve liberal policy ends. The Ford Foundation funded legal clinics in many leading law schools aimed at advocacy of legal services for the poor and for social change (ibid., 38–41). Congress responded to President Johnson's request for a new federally funded Legal Services Program (LSP) to provide legal help to the poor. The previously conservative American Bar Association endorsed new liberal initiatives, becoming a strong advocate of the LSP. The LSP proved effective at liberal advocacy in federal courts. Between 1966 and 1974, the LSP submitted 169 cases to the Supreme Court and had 73 percent accepted for court action, a rate higher than the President's own Solicitor General during that time (Lawrence 1990, Appendix C).

The Liberal Legal Network developed into a dominant player in federal judicial policymaking just as the liberal Democratic governance of the mid-1960s was receiving a rebuke from voters at the ballot box in the 1966 and 1968 elections. Despite this, several factors allowed the LLN to entrench itself in judicial politics. Political scientist Steven Teles lists several reasons why the LLN was able to entrench itself. First, the legal profession—from law schools to the ABA—embraced new modes of liberal legal activism. Second, liberal legalism seemed a civilized alternative to violent protest erupting in the late 1960s. Third, the federal courts, with the Warren Court at the lead, and the federal government through the Legal Services Program, created new resources and venues for liberal activism. Fourth, the rhetoric of "rights" gained great moral sway in the 1960s. Fifth, elite foundations, led by the Ford Foundation, funded a new "liberal legal support structure" in law schools and public service law programs (Teles 2008, 56). In all, a powerful faction of legal professionals found the new avenues of federal judicial policymaking very suitable to the pursuit of liberal ends. Increasing the scale and complexity of judicial policymaking served the Liberal Legal Network's policy goals well. The concurrent rise in federal court lawsuits, cases in federal courts of appeals, and appeals to the Supreme Court has persisted since the rise of the LLN in the 1960s (ibid., 265–274).

One reason for the continued high level of activity in federal courts was that, perhaps inevitably, the liberal initiative toward the federal courts generated a conservative response. Judicial policymaking became, in the decades since the 1960s, an enduring battlefield of polarized liberal and conservative legal elites. Conflicts over judicial policymaking continued in federal court but also spilled over into congressional appointment battles and electoral politics. The first filibuster against a Supreme Court nominee in American history came against Abe Fortas, a judicial liberal nominated by President Johnson in 1968. Richard Nixon during that year's presidential campaign pledged to appoint "law and order" judges who shared his judicial philosophy—one much more conservative than that evident in the Warren Court. Nixon pursued this by appointing the more conservative Warren Burger as Warren's successor as Chief Justice. The Democratic majority Senate rejected other conservative nominees to the court, Clement Haynsworth and G. Harold Carswell, the first time since 1894 that two consecutive Supreme Court nominees had been turned down.

The Burger court, however, gradually earned a reputation as "the counterrevolution that wasn't" by producing large-scale, liberal policy change in three landmark decisions: *Swan v. Charlotte-Mecklenburg Board of Education* 402 U.S. 1 (1971) endorsing school busing as a structural remedy to de jure segregation, *Roe v. Wade* 410 U.S. 113 (1973) establishing a woman's abortion decision as part of a constitutionally protected right to privacy and *University of California Davis v. Bakke* 438 U.S. 265 (1978) permitting race to be considered as a factor in college admissions as "affirmative action." Justice Harry Blackmun authored the *Roe* majority opinion and Justice Lewis Powell the *Bakke* majority opinion; both were Nixon appointees. Only Nixon's last appointee, William Rehnquist, proved to be a reliably conservative justice. His conservative fidelity gained him appointment as Chief Justice by Ronald Reagan in 1986 upon Burger's retirement.

While the Nixon administration attempted to stock the federal courts with more ideological conservatives, right-leaning legal professionals began organizing in ways to rival the Liberal Legal Network. In the 1970s, initial attempts to create conservative legal foundations funded by business proved of limited effectiveness because of their regional focus and emphasis on parochial business concerns (Teles 2007, 75–78). The next major step in the brewing conservative counterrevolution came with the election of Ronald Reagan in 1980. Reagan's Justice Department made ideological screening of federal judicial candidates a top priority. The cumulative impact of Reagan and Nixon Supreme Court appointments became evident in the late 1980s, when the court moved in a more conservative direction.

Conservative "legal entrepreneurs" founded the Federalist Society in 1982, an organization that since that time has challenged legal liberalism and provided a pipeline of conservative nominees for GOP presidents. Current Supreme Court Chief Justice John Roberts and Associate Justice Samuel Alito are members. On its website, the organization claims:

> Law schools and the legal profession are currently strongly dominated by a form of orthodox liberal ideology [. . .] founded on the principles that the state exists to preserve freedom, that the separation of governmental powers is central to our Constitution, and that it is emphatically the province and duty of the judiciary to say what the law is, not what it should be.
>
> (Federalist Society 2012)

Other interest groups formed in the 1970s and 1980s to enlist in ideological battle over the courts. Conservatives formed organizations such as Judicial Watch and the Institute of Justice; liberals countered with the Alliance for Justice, People for the American Way and National Organization for Women, alongside the longstanding liberal mainstay, the American Civil Liberties Union. Prime focuses for interest group battle were the federal judicial appointments. The groups testified during nomination hearings, ran television ads against Supreme Court nominees, directly lobbied legislators, and filed briefs in court cases. Interviews with judicial interest groups leaders revealed a common belief on their part "that the federal courts wield significant power in implementing public policy" (Scherer 2005, 195). Beyond these core judicial groups, interest group involvement in federal judicial appointment politics became vast. One study found that 448 groups expressed formal opinions about one or more federal judicial nominees in just one two-year period, 1998–1999 (Bell 2002, 88).

Growing Conflict over Federal Court Appointments

Senate opposition of presidential nominees to federal district and appeals courts began during the Reagan presidency (Scherer 2005, 148–150). Democrats throughout the 1980s began to employ a variety of strategies to derail objectionable federal court nominees: inaction, delay, filibusters and refusing to bargain with the White House. Confirmation conflicts, however, first erupted into total warfare surrounding the Reagan administration's nomination of Robert Bork to the Supreme Court in 1987. President Reagan's first two appointees, Sandra Day O'Conner and Antonin Scalia, sailed through the nomination process in the customary way—with little discussion of their substantive views about constitutional interpretation. Bork had served in Nixon's Justice Department as Solicitor General and was an outspoken opponent of liberal judicial policymaking. The Senate Judiciary Committee held widely televised hearings at which Bork himself discussed at length his judicial philosophy. Interest groups ran ads against Bork, asking citizens to call their Senators to register their opinions on the matter; subsequently the phone lines were jammed. The Democrat-majority committee ultimately rejected Bork's nomination on a party-line vote. Reagan's next nominee, Anthony Kennedy, was a much less outspoken conservative and won Senate confirmation with less fanfare.

The Bork battle was tepid compared to the conflict over the nomination of black conservative Clarence Thomas to the court in 1991 by George Herbert Walker Bush. Bush's first appointment was the relatively obscure David Souter, who said little about his judicial philosophy during the appointment process and proved to be a far more liberal judicial policymaker on the bench than Bush had desired. Thomas, in contrast, was a well-known conservative figure. Interest groups on both ideological sides testified, ran ads and urged public contact of lawmakers. Anita Hill, a former employee of Thomas at the Equal Employment Opportunity Commission, charged Thomas with sexual harassment during public hearings. No conclusive proof of the charges ever surfaced, and Thomas was confirmed by a narrow 52–48 margin by a Senate controlled 56–44 by Democrats.

Bill Clinton's two nominees, Ruth Bader Ginsburg and Stephen Breyer, won confirmation from the Democratically-controlled Senate with little difficulty. After the GOP gained control of Congress in 1995, conflict over judicial appointments expanded to include several battles over federal district and appeals court nominees. GOP Senators resorted to inaction, delay, filibusters and refusing to bargain with the White House to stop unacceptable Clinton federal court nominees. Conflict within the Senate continued during George W. Bush's presidency, as lower federal court nominations faced unprecedented difficulties gaining Senate approval as the use of filibusters increased. By the spring of 2005, Democrats had successfully filibustered several nominees for federal appeals courts. GOP leaders in response proposed a number of ways to curtail the use of filibusters regarding judicial confirmations. Most dramatic was Senate Majority Leader Bill Frist's proposal, dubbed by Democrats the "nuclear option," in which a series of parliamentary rulings would declare filibusters against nominations unconstitutional. Democrats threatened to shut down the Senate completely in response, and Frist withdrew his proposal (Binder and Maltzman 2009, 100). With the Democratic takeover of Congress in 2007, G. W. Bush's success in obtaining federal court confirmations fell to 77 percent, well below the 90 and above levels registered by Presidents Carter through Clinton. Barack Obama's first two years in office yielded a much lower success rate of 58 percent (Alliance for Justice 2011, 21). Confirmation wars have reached new levels of intensity in a Senate strongly polarized by two overlapping factors: ideology and partisanship. The advent of partisan media, discussed in Chapter 4, contributes to the bitter confirmation wars as website, cables news channels, and radio programs take sides and rally the party faithful in support or opposition of nominees.

Patterns of Conflict over Judicial Nominations

Because of the widely acknowledged policymaking role of federal courts, partisan and ideological Senate battles over nominees have now become commonplace. The number of federal appeals and district court nominees confirmed dropped from nearly 100 percent in the 1960s to below 50 percent in recent Congresses, particularly for Appeals Court nominees (Binder and Maltzman 2009, 3). Federal Appeals Court confirmation battles have grown with the decline in annual cases heard by the Supreme Court, from well over 150 in the 1960s to fewer than 100 in the twenty-first century. With less Supreme Court review of Appeals Court decisions, the Appeals Courts have gained authority as final policymakers in many areas of law.

The correlations in Table 8.2 reveal that partisan polarization and the rise of interest groups have made confirmation of Appeals Court nominees more difficult from 1952 to 2008. The incidence of votes that are party line—with all Democrats opposing all Republicans—and the frequency with which Senators vote with their own party on roll calls share a common pattern with Appeals Court nominations. As party line voting and party unity in voting increased, appeals nomination success dropped and the length of the confirmation process increased. Partisan polarization surrounding the president had a similar relationship to Appeals Court nominations. The more polarized partisan support for the president was in the Senate and among the public, the lower the level of Appeals Court confirmation success and the longer the process. The number of interest groups had a strongly negative relationship with appeals nomination success and correlates positively with longer confirmation processes. The number of lower federal court nominations opposed by interest groups stood at zero until 1973 and then rose steadily to reach 33 percent by 2004 (Scherer 2005, 4). In all, partisan polarization and interest group proliferation have raised the stakes in battles over judicial policymaking.

The trends of partisan polarization in the Senate and the course of Appeals Court nominations appear in detail in Figure 8.1. Appeals Court nomination success was virtually certain until the late 1970s and early 1980s, when

Table 8.2 Systemic correlates of Appeals Court nominations, 1952–2008

	Nomination success	Duration of successful nomination
Percentage of Senate votes party line	−.45	+.70
Party unity in Senate vote	−.56	+.49
Senate partisan support gap for president	−.73	+.63
Public partisan support gap for president	−.73	+.51
Number of associations	−.92	+.57

Source: See Appendix.

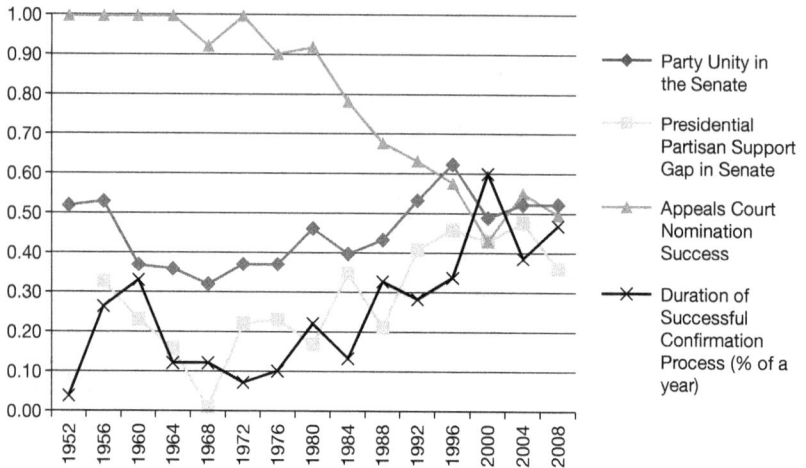

Figure 8.1 Senate party polarization and Federal Appeals Court nominations, 1952–2008

contestation began and rose to steadily higher levels by the twenty-first century. At the same time, party unity in Senate roll calls steadily grew and the partisan support gap for presidents also rose. After 2000, the confirmation environment hardly resembles that of the 1950s and 1960s.

Partisan polarization and less certain confirmation outcomes had become the rule of the day. A causal analysis of Appeals Court nominations from 1947–2006 found that partisan polarization, measured as the absolute difference in the average ideology of each Senate party each year, had a strongly negative effect on both the length and success of Appeals Court nominations (Binder and Maltzman 2009, 92–96).

As with so many aspects of American national governance, the politics of the federal courts altered dramatically after 1960. Supreme Court decisions and changes in judicial rules created new modes of judicial policymaking. Interest groups organized to press the courts for favorable policies and to populate the courts with judges who would create those policies. Congress passed a raft of laws permitting enforcement via lawsuits. The courts became a battleground of rival professional legal elites, making policy at a considerable remove from the public and its wishes. The stakes in judicial policymaking are frequently high, as the following example of the Supreme Court's policymaking about college admissions demonstrates.

Judicial Policymaking Regarding College Admissions

For most of American history, the undergraduate and graduate admissions processes of colleges and universities remained entirely private affairs, with institutions having total control over whom they admitted. Now, elaborate federal regulations and federal judicial decisions guide the admissions process. The increased federal role began in the 1960s. The 1964 Civil Rights Act contained a provision that would produce much judicial policymaking in subsequent decades. Section 601 states:

> No person in the United States shall, on the ground of race, color, or national origin, be excluded from participation in, be denied the benefits of, or be subjected to discrimination under any program or activity receiving Federal financial assistance.

The Act established elaborate regulatory procedures to prevent discrimination on the basis of race and sex in hiring, promotion and firing and created the Equal Employment Opportunity Commission to find ways to combat discrimination. President Johnson then issued Executive Order 11246 calling on federal contractors to take "affirmative action" in the employment of minorities. Under the EEOC, the term "affirmative action" came to be employed in the 1970s to describe programs aimed at diversifying occupations in which members of underrepresented groups—particularly African-Americans and Latinos—had been the subject of societal discrimination.

How far could the government go in ending such discrimination? The Supreme Court decided that in 1971 in *Griggs v. Duke Power* 401 U.S. 424. A unanimous court adopted a "disparate impact" test for affirmative action. The burden of proof would rest with the employer if hiring produced underrepresentation of one of the "protected classes" of the 1964 Civil Rights Act. In 1972, Congress adopted this approach to discrimination in the Equal Employment Opportunity Act. Going farther, Congress' 1977 Public Works Employment Act required government contractors to set aside 10 percent for minority contractors. Since 1977, however, federal policy on affirmative action—including that practiced by colleges and universities—has resided primarily with the courts.

The Supreme Court first addressed affirmative action in higher education in *Regents of the University of California v. Bakke* 438 U.S. 265 in 1978. Alan Bakke, a white medical school applicant, brought litigation, arguing that he was passed over for less qualified minority applicants. Of the 100 admission positions at the medical school, 16 were reserved for minority applicants. Bakke argued that since minority applicants were eligible for any of the 100 positions but white applicants for only 84, the medical school had violated both Title VI of the 1964 Civil Rights Act and the Equal Protection Clause of the Fourteenth Amendment.

The *Bakke* decision split the Court three ways. Four liberal justices (Blackmun, Brenna, Marshall and White) held the Davis plan violated neither the Civil Rights Act or the Fourteenth Amendment, arguing the numerical quotas were a legitimate way to "take race into account" to rectify "dis-advantages cast on minorities by past racial prejudice." Four conservative justices (Rehnquist, Stevens, Stewart and Burger) argued that the Davis program clearly violated Title VI of the Civil Rights Act by discriminating on the basis of race. It was left to Justice Lewis Powell to create a majority opinion by agreeing in part with both the liberal and conservative judges. Powell created a 5–4 majority with the conservatives disallowing minority quotas, but Powell varied from the conservatives in grounding his objection in the Fourteenth Amendment, not Title VI. To Powell, the Davis program violated Bakke's entitlement to "equal protection of the laws." Powell, however, sided with four liberals in asserting that race could be used as a factor in college admissions. Powell endorsed "competitive consideration of race" without numerical quotas. He supported this with a "diversity" argument, holding that a university's "atmosphere of speculation, experiment and creation . . . is promoted by a diverse student body." Hence, universities had a First Amendment "diversity" justification for considering race when admitting students. Powell specifically praised Harvard University's admissions procedure, in which the race of an applicant was known and weighed in the admission process without resort to numerical quotas.

Though the Court addressed many other affirmative action cases in the 1980s and 1990s, national policy on college admissions was set by the *Bakke* decision. Congress and the president took no initiatives to intrude on this policy area in a way that materially affected the court's decision. Colleges and universities operated their undergraduate and graduate admissions process in reference to the Court's opinion. In this area, Supreme Court policymaking did indeed reign supreme.

Beginning in 1989, though, the Court became more conservative in its other affirmative action decisions concerning the proper use of race in hiring, promotion and termination decisions by companies, school districts and universities (Naff 2004, 412–418). This led to speculation that the Court might reverse college admissions policy as promulgated in *Bakke*. Would the creation of a diverse student body continue to justify employing race as a factor in college admissions, and if so, how? The answer came in two related Court opinions in 2003 concerning the University of Michigan. One, *Gratz v. Bollinger* 539 U.S. 244, concerned its undergraduate admissions process and another, *Grutter v. Bollinger* 539 U.S. 306, dealt with its law school admissions.

The Court by 5–4 upheld the law school admissions process, reaffirming the decades-old *Bakke* policy. Writing for the other members of the majority (Ginsburg, Souter, Stevens and Breyer), Justice Sandra Day O'Connor upheld the "diversity" argument of *Bakke*, lauding "the important purpose of public education and the expansive freedoms of speech and thought associated with the university environment." So the Court deferred to "the Law School's educational judgment that such diversity is essential to its educational mission." Absent a strict numerical quota the university could continue to use race as a factor in admitting law students. The university's undergraduate admissions process employed race in a fashion differing from the law school's methods. For undergraduates, the university awarded a specific number of points to students who were members of "underrepresented groups." The court struck down the points system as not "narrowly tailored" but Chief Justice Rehnquist, writing for the 6–3 majority (also including Scalia, Kennedy, Thomas, Breyer and O'Connor), specifically declined to overrule the "diversity" logic of *Bakke*, ensuring that the previous decision's admissions policy would be the law of the land.

But for how long? That would depend on the shifting majorities on the closely divided Court. Justice O'Connor served warning in her *Gratz* majority opinion that, "The court expects 25 years from now, the use of racial preferences will no longer be necessary to further the interest approved today." Whether this comes to pass seems to depend entirely on the future composition of the Supreme Court. Another change in college admissions policy may be looming. The Court agreed to hear a case concerning race-conscious admissions at the University of Texas during its October 2012 arguments.

Because of the absence of Congress and president, the nine justices remain in charge of college admissions policy. Supreme Court policymaking about affirmative action, however, extended far beyond college admissions over the past 30 years. The Court has asserted final say on the proper role of race in hiring, promotion and hiring in both the public and private sectors.

> Thus, an examination of congressional and presidential actions since the Supreme Court began to rule on affirmative action programs in the late 1970s suggests that it was the court that set the agenda and formulated the policy, with Congress and the president doing little more than sniping from the sidelines.
>
> (Naff 2004, 425)

Major avenues of social mobility and opportunity remain under the sway of Supreme Court policymaking.

Conclusion

The rise of policymaking by the federal judiciary "is a change that emerged prominently after World War II and then mushroomed after 1960" (Mackenzie 1996, 155). Consider the many areas of policy directed and controlled by federal courts at present, with most of this expanded jurisdiction resulting in the past 50 years. These include criminal justice (police searches, a right to a lawyer in a criminal trial, the right to be informed of one's rights when arrested), reproductive freedom (abortion, birth control), prayer in school and other church/state issues, affirmative action in hiring, promotion, firing and university admissions, terrorist detainment and treatment, the racial composition of elementary and secondary schools and other controversies regarding discrimination concerning race, gender and sexual orientation. The federal courts also hold great sway over the economy by determining the appropriate powers of Congress to "regulate interstate and foreign commerce" under the Constitution. They also now determine the rules for the apportionment of legislative districts for state legislatures and the House of Representatives and the rules for funding federal legislative and presidential campaigns. Further, Congress beginning in the 1960s, created many regulatory laws concerning consumer protection, racial and gender discrimination, environmental protection and disability access that depend on litigation in federal court for thorough enforcement. "Whether we like it or not . . . court judges are policymakers and litigation is a form of policymaking" (Barnes 2009, 108).

Accompanying broader policymaking power was the emergence of federal judicial confirmations as ideological battlefields. Nancy Scherer summarizes the steps that led to this outcome. First, political parties became dominated by issue activists, ending the patronage basis of judicial selection and inserting ideological concerns into the selection process. This led to presidents, beginning with Johnson and Nixon, using ideological litmus tests in judicial appointments, and prompted interest groups to form and make judicial confirmations arenas of ideological warfare. Both parties in the Senate began to obstruct confirmation of unacceptable nominees and at times the confirmation process became the locus of sensational political conflict, as in the Bork and Thomas confirmation hearings (Scherer 2005, 195–195). The warfare seems an enduring aspect of the new national political system because it is the product of "effective conservative mobilization without significant displacement of liberalism" (Teles 2008, 274). The current "no party majority" electoral system coupled with a frequently polarized and partisan media environment portends endless and closely fought judicial confirmation battles.

Federal courts since 1960 have effectively "judicialized politics." They "have been increasingly able and willing to impose substantive limits on the power of legislative institutions . . . have increasingly become places where substantive policy is made" and "have been increasingly willing to regulate the conduct of political activity itself—by . . . interest groups, political parties, and both elected and appointed officials" (Ferejohn 2002, 41). The courts' new power seems here to stay.

This is not to say that the federal judiciary runs every aspect of our national political system. They have limited agenda power, in that they must wait for a dispute to be brought before them by others before a policy judgment can be made. They also are bound by past precedents, and overturning a prior precedent, as the Supreme Court notably did in *Brown* is a major, rare and controversial event. Federal courts also must depend on the Congress and president to formally comply with their decisions. In one notable case in 1985, *Immigration and Naturalization Service v. Chadha*, 462 U.S. 919, the Supreme Court produced a sweeping decision invalidating hundreds of congressional laws that both Congress and the president ignored. That case involved the legislative veto, statutory language allowing Congress by a vote of a committee, one chamber, or both chambers to block a presidential action. The court in *Chadha* held that all forms of legislative veto were unconstitutional because they had the force of law and all laws must, according to the Constitution, be presented to the president for his signature. In response, the national legislature and executive nevertheless agreed to continue observing most forms of legislative veto because they found them mutually convenient (Fisher 2005).

If federal courts do not make policy with impunity, the new judicial system that evolved in the 1960s and 1970s gave courts more policymaking clout than ever before in American history. It is fair to ask if courts are well designed for their expanded policymaking functions. To make policy well, one must have a command of all relevant facts, understand a wide variety of related controversies, address problems as they arise and review present policy in an appropriately timely manner. Legal scholar Donald Horowitz holds that courts are poorly designed to create policy in this fashion, for several reasons. First, adjudication focuses on one particular adversarial controversy and does not more broadly consider facts and principles of related controversies. Courts cannot fully consider an array of alternatives and thoroughly match benefits and costs among them. Second, a court opinion is "piecemeal" in that it can only address the specific issues in the controversy before the court. It can take a lengthy parade of decisions to fashion a comprehensive policy. For example, federal policy regarding school integration evolved over several decades as the Supreme Court dealt over time with specific controversies. Third, courts can only rule when litigation arrives before them, not in timely response to the onset of public problems. Courts "only act when litigants call" and so must depend upon the chance appearance of policy problems on their dockets. A lack of control and coordination across cases often results. Fourth, judicial fact-finding is narrow and often is not based on a broad consideration of necessary evidence. "The potentially unrepresentative character of the litigants makes it hazardous to generalize from their situation to the wider context" (Horowitz 1977, 34–45).

There is also the question of democratic accountability. If federal judges are appointed for life and are making policy, are they operating democratically in such policymaking? As a leading text on American courts puts it:

> In a democracy broad matters of public policy are, at least in theory, presumed to be left to the elected representatives of the people—not to judicial appointees with life terms. In principle, U.S. judges are not supposed to make policy, but in practice they cannot help but do so to some extent.
>
> (Carp, Stidham, and Manning 2011a, 31)

A key consequence is that much policy previously decided by popular participation in elections is now determined by legal professionals. With courts, litigious interest groups and legal professionals controlling important policy areas, a result is "a diminished systemwide ability to construct proper foundations of popular support for new policy initiatives" (Mackenzie 1996, 159). Popular discontent with government rises.

Federal court policymaking is another triumph of professional government. It is well entrenched because it is supported by interest groups of the Left and Right, the many ideological activists populating both major parties, and compliant Senators who respond to kindred activists and interest groups by making federal judicial confirmations an ideological and partisan battle zone. Conservatives argue for judicial "restraint" meaning a more conservative turn in federal court policymaking. Liberals, seeking judicial activism for "social justice," in contrast, promote a liberal turn. But everyone involved knows the federal courts make much important national policy. Most of the public is not involved. The courts' expansion of professional government reinforces many Americans' distrustful distance from their national rulers.

9 The Road from Here

An Unsustainable Path and
an Uncertain Future

The central features of the post-1960 American political system, detailed in
our previous chapters, have attracted notice from other contemporary
political analysts. *New York Times* columnist Thomas Friedman, writing in a
recent book with Johns Hopkins professor Michael Mandelbaum, drew an
ominous implication from several traits we have explained here:

> Our political system is stuck. It is under the sway of powerful special
> interests that work for policies that are at best irrelevant to and at worst
> counterproductive for the urgent present and future needs of the United
> States. The two parties are so sharply polarized that they are incapable
> of arriving at the deep, ideologically painful compromises that major
> initiatives, of the kind required to meet the major challenges America
> faces, will require.
>
> (Friedman and Mandelbaum 2011, 331)

At the root of the system's inability to address policy challenges is widespread
public distrust of professional government, a force highlighted by Nicholas
Hayes in his recent book critical of America's governing elites. Hayes notes
that this problem reaches back to the 1960–1980 period we identify as crucial
in the formation of America's contemporary political system:

> Writing in the *New York Times* on April 8, 1970, James Reston observed:
> "Behind all of the questions of politics, ideologies and personalities . . .
> lies the larger issue of public confidence and trust in the institutions
> of the nation . . . That trust does not exist now. The authority of the
> government . . . is under challenge all over the republic, and men of all
> ages, stations and persuasions agree that this crisis of confidence is one
> of the most important and dangerous problems of the age." But what
> was viewed at the time as a nadir of public trust turns out to have been
> its high-water mark . . . We are in the midst of a broad and devastating
> crisis of authority.
>
> (Hayes 2012, 11, 13)

Hayes overstates this a bit. Trust, as we have shown, began to drop in the middle 1960s and was not at its high water mark in 1970. His broader point, however, is spot on. The decline of trust is central to America's current politics and problems. Restoring trust is a signal priority. In this chapter we summarize our findings and discuss ways the nation can restore trust and improve its political system's functions.

Let's begin with a summary of our findings.

- We began by sketching the seven key transformations of America's political system occurring from the 1950s to the 1980s. First, the Democrats lost their status as the nation's majority party due to the collapse of their supporting electoral coalition forged during the New Deal era of the 1930s. Second, an anti-majority party realignment occurred in the electorate, featuring no "normal" majority party. Third, the transformation of the American media allowed partisan and engaged voters to gain access to information sources tailored to their views. Fourth, as more members of the electorate became either politically independent or began to evidence weak and variable partisan ties, polarization between the two parties and among actual voters increased. Fifth, trust in government plummeted from 1965–1976 and remained at lower levels thereafter. Sixth, the rise of professionalism among elected officials, judges and bureaucrats contributed to low public trust and electoral volatility. Seventh, changing behavior in Congress, the presidency, the courts and bureaucracy transformed governance as professional routines became entrenched in these institutions and interest groups became more numerous and active in national policymaking.
- The underlying forces shaping the seven trends were the rise in popular discontent and the expansion of professional government. Professional government features congressional job security and legislative careerism, thousands of professional advocacy groups in Washington, a bigger and more elaborately organized presidency, a thicker bureaucracy with more complex organization and policymaking authority, and expanded judicial policymaking by judges with professional legal, rather than political, backgrounds. Widespread popular suspicion of elites accompanied this growing professionalization.
- The dynamic element in the current no-majority party system is the growing number of independent and unreliable independent partisans. The arrival of this volatile faction occurred during the late 1960s when the New Deal coalition fractured as southern white voters left the Democratic Party. The proliferation of new media contributed to lower levels of participation by these less partisan voters and greater participation by their more partisan counterparts. Each party's primary electorates became ideologically more uniform, comprised of conservative Republicans and liberal Democrats, which produced more ideologically extreme candidates and more partisan polarization in

government. The result is a more polarized voting electorate and more partisan politics. However, during highly contentious elections, less partisan voters are drawn back into the process and they contribute to the volatility that is a hallmark of the present era.

- From the late 1950s through the 1970s, Congress evolved into a body of professionalized and highly partisan members. This gradually produced more resources for congressional party leaders and an increased reliance upon unorthodox procedures for passing legislation. Congress became more difficult to manage due to intense partisan polarization. Legislative dysfunction is the fault of both congressional parties. Polarization, combined with the great proliferation of professional interest groups in Washington, made legislating more difficult and obstructing legislation easier.

- After 1965, presidents possessed less "political capital", particularly due to lower public and congressional support. Shrinking presidential clout correlated with the rise of a more independent electorate, the decline in public trust, and the rise of resourceful professional interest groups and a larger and more complex bureaucracy. In response, presidents have relied more on expansive definition of their formal powers, which paradoxically often ensnares them in political controversies and further weakens their political capital. Presidents, given the frustrations of governance, at times embrace executive unilateralism as an inviting tactical option, but it becomes a power trap that often relegates chief executives to positions of permanently shrunken influence.

- In the 1960s, the bureaucracy expanded its regulatory and administrative authority as domestic government expanded. Divided government produced pitched partisan battles over control of the bureaucracy. Closely contested partisan warfare in Congress in subsequent decades produced more legislative delegation of policymaking decisions to bureaucrats. Yet the bureaucracy finds itself often ensnared in Congress' partisan conflicts, a volatile environment that can produce policy changes as partisan control of the legislature shifts. This zigging and zagging occurs in a dense forest of well-established "issue networks" comprised of interest groups, bureaucrats and their agencies and legislative specialists populating congressional committees. Policymaking and policy decisions thus became ever more complex and confusing, stoking popular discontent.

- Federal courts from the 1950s through the 1970s adopted doctrines and procedures that greatly increased their policymaking power, producing an increasing judicialization of politics. Courts now predominate in policy areas such as reproductive freedom, church/state issues, affirmative action, terrorist detainment and the commerce power of the national government. Because of the policy consequences of federal judicial decisions, judicial confirmations in the Senate have become bitterly contested partisan battlefields. Judicial policymaking is a new form of professional government. Federal judges today tend to come from careers in the legal profession and have little, if any, experience with electoral or legislative politics.

One of the biggest consequences of the traits and trends summarized above is the expansion of the national agenda. Many interest groups and government professionals invent issues and proposed solutions for consideration in the halls of national government. But despite the great expansion of the agenda, progress on many issues remains stagnant. Why is that?

A Big Agenda Yields Little Action

Political scientist James Q. Wilson identifies the forces behind national agenda expansion, several mentioned in our previous chapters:

> Once politics was about only a few things; today, it is about nearly everything. There has been . . . a drastic reduction in the cost of using the political process relative to the cost of using, for similar results, the market. That reduction has been the result of easier access to the courts (by fee shifting and class-action suits), the greater ease of financing interest groups with foundation grants and direct-mail fundraising, and the multiplication of government agencies and congressional staffs.
>
> (Wilson 2010, 8)

Wilson's constellation of forces promoting agenda expansion closely resembles Mancur Olson's "distributional coalitions" introduced in our earlier chapters. Olson notes how a stable society like that of the United States produces "crowded agendas" and "cluttered bargaining tables" fueled by lobbying and a government populated by professionals seeking to further their careers (1984, 56). Lobbying "increases the complexity of regulation and the scope of government by creating special provisions and exemptions" (ibid., 69). The result?

> The growth of coalitions with an incentive to try to capture a larger share of the national income, the increase in regulatory complexity and governmental action that lobbying coalitions encourage . . . alter the pattern of incentives and direction of evolution in a society. The incentive to produce is diminished; the incentive to seek a large share of what is produced increases.
>
> (ibid., 72)

Perhaps it is no surprise that national economic growth has trended downward since the 1960s and now proceeds at its slowest pace since the Great Depression of the 1930s.

Stalemate is now the norm in many areas of national policy. A recent comprehensive study of interest groups' role in 98 policymaking cases concluded: "in any given year, the typical issue lobbyists are working on doesn't move at all. Instead, the status quo usually triumphs . . . it's stalemate" (Baumgartner et. al. 2009, 244). This occurs, according to the study's authors, for five reasons. First, "the scarcity of attention, the crush of other problems, is obstacle number one that advocates face" (ibid., 248). Agenda expansion promotes agenda inaction. Second, defenders of the status quo have the easier task of sowing doubts about possible policy changes. Third, in a polarized environment, creating bipartisan coalitions to push for policy change is now more difficult. Fourth, the gatekeepers of current policy frequently are stakeholders who created current policy and "it takes a lot to convince them that 'their' policy doesn't work" (ibid., 249). Finally, shared information among players in Washington's many issue networks induces policy stability "because individual policy makers typically do not have the ability single-handedly to change the collective understandings of entire policy communities" (ibid., 250).

Stalemate ensues from the proliferation of Olson's "distributional coalitions" that produces a crowded agenda and multifarious stakeholders in established arrangements. At the heart of this is the interaction of so many well-established interest groups with government decision-makers in the Congress, bureaucracy and courts. As journalist Jonathan Rauch puts it:

> We created a government with vast power to reassign resources . . . we created countless new groups. What we did not create . . . was a way to control the chain reaction set off when activist government and proliferating groups began interacting with each other.
>
> (1999, 165)

Political scientist Stephen Skowronek believes government's current crisis of popular legitimacy results from

> [The] growing disconnect between the scale of the problems now commanding the attention of policy makers—health care, climate change, globalized economic competition—and the responses a state can generate after it has so vastly expanded access to the policymaking process. This disconnect poses a fundamental challenge to progressive standards of political legitimacy. Justified as a problem solving machine, the policy state now strains under its own weight to make any convincing show of actually solving a problem.
>
> (2011a, 41–42)

The proliferation of skilled professionals pursuing disparate causes and often working at cross-purposes has ground national policymaking to a near halt.

Yet governmental rigidities and inaction have not spawned widespread popular unrest and political instability. The public's support of the Constitution continues, despite widespread discontent with the operation of national institutions and politics (King 2012, 207). Citizens are not particularly interested in devoting more time and effort to directing politics and policy in more constructive directions. A study of public attitudes concluded:

> The notion that people are champing at the bit to get back into politics on a personal level is simply wrong . . . A large number, in fact, would prefer to have nothing to do with politics and therefore readily admit that they opted out.
>
> (Hibbing and Thiess-Morse 2002, 125–126, 127)

The usual national policy inaction is occasionally "punctuated" by large policy changes, most often occurring with the arrival of a new presidential administration (Baumgartner et al. 2009, 34–38). Recent examples include the George W. Bush tax cuts and "No Child Left Behind" education policies of 2001 and Barack Obama's economic stimulus, financial reform and health care legislation of 2009–2010. The usual effect of occasional large-scale reforms, however, is to layer on additional complex organizations, policy routines and regulatory responsibilities on our baroque national governmental structure. Complex problems, addressed by diverse professionals in government and interest groups, do not result in simple solutions.

The Obama financial and health care reforms provide examples of increased organizational layering and policy complexity. The financial crisis of 2008 had its roots in the splintered authority and policy complexity involving five regulatory bodies: the Commodities Futures Trading Commission, the Federal Reserve Board, the Securities and Exchange Commission, the Federal Deposit Insurance Corporation, and the Office of Thrift Supervision. The Dodd-Frank financial regulatory reform law complicated this situation yet further, its text running to 864 pages with hundreds of additional pages of appended rules. Jonathan Macy of Yale Law School notes its impact: "Laws classically provide people with rules. Dodd-Frank is not directed at people. It is an outline directed at bureaucrats and it instructs them to make still more regulations and to create more bureaucracies" (*Economist* 2012, 2). Similarly, the Obama health care reform law contains some 450 policy changes in its 2700 pages. It creates many new bureaucratic organizations, such as the Health Choices Administration, the Health Benefits Advisory Committee, the Bureau of Health Information, the Public Plan Ombudsman, the Health Insurance Exchange Trust Fund, and the Clinical Preventative Services Task Force. It is a massive series of policies and regulations and subsidies and mandates. Public concerns about the law's impact on personal health insurance probably lie behind its enduring unpopularity (Levey 2012).

Management consultant Peter Drucker, who guided the restructuring and resurgence of Japanese industries after World War II, noted the problems resulting from America's complex stalemate in national governmental institutions and policymaking. Efforts at partial reforms, "are trying to patch and to spot-weld here, there and yonder—and that never accomplishes anything" (1995, 3). The broader problem, he suggested, is the complex, structural stasis supported by governing professionals. Government has expanded greatly in size since 1960, but has done so willy-nilly, without serious attempts at comprehensive restructuring to improve performance.

> Any organization, whether a business, a nonprofit, or a government agency, needs to rethink itself once it is more than forty or fifty years old. It has outgrown its policies and its rules of behavior. If it continues in its old ways, it becomes ungovernable, unmanageable, uncontrollable. The civilian part of the U.S. government has outgrown its size and outlived its policies.
>
> (Drucker 1995, 4)

Drucker wrote this almost 20 years ago. More recently, Christopher Howard, a professor of government and public policy at the college of William & Mary, noted the tendency for institutional layering in American bureaucracy and policy. Rather than rethink or redesign existing policies or agencies when new problems arise, we instead add new policies and agencies. We are engaged in an ongoing process of making additions as opposed to making renovations (Howard 2006). It should come as no surprise then that since Drucker first made his observation, no comprehensive "rethinking" of our national government's size structure and mission has occurred. It is time that it did.

Changes Needed

Drucker's rethinking is needed because the current policy path of national government is unsustainable. For decades, America's budget and tax policies have been seriously out of whack, with trends growing increasingly ominous since 2008. Since then, federal deficits for the first time have totaled over one trillion (that's one thousand billion) dollars per year, amounting to over 8 percent of GDP each year. In no other three-year period since 1945 has the deficit loomed so large. The national debt has mushroomed as well, now totaling more than 100 percent of America's Gross National Product, a proportion topped only once before, at the end of World War II (Associated Press 2012). The long-term trends are equally ominous. In June 2012, the Congressional Budget Office released a projection of the national debt and deficits if current policies now in place persist into the future. The CBO predicted that the national debt would continue to expand rapidly over the next 15 years, fueled by historically large and persistent budget deficits.

The result? "Large budget deficits and growing debt would reduce national saving, leading to higher interest rates, more borrowing from abroad and less domestic investment—which in turn would lower the growth of incomes in the United States" (Congressional Budget Office 2012). The national government's structural rigidities and policy stasis must and will change because of our untenable fiscal future. Either the changes will be endogenous, involving reforms from within, or exogenous, resulting from crises imposed from without due to the national government's unsustainable financial path.

The Ways of Change

What is to be done? A host of recent books have proposed all manner of institutional changes of varying scope, from constitutional conventions to new electoral systems to changes in congressional rules. We do not present such a list here, for two reasons. First, the systemic impediments to sweeping institutional change are formidable. Constitutional amendments require two-thirds support from each house of Congress and majority approval by each chamber of 34 of the 50 state legislatures. Electoral system reform primarily is a matter for state and local governments. So American federalism minimizes the likelihood of uniform changes in how we elect our governmental officials. Changes in specific institutional rules also can produce perverse and unexpected consequences.

For example, many reformers urge changes in U.S. Senate rules to curtail the growing number of filibusters. The current cloture rule, requiring 60 votes to end debate, might be reduced to a bare majority requirement to lessen unlimited debates. But it could be that removing the 60-vote cloture rule might make matters worse. A simple majority requirement might cause narrow ideological majorities to push through controversial and unpopular legislation. The unpopular health care reform of 2010, for example, avoided a filibuster because it was attached to budget reconciliation legislation that by Senate rules cannot be filibustered. The legislation likely would have been undone via a similar process if Republicans had reclaimed the Senate and the White House in the 2012 election. Absent the filibuster, this sort of ideological zigzag would produce a cycle of passage and repeal of programs. Without filibusters, narrow Senate majorities will appoint more ideologically extreme judicial and executive branch nominees. Given the sharp partisan polarization in Congress and party activists, the filibuster offers protection against immoderate majorities.

Protection against partisan majorities is necessary because, as we noted in previous chapters, America's two major parties are polarized and neither commands close to majority popular support. The less-polarized public vacillates between two ideologically extreme parties and at times frustrates both parties by voting in a divided government, most recently in 2010 and 2012. If popular majority preferences consistently were frustrated by arrangements like the Senate cloture rule, then perhaps majoritarian reforms would be in order. But that is not the case. The cloture rule prevents either party from readily enacting an agenda that does not reflect the popular will.

Instead of institutional tinkering, the national government's large and immediate fiscal problems require a more comprehensive "rethinking" of what government can and should accomplish for its citizens. It's our bet that this will be forced on national politicians in the coming years. Peter Drucker describes a sound way to go about it:

> Every agency, every policy, every program, every activity, should be confronted with these questions: "What is your mission?" "Is it still the right mission?" "Is it still worth doing?" "If we were not already doing this, would we now go into it?" . . . The overall answer is almost never "This is fine as it stands; let's keep on." But in some—indeed a good many—areas the answer to the last question is "Yes, we would go into this again, but with some changes. We have learned a few things."
> (1995, 5)

Another way of putting this is that national government, given its parlous finances, can only afford to "look before it leaps" in the future. In the private sector, this is a daily occurrence and it must become so in government. Corporate management consultant Jim Manzi recently proposed reforms to improve government's ability to learn about its past and proposed actions. Manzi proposed a new government agency "to develop, promulgate, and enforce standards for designing and interpreting social policy experiments" (2012, 245). Only by rigorous scientific experimentation, he argues, can we reliably determine which present and proposed government programs can achieve their goals and which cannot. As a result, government will "up its standards" when deciding whether or not to spend money on present or existing programs: "Though almost any reasonable-sounding program will probably work under some conditions, most fail most of the time. The burden of proof should always be on those who claim that some new program is worth the investment" (ibid., 202). America's fiscal problems require sound spending decisions in the future. Reliable experimental evidence would permit the national government to determine how to get the right results with its money.

We do not suggest that government needs to be run more like a private business. Important differences exist between the two. Unlike a business, a representative government lacks the efficiency of centralized decision-making and must make decisions that are inclusive of multiple perspectives. Likewise, individuals can choose to patronize a particular business but participation in government—whether through taxation, program partici-pation, or regulatory adherence—is largely involuntary. The federal government also is, by design, a monopoly. Private businesses must compete for customers and this competition forces upon them a need to improve services, to innovate, to be more efficient. Differences notwithstanding, there are areas where government can and should learn from business and it should be open to doing so. This would not undermine the purpose of government; rather it would enhance government's ability to fulfill its purpose, given the realities and limitations of the present era.

Obstacles to Change

We would be naïve indeed, if we failed to note the many obstacles to Drucker's rethinking and Manzi's experimentation. Politicians and entrenched interests often do not want careful scrutiny of established programs they support. Voters, for their part, typically cast their ballots retrospectively but not in reference to the results of social science experiments. Instead, electoral majorities, prompted by a general dislike of national conditions, have frequently rejected the party in power. Widespread popular discontent since the 1960s makes that a regular occurrence, contributing to governmental instability and policy stagnation. Another obstacle is our congressional redistricting system, which in the U.S. House has produced about 370 electorally "safe" seats out of that chamber's 435. About 190 seats are safe for Democrats and 180 for the GOP. After each election, either party is in a reasonable position to take back the House. The recent cycling of partisan control feeds the problem of politics and policy driven by the election cycle. So leaders look at the short term and not at the long term. In addition, the campaign finance system allows large amounts of sums from well-heeled interests and individuals to shape electoral politics. Record spending characterized the 2012 presidential and congressional races. The partisan media explosion on television, radio, and the internet is unlikely to subside and these partisan outlets further fuel a sense of division within the nation. These groups and individuals focus on short-term outcomes and seek specific benefits from government instead of broad rethinking or sound social scientific experimentation.

All this produces a composite shape resembling Stephen Skowronek's description of contemporary American politics as a "politics of preemption" (2008, 105). Preemptive politics has two main characteristics. First, no "normal" majority coalition dominates national politics, as had been the case before the 1960s. Second, national government is subject to "institutional thickening" defined as "a proliferation of organized interests and independent authorities" constituting "a political universe which is in every way more fully organized and more densely inhabited" (Skowronek 1996, 29–30). Karen Orren notes that policymaking power is now so far-flung in this thick environment that virtually all major governing bodies have become deeply and explicitly involved in lawmaking (Orren 1991). That is the picture we have sketched in this book. American government's expansive policy commitments constitute a third aspect of our thicker government. Among them, the large and growing spending obligations for our national government's entitlement programs—the biggest being Social Security, Medicare, Medicaid—produce a set of untenable governmental promises. Everyone is at work making policy, resulting in aggregate national spending that is fiscally unsustainable.

The intense level of electoral competition and (we argue) the related increases in partisan polarization between the two parties make matters worse. Most independent analysts agree that only a combination of revenue increases and entitlement reforms can alter our nation's unsustainable fiscal path. However, the refusal to raise taxes and a commitment to shield entitlement programs from reforms that would reduce benefits are central tenets of Republican and Democratic Parties' orthodoxy respectively. So long as both parties are beholden to their ideological bases and the competition for control of the mechanisms of government remains so tight, it is unlikely that either party will be willing to compromise and make concessions. Such concessions would require long-term thinking in a system currently driven by short-term, election-cycle politics.

In the End

Economist Herbert Stein once remarked, "Unsustainable trends tend not to be sustained" (Stein 2012). That is the likely outcome of America's fiscal policy problems. Will the demise of America's current national spending trends also produce a transformation of the national political system like that occurring from the 1950s to the 1980s? The system depicted in this book probably will remain remarkably durable for the reasons we noted in previous chapters. If history is any guide, broad systemic change would come with the rise of a stable majority party coalition that transforms national institutions, electoral processes and public policy. The rise and persistence of our no-majority party system seem to preclude that outcome. The "micro" incentives of power holders will probably keep the current national political system in place. Representatives and Senators will continue to seek to distribute benefits and seek reelection; presidents will continue to press for expanded powers in the wake of political frustrations; federal judges will pursue policymaking when they can get away with it; bureaucrats will regulate and make policy amidst political conflicts with Congress and courts. Our politics will remain dominated by professionals. America's higher educational institutions will continue to create a steady stream of professional replacements for current power holders.

It is our guess that the present system will persist and will have to be the source of solutions for America's fiscal and economic problems. The solutions will either come from endogenous leadership "from within" or will be imposed by exogenous crises "from without." Internal leadership occurs only with a new president and a supportive Congress—think Reagan in 1981 or Obama in 2009—but those circumstances are fleeting. If the crisis comes from without, we can only guess at its timing and scale.

Will Americans ever come to trust this thick national political system dominated by professionals? Ultimately, it depends on the system's results. If the nation's fiscal and economic problems produce broad rethinking and the use of experimental evidence as the basis for policy, better results are likely to ensue. Better policy results may boost popular trust. And if trust resurges, a new American political system will again be born.

Afterword
Stability and the 2012 Election

Throughout the preceding chapters, we make repeated reference to the present, stable system. In Chapter 1, we argue the present system has persisted despite sporadic populist eruptions and its stability rests upon a paradoxical entrenchment of professionals in government and interest groups and a persistent popular disaffection with government and parties. These entrenchments prevent a reorientation of the system through party realignment. The present system has persisted despite witnessing frequent shifts in party control of the institutions of government at the state and national level.

As discussed in Chapter 2, many viewed the tremendous electoral gains enjoyed by Democrats in the mid-term election of 2006 and the election of 2008 as evidence of a new realignment. In Table 2.1 we updated the seminal realignment work of Gerald Pomper and revealed no such evidence of a new party system emerging. Our update to Aldrich and Niemi's work expands their examination beyond the party system to the larger political system. Our examination of critical system variables confirmed maintenance of a stable political system through 2008.

The significant Republican victories in the mid-term election of 2010 quashed most discussion of realignment because the election signaled a return to divided government and close party competition. However, the discussion soon resumed. As the 2012 election approached, Obama's re-election was anything but a certainty. U.S. unemployment was high at 7.9 percent and job and economic growth were weak. The president's approval rating was just under 50 percent and national and state polls showed a close race between President Obama and Republican Nominee Mitt Romney.

In November 2012, Barack Obama comfortably gained re-election to a second term as president. President Obama carried every state he carried in 2008 except for Indiana and North Carolina. His victory margin declined in every state that he had carried in 2008 and nationally his margin declined from 7.2 percent to 2.5 percent. Turnout in the 2012 election declined as well; marking the first turnout decline since 1996. The lower turnout and diminished margins were perhaps less important than the president's 332–206 Electoral College victory.

Overwhelming support from the same coalition that elected Obama in 2008 fueled his re-election. Though overall turnout was down, African-American turnout matched its historic 2008 levels. Turnout by Hispanic voters and voters aged 18–29 increased as a share of all voters. The president won each group by commanding margins. Those votes, coupled with his strong performance among women, delivered victory. Within days of his re-election, talk of a political realignment re-emerged: "With his clear Electoral College and national popular vote majorities, President Obama has arguably created a genuine realignment at the national level that could continue to shape American politics for years to come" (Teixeira and Halpin 2012). Realignment advocates dismissed the 2010 mid-terms as anomalous and focused on the "progressive majority—built on a multi-racial, multi-ethnic, cross-class coalition in support of an activist government that promotes freedom, opportunity, and security for all" (ibid.).

Such rhetoric is reminiscent of similar realignment claims made following Republican George W. Bush's re-election in 2004 and Obama's election in 2008. We refuted those claims in Chapter 2. As of this writing, little of the data used in our Aldrich and Niemi update is available through 2012. Crucial party system data, however, is available. Given the clear relationship, established in Chapter 2, between the party system and the political system we can draw some conclusions regarding 2012 in the broader context of American politics.

Figure A.1 presents an update to the Pomper correlations discussed in Chapter 2 and shown in Figure 2.1. We have used preliminary election results for all 50 states and the District of Columbia to calculate the Democrats' two-party vote share by state in the 2012 election. We paired successive elections by comparing the Democratic share of the total two-party vote by state. The state-by-state comparison generates a Pearson correlation co-efficient with a low or negative value indicating a disruption or cleavage point and a higher positive value indicating continuity or electoral stability.[1]

The results are not surprising. The election of 2012 was highly correlated with the election of 2008. Only two states switched party columns between 2008 and 2012 and as Obama's margins shrank in many of the so-called swing states discussed in Chapter 2, his impressive victories in 2008 slipped to the more narrow margins witnessed in the election of 2004. President Obama's re-election in 2012 did not represent a break in our long enduring era of political stability, nor did it represent the emergence of a new geographic electoral coalition. Note the clear evidence of such a break in 1964 with the election of Lyndon Johnson.

Evidence of the stability of the present era also appears as one looks beyond the contest at the top of the ballot. Republicans secured a majority in the House of Representatives in the 2010 mid-term election. Former Speaker and Democratic House Minority Leader Nancy Pelosi (D-CA) vowed Democrats would reclaim that majority in 2012. To that end, Democrats emphasized the budget proposal put forward by Republican House Budget

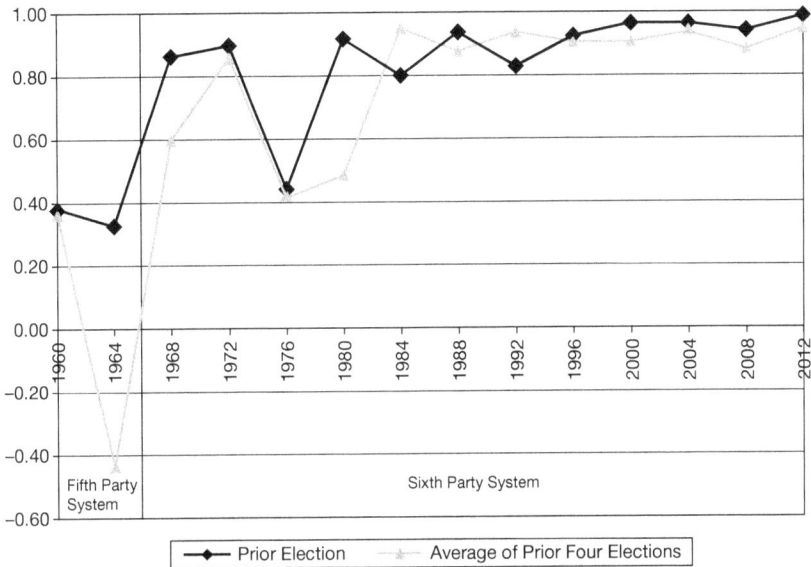

Figure A.1 Correlation of successive presidential elections with prior election, 1968–2012, and the average of four prior elections, 1968–2012[1]

Source: State by state election data retrieved from Leip (2010).

Committee Chair Paul Ryan (R–WI). Ryan proposed fundamental reforms to the Medicare program, including a voluntary transition to publicly funded private insurance for America's seniors. When Mitt Romney chose Ryan to be his running mate, many Democrats believed they would be able to nationalize the House elections by focusing on the Medicare reform. In the end, however, Republicans successfully defended their majority and surrendered fewer than 10 seats to Democrats.

The effects of partisan redistricting were evident in the 2012 House elections. Republicans capitalized on their tremendous victories in guber-natorial and legislative elections in 2010 by controlling the redistricting process in most states. Republicans redrew district lines in an effort to protect newly elected House members and to endanger existing Democratic members. Their success was evident in many states, especially Pennsylvania. President Obama won Pennsylvania by 52 to 47 percent, but despite that comfortable margin of victory Republicans won 13 of the state's 18 seats in the House of Representatives. Republicans were not alone among those to benefit from partisan redistricting. Of the seats Democrats did win, many came as the result of their own redistricting efforts in Illinois and Maryland.

In the Senate, Republicans began the 2012 cycle confident they would reclaim majority control of the chamber. Party efforts were undermined throughout the election season by controversial comments regarding rape and abortion made by male Senate candidates in Missouri and Indiana. In the end, Democrats picked up two seats to add to their existing majority.

At the state level, the election found Republicans holding 30 governorships, representing a net gain from the 2010 mid-term elections. The party maintained the state legislature advantage it acquired in 2010 as well. Going into the election, Republicans enjoyed unified control of 26 legislatures compared to 15 for the Democrats. Another 8 legislatures had divided control. After the election, Republicans still controlled 26 legislatures, while Democrats boosted their total to 19 after winning unified control of several legislatures previously divided. Though 2012 saw a decline in divided government at the state level, it did not witness a change in the close balance of power between the two parties.

In many respects, the 2012 election yielded a government little changed from the one produced in 2010. Democrats held the White House and the Senate while Republicans controlled the House of Representatives and enjoyed advantages in State Houses and State Legislatures. ABC News' Political Director Amy Walter summed up the results as thus,

> In 2006, 2008 and 2010 voters punished the party it saw as too consumed with its own agenda and unfocused on the concerns of average Americans. But each "wave election" only served to convince the winning party that they had a mandate for their ideological agenda. Ironically, it took a "status quo" election to finally convince the two sides to hear what voters have been telling them along: stop the posturing and work together to get something done to fix the many problems this country is facing.
>
> (Falcone and Walter 2012)

We are inclined to agree.

Even with the present political order maintained, however, there are important undercurrents worth noting. Perhaps the most important is the changing demographic landscape of American politics. In 2008, Barack Obama was carried to victory in part by the record turnout by African-American and youth voters as well as by the overwhelming support he enjoyed among both groups and Hispanic voters. It was an open question whether that coalition would hold together and whether turnout by these key groups in 2012 would rival that of 2008. The answer to the question was an unequivocal "yes." In 2012, African-American turnout matched 2008 levels, while youth and Hispanic turnout increased. Though Obama's support among young voters declined, a significant increase in support among Hispanic voters offset the decline.

The shifting demographics of the American electorate suggest an advantage for Democrats for the near future at least. There are other warning signs for the Republicans and their party's presidential aspirations. In the five elections from 1972 to 1988, Republicans won all but one in 1976. During that time, the GOP enjoyed a clear advantage in the Electoral College, averaging 440 electoral votes to the Democrats' 98. Over the six elections from 1992 to 2012, however, Democrats have won six of the eight and averaged 327 electoral votes to the Republicans' 211. Though the GOP has solidified its base of the support in southern states, it has witnessed significant erosion in the southwest as well as Florida and Virginia. Much of that erosion links to demographic changes in the electorate.

Though some continue to forward the notion of an emerging Democratic majority driven by demographic change, the supposed majority has been "emerging" for well over a decade (Judis and Teixeira 2002). Similar proclamations of an emerging Republican majority were made in the late 1960s (Philips 1969), but a clear governing majority for the GOP never arrived. Rather, a period of intense two-party competition emerged. Demographic change notwithstanding, the results of the 2012 election suggest the period of intense competition is likely to continue.

The histories of the Democratic and Republican Parties demonstrate adaptation not stasis. A changing nation will always face new challenges as well as new issues of interest to the public. The two parties have weathered myriad changes by adapting to new political realities. Likewise, voters in recent decades have demonstrated that partisan loyalty is not permanent. Whether any adaptation takes place within the structure of our current and stable system, or whether it brings about a reordering of the political system remains to be seen. At present, however, there is scant evidence of any such reordering. The Sixth Party System and the broader political system it supports and that we have described in this book remain in place.

Appendix
Variables and Sources

Variables

The original macropattern included three measures of race/segregation as well as one variable of voters linking issues to candidates and not parties. Data for these variables are not available beyond the 1970s so we opted to exclude them from our analysis and update of the original Aldrich and Niemi work. The authors' original macropattern is available in Aldrich and Niemi (1996, 87–109).

For our update, we excluded one variable from the original Aldrich and Niemi study, "Clarity of Party Racial Issue Stands," as data were not available post 1980. Our variables are all on interval scales and include electoral and institutional variables with values for every presidential election year since

Shown are mean and +/– Standard Deviation of 22 Standardized Variables

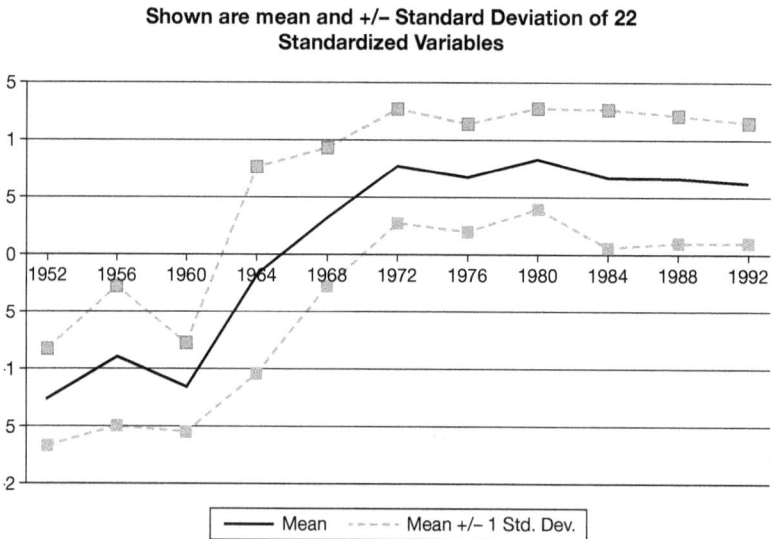

Figure Appendix 1 Schier and Eberly's update to Aldrich and Niemi macropattern, 1952–2004
Source: Adapted from: Aldrich and Niemi (1996).

1952, a total of 16 cases for each variable, with one exception, state and local split ticket voting, for which we have data only for 1952–1968 and 1980–1984.

Micro and Macro-Pattern Variables Included in Figures 1.4–1.7

The variables are grouped into three categories: those concerning partisanship, the electorate, and institutional behavior.

*   *The micro-pattern partisanship variables*: percentages of blacks apolitical; blacks identifying as Democrats; whites who are pure independents; whites who are pure or leaning independents; whites who are strong partisans; southern white support for the Democratic Party; Democratic coalition that is working class; percentage of Democrats in the electorate; percentage neutral to parties; split ticket voting for state and local elections; president and House split ticket voting; House and Senate split ticket voting; presidential party line voting in Congress; House party line voting in Congress; Senate party line voting in Congress; Percentage of Congressional districts carried by presidential candidate of one party and House candidate of another; and presidential partisan approval gap among the public.
*   *The micro-pattern electorate variables*: turnout in presidential elections; turnout in mid-term elections; percentage agreeing "public officials don't care what I think"; average presidential approval rating; states with ballot initiatives each election year; total number of ballot initiatives each election year; percentage naming most important problem as domestic annually; and percentage naming most important problem as foreign annually.
*   *The micro-pattern institutional variables*: House incumbent electoral security; Senate incumbent electoral security; percentage of House votes that are party unity votes; percentage of Senate votes that are party unity votes; presidential success in Congressional voting; gap between House parties in presidential voting support; gap in Senate parties in presidential voting support; percentage of Appeals Court nominees approved by Senate; duration of successful court confirmation processes (percentage of the year); number of restrictive House rules; number of Senate cloture motions filed to end filibusters; total pages of regulations published in the Federal Register; and David Mayhew's list of major enactments.

Sources

Sources and descriptions for all variables included in the micro/macro-pattern analyses, as well as additional variables presented in other figures and tables, are provided below.

List of Variables Organized by Source

- The American National Election Studies. *The ANES 2008 Time Series Study.* Stanford University and the University of Michigan. Online. Available http://www.electionstudies.org (accessed 15 July 2012).
- Blacks Identifying as Democrats: Based on self-identification of partisan preference. Variable = VCF0106A: Respondent Race 6-category X VCF0303: Party ID Collapsed.
- Ideological Distribution of Activists and Non-Activists: Cross-tabulations of VCF0803: Respondent self-identification on a liberal–conservative scale with variables VCF0719: Respondent did "any other campaign work for party/candidate", and VCF0721: Respondent "contribute to candidate". Moderates include respondents who self-identified as "slightly liberal," "moderate," and "slightly conservative." Party activists defined as those who answered "Yes" to VCF0719 and VCF0721.
- Percentage of Blacks Apolitical: ANES defines "apolitical" as someone who expresses neither independence nor a partisan preference. Such people tend to be less interested and less involved in politics. Variable = VCF0106A: Respondent Race 6-category X VCF0301: 7-pt Scale Party Identification.
- Share of the Democratic Coalition Working Class: Percentage of self-identified Democrats also identifying as members of the working class. Variable = VCF0148A: Respondent Social Class 6-category X VCF0303: Party ID Collapsed.
- Share of Democrats in the Electorate: Based on respondent self-identification, include independents who lean toward the Democratic party. Variable = VCF0303: Party ID Collapsed.
- Share Neutral to Parties: Variable = VCF0322: Affect Toward Major Parties.
- Share of Whites Any Independent: Based on self-identification of partisan preference, including those who claim to be independent but lean toward one party. Variable = VCF0106A: Respondent Race 6-category X VCF0301: 7-pt Scale Party Identification.
- Share of Whites Pure Independents: Based on self-identification of partisan preference, excluding those who claim to be independent but lean toward one party. Variable = VCF0106A: Respondent Race 6-category X VCF0303: Party ID Collapsed.
- Share of Whites Strong Partisans: Among those initially identifying as a partisan, ANES then asks if they are a strong or weak partisan. Variable = VCF0106A: Respondent Race 6-category X VCF0305: Strength of Partisanship.
- Southern Whites Support for the Democratic Party: Share of Southern Whites identifying as a member of the Democratic Party. Variable = VCF0113 - Political South/Nonsouth X VCF0106A: Respondent Race 6-category X VCF0303: Party ID Collapsed.

List of Sources

American National Election Studies. *The ANES Guide to Public Opinion and Electoral Behavior: Support for the Political System*. Ann Arbor, MI: University of Michigan, Center for Political Studies. Online. Available at: http://www. electionstudies.org/nesguide/gd-index.htm#5 (accessed 15 July 2012).

- Popular discontent: Table 5B-3: Public Officials Don't Care What People Think, 1952–2008.
- Trust Index: Table 5A-5: Trust in Government Index, 1958–2008.

Carroll, R., Lewis, J., Lo, J., McCarty, N., Poole, K. and Rosenthal, H. *DW-NOMINATE Scores with Bootstrapped Standard Errors*. Voteview.com and the University of Georgia. Online. Available at: http://voteview.com/downloads. asp (accessed 15 July 2012).

- Party Means on Liberal-Conservative Dimension;
- Party Polarization.

Gallup Organization. *Presidential Approval Ratings: Gallup Historical Statistics and Trends*. Washington, DC. Online. Available at: http://www.gallup.com/ poll/116677/presidential-approval-ratings-gallup-historical-statistics-trends. aspx (accessed 15 July 2012).

- President Average Approval Rating

Gallup Organization. Washington, DC: Data compiled by authors.

- Presidential Partisan Approval Gap: Gap between presidential approval rating among Democrats and Republicans.

Initiative & Referendum Institute at the University of Southern California. *IRI Historical Database*. Los Angeles: USC School of Law. Online. Available at: http://www.iandrinstitute.org/data.htm (accessed 15 July 2012).

- Ballot Initiative Success rate: Initiatives (number, approval rate) by state and year, 1904–2010;
- States with Ballot Initiatives: Initiatives (number, approval rate) by state and year, 1904–2010;
- Total Ballot Initiatives in States: Initiatives (number, approval rate) by state and year, 1904–2010.

Mayhew, D. (2009) *Updates to Divided We Govern*. New Haven, CT: Yale University. Online. Available http://pantheon.yale.edu/~dmayhew/data3. html (accessed 15 July 2012).

- List of Important Enactments

Policy Agendas Project. *Gallup's Most Important Problem.* The University of Texas at Austin. Online. Available http://www.policyagendas.org/page/datasets-codebooks#gallups_most_important_problem (accessed 15 July 2012).

- Most important problem Domestic: Gallup's long-term "most important problem" question in which respondents, unaided, are asked to name what they think is the most important issue facing the country. All responses related to the economy generally (including the economy, unemployment, and the recession) and all mentions related to international matters (including war, terrorism, U.S. relations with other countries, and national defense) are collapsed into two categories.
- Most important problem Foreign: Gallup's long-term "most important problem" question in which respondents, unaided, are asked to name what they think is the most important issue facing the country. All responses related to the economy generally (including the economy, unemployment, and the recession) and all mentions related to international matters (including war, terrorism, U.S. relations with other countries, and national defense) are collapsed into two categories.

Sinclair, B. *Unorthodox Lawmaking.* 4th ed. Los Angeles: Sage/CQ Press, 2011, Table 6.3.

- Committee bypassed in the House;
- Committee bypassed in the Senate;
- Post-committee adjustment in the House;
- Post-committee adjustment in the Senate.

Stanley, H.W. and Niemi, R.G. *Vital Statistics on American Politics, 2009–2010.* Washington, DC: CQ Press, 2009.

- Turnout presidential elections: Table 1-1: Voter Turnout Rates, United States, South, and Non-South, 1789–2008;
- Turnout House mid-term elections: Table 1-1: Voter Turnout Rates, United States, South, and Non-South, 1789–2008;
- House incumbent security: Table 1-19: Incumbent Reelection Rates: Representatives, Senators, and Governors, General Elections, 1960–2008;
- Senate incumbent security: Table 1-19: Incumbent Reelection Rates: Representatives, Senators, and Governors, General Elections, 1960–2008;
- House party line voting: Table 3-9: Party-Line Voting in Presidential and Congressional Elections, 1952–2008;

- Senate party line voting: Table 3-9: Party-Line Voting in Presidential and Congressional Elections, 1952–2008;
- Presidential party line voting: Table 3-9: Party-Line Voting in Presidential and Congressional Elections, 1952–2008;
- State and Local split ticket voting: Table 3-10: Split Ticket Voting, 1952–2008;
- President and House split ticket voting: Table 3-10: Split Ticket Voting, 1952–2008;
- House and Senate split ticket voting: Table 3-10: Split Ticket Voting, 1952–2008;
- Percentage of Congressional districts carried by presidential candidate of one party and House candidate of another: Table 1-14: Split Presidential and House Election Outcomes in Congressional Districts, 1900–2008;
- Party unity House: Table 5-10: Party Unity in Congressional Voting, 1954–2008;
- Party unity Senate: Table 5-10: Party Unity in Congressional Voting, 1954–2008;
- Total pages Federal Register: Figure 6-1: Total Pages in the Federal Register, 1940–2008;
- Presidential success in Congress: Table 6-7: Presidential Victories on Votes in Congress, 1954–2008;
- Presidential support party gap in House: Table 6-8: Congressional Voting in Support of the President's Position, 1954–2008;
- Presidential support party gap in Senate: Table 6-8: Congressional Voting in Support of the President's Position, 1954–2008.

United States Office of Personnel Management. *Historical Federal Workforce Tables.* Washington, DC. Online. Available at: http://www.opm.gov/feddata/HistoricalTables/index.asp (accessed 15 July 2012).

- Executive Branch civilian employees (bureaucracy);
- Legislative and Judicial Branch employees.

United States Senate. *Senate Action on Cloture Motions.* Washington, DC. Online. Available at: http://www.senate.gov/pagelayout/reference/cloture_motions/clotureCounts.htm (accessed 15 July 2012).

- Cloture Motions Filed;
- Cloture Invoked;
- Cloture Votes.

Published/Unpublished Data Provided By Others, Compiled by Authors

- Frank Baumgartner
  - Total Associations

- Sarah Binder
  - Appeals Court nomination success;
  - Duration of successful confirmation process.

- Barbara Sinclair and John E. Owens
  - Restrictive rules in the House

Notes

1 The New American Political System

1 For example, see Aldrich and Niemi (1996, 87–109).
2 See, for example, the discussion of conflicting theories in Paulson (2007), or Walter Dean Burnham's defense of realignment theory against Everett Carll Ladd's (1991) critique.
3 Such declines are evident in reports from the American National Election Study "Party Identification 7-Point Scale," available at: http://www.electionstudies. org/nesguide/toptable/tab2a_1.htm and a recent report by the Pew Center for People and the Press, "Trends in Political Values and Core Attitudes." May, 2009.
4 A full discussion of party sorting can be found in Fiorina (2009) and Fiorina and Levendusky (2006).
5 For a discussion of the increasing influence of special interests and activists in the judicial nomination and confirmation process see Bell (2002) and Scherer (2005).

2 The Current Stable System

1 See, especially, Sundquist (1983). Though there is quite a deep body of work demonstrating the rise and fall of party systems, many scholars dismiss the notion that American political history can be so neatly categorized (Mayhew 2005). Perhaps much of the criticism of the party system and realignment concept stems from the lack of a single accepted definition of either (Campbell 2006). Our discussion of the contemporary political system (as opposed to party system) may add to the confusion, but we see merit in the work.
2 In 1848, 1860, 1892, 1904 to 1924, and 1948 Pomper added the third-party vote to the Democratic total premised on the assumption that the vote would have otherwise gone to the Democratic candidate.
3 As noted in Chapter 1, Pearson correlations vary on a scale from -1 indicating a perfect inverse tendency to +1 a perfect positive tendency. The closer to zero on the scale, the weaker the tendency of the relationship.
4 We provide an updated chart inclusive of the 2012 election in Figure A.1 in the Afterword. We chose not to include the 2012 election in Figure 2.1 because much of the 2012 data was preliminary at the time of this writing.
5 For further discussion of the unique nature of the 1976 election, see Knuckey (1999) and Paulson (2007).
6 States were defined as reliable if they voted with their respective party's candidate

in at least four of the five elections between 1988 through 2004. Reliably Republican States include Alabama, Alaska, Arizona, Colorado, Georgia, Idaho, Indiana, Kansas, Mississippi, Montana, Nebraska, North Carolina, North Dakota, Oklahoma, South Carolina, South Dakota, Texas, Utah, Virginia, and Wyoming. Reliably Democratic States: California, Connecticut, Delaware, District of Columbia, Hawaii, Illinois, Maine, Maryland, Massachusetts, Michigan, Minnesota, New Jersey, New York, Pennsylvania, Oregon, Rhode Island, Vermont, Washington, Wisconsin. Swing States: Arkansas, Florida, Iowa, Kentucky, Louisiana, Missouri, Nevada, New Hampshire, New Mexico, Ohio, Tennessee, West Virginia.

7 As with the national results previously discussed, a high degree of correlation between successive elections would indicate stability while lower correlations would suggest discontinuity. The case of the swing states, however, is unique. Swing states are swing states because they are not predictable, they do not follow the stable electoral pattern evident in Republican and Democratic states. As such, one would expect high levels of correlation from one election to the next when a president is re-elected, or succeeded in office by a member of the same party. Conversely, elections that witness the defeat of an incumbent or a shift in party control of the White House should be marked by lower correlations.

8 A variable representing voter clarity of party stands on issues of race was excluded, as values were not available post 1980.

9 Information on each of these variables is included in the Appendix.

10 Data on ballot initiatives was retrieved from the Initiative & Referendum Institute at the University of Southern California. We exclude measures placed on the ballot by legislatures.

11 As explained by Aldrich and Niemi (1996), this is a common form of standardization, used to make items comparable when they are measured on different scales. We use the formula $X = (x_i - ?)s_x$ where x_i stands for each of the values across the 15 elections and s_x = the square root of $(1/(n-1))(x_i -x)$. The values are thus measured in terms of standard deviations above or below the mean of that variable across time.

12 Aldrich and Niemi's 1952–1992 findings are presented in the Appendix.

13 How long lasting was the pre-1964 system? We cannot be certain of this, because the data in our analysis only reach back to 1952.

14 See, for example, the discussion of conflicting theories in Paulson (2007), or Burnham's (1991) defense of realignment theory against Everett Carll Ladd's critique.

15 See Pomper (1967).

3 Popular Discontent and Professional Government

1 Pearson correlations vary on a scale from -1 indicating a perfect inverse tendency to +1 a perfect positive tendency. The closer to zero on the scale, the weaker the tendency of the relationship. For example, when the Trust Index increases on its scale, the indicator for popular discontent decreases on its scale. But how strong is the pattern of change on the two scales? If the two patterns vary strongly together, with movement on one closely associated with movement on the other, the correlation is a strong one. In this case, it's a very strong -.81, close to a perfect negative correlation of -1.0. So as Trust Index scores for the public increase over time, popular discontent scores decrease in a strong pattern. Conversely, the Trust Index correlates with presidential election turnout since

1964 at +.60, not far from a perfect positive correlation of +1.0. This indicates a fairly strong tendency for the Trust Index and presidential election turnout to vary in the same direction since 1964, the first year both were measured. So as Trust Index scores increase, so does presidential election turnout and as the Trust Index score decreases, so does turnout. If movement on two variable scales seems to vary randomly, however, there is no correlation and the Pearson coefficient registers zero. The closer to zero the Pearson correlation coefficient, the weaker the relationship between the variables.

2 Similar research suggests that the reason the courts remain popular is that people do not see the sausage-making involved in court decisions. See Baird and Gangle (2006).

4 The Puzzle of Contemporary Party Politics

1 See Brady et al.'s *Red and Blue Nation* volumes (2006) or more recently Alan Abramowitz's *The Disappearing Center* (2010).

2 See, for instance, Abramowitz (2010) and Abramowitz and Saunders (2008), and Bafumi and Shapiro (2009).

3 See Beckman (2009) and Fiorina, Abrams, and Pope (2008), and McGhee and Krimm (2009).

4 Leaning Independent includes respondents who indicated that they were an Independent Democrat or Independent Republican. These "independent partisans" are often referred to as "Leaners."

5 See Keith et al. (1992).

6 See McGhee and Krimm (2009).

7 See Abramowitz (2010) and Petrocik (2009).

8 Kurlowski found that Petrocik's decision to consider Republican and Democratic leaners collectively and to pool data from elections spanning 1952 to 1972 masked significant variations across parties and individual elections. Petrocik chose to pool data to boost sample size and produce significant results.

9 We theorize the loyalty of Republican leaners in 2002 was a reflection of the strong Republican year in the first mid-term election following the attacks of September 11 or the ongoing national debate over the pending war with Iraq. President Bush was the first president since Franklin Roosevelt to see his party gain seats during his first term.

6 The Presidency

1 It is important to note another aspect of political capital—the number of presidential appointments—that does not comport with the predicted direction of our argument. In his recent book on presidential appointments, David E. Lewis presents data indicating that the number of presidential appointments and the percentage of all federal appointees appointed by the president has held largely constant and declined only slightly since 1980 (2008, 98, 100). Though both the number and percentage rose steadily from 1960 to 1980—the number doubling from 1700 to 3500 and the percentage rising from .06 to .12 of all federal employees—since 1980 both measures have been largely static. Lewis concludes:

> In sum, it is not a fair characterization to say the number of appointees is increasing steadily over time. While the number of appointees is higher today

than in 1960, a then–versus–now comparison ignores substantial variation over time and across types of appointees.

(ibid., 99)

If recent presidents have faced problems with political capital, it probably has been located elsewhere.

2 The standard deviation is a measure of the dispersion of numerical values around the average value in a series measured on a scale with a fixed unit of measure. It is the square root of the variance, which is the squared sum of the distance of all values in such a series from the average. The larger the standard deviation, the bigger the dispersion of values from the average value.

3 Data on presidential terms is not presented in tabular form here but is available from the authors upon request.

4 In David Mayhew's data, based on media reports on congressional legislation at the end of annual congressional sessions, Congress annually averaged 1.2 "highly important" policy changes and 7.9 "important" policy changes from 1995 to 2004, but only .68 "highly important" and 6.1 "important" policy changes from 1947 to 1966 and .47 "highly important" and 6.3 "important" policy changes from 1967 to 1994. Source: http://pantheon.yale.edu/~dmayhew/data3.html (accessed November 10, 2010).

Afterword

As noted in Chapter 1, Pearson correlations vary on a scale from -1 indicating a perfect inverse tendency to +1 a perfect positive tendency. The closer to zero on the scale, the weaker the tendency of the relationship.

Bibliography

Abramowitz, A.I. (2010) *The Disappearing Center: Engaged Citizens, Polarization and American Democracy.* New Haven, CT: Yale University Press.

Abramowitz, A.I., Alexander, B., and Gunning, M. (2006) "Incumbency, Redistricting, and the Decline of Competition in U.S. House Elections." *The Journal of Politics,* 68(1): 75–88.

Abramowitz, A.I. and Saunders, K.L. (1998) "Ideological Realignment in the U.S. Electorate." *Journal of Politics,* 60 (3): 634–52.

—— (2008) "Is Polarization a Myth?" *The Journal of Politics,* 70(2), 542–555.

Ackerman, B. and Hathaway, O. (2011) "Death of the War Powers Act?" *Washington Post.*

Administrative Office of the U.S. Courts. (2012) "Civil Cases Commenced, by Nature of Suit, During the 12-Month Periods Ending September 30, 2007 Through 2011." Table C-2A. Available at: http://www.uscourts.gov/uscourts/Statistics/JudicialBusiness/2011/appendices/C02ASep11.pdf (accessed May 31, 2012).

Agence France-Presse. (2012) "Republicans Join Suit over Obama Recess Appointments." Available at: http://news.yahoo.com/republicans-join-suit-over-obama-recess-appointments-233115947.html (accessed May 16, 2012)

Aldrich, J. and Niemi, R. (1996) "The Sixth American Party System", in S. C. Craig (ed.) *Broken Contract: Changing Relationships Between Americans and Their Government,* Boulder, CO: Westview Press, pp .87–109.

Aldrich, J. and Rohde, D. (2009) "Congressional Committees in a Continuing Partisan Era." In L. Dodd and B. Oppenheimer (eds.) *Congress Reconsidered.* Washington, DC: CQ Press, pp. 217–240.

Alliance for Justice. (2011) *The State of the Judiciary: President Obama and the 111th Congress.* Washington, DC: Alliance for Justice.

Arbuckle, D. (2008) *OIRA and Presidential Regulatory Review: A View from Inside the Administrative State. Selected Work,* Berkeley, CA: bepress.

Arnold, P. (1998) *Making the Managerial Presidency: Comprehensive Reorganization Planning 1905–1996.* Lawrence, KS: University of Kansas Press.

Associated Press. (2009) "Obama's Signing Statements Draw Fire for Mimicking Bush." Available at: http://www.startribune.com/politics/51359172.html (accessed December 9, 2010).

—— (2012) "Federal Deficit Totals $844.5b Through 8 Months." *USA Today.*

Bafumi, J. and Herron, M. (2010) "Leapfrog Representation and Extremism: A Study of American Voters and Their Members in Congress." *American Political Science Review,* 104(3): 519–542.

Bafumi, J. and Shapiro, R. (2009) "A New Partisan Voter." *The Journal of Politics*, 71(1): 1–24.

Baird, V. and Gangle, A. (2006) "Shattering the Myth of Legality: The Impact of the Media's Framing of Supreme Court Procedures on Perceptions of Fairness." *Political Psychology*, 27(4): 597–614.

Baker, R. K. (2010) "Touching the Bones: Interviewing and Direct Observational Studies of Congress." In E. Shickler and F. Lee (eds.) *The Oxford Handbook of the American Congress*. Oxford: Oxford University Press.

Barnes, J. (2009) "U.S. District Courts, Litigation, and the Policy-Making Process." In M.C. Miller (ed.) *Exploring Judicial Politics*. Oxford: Oxford University Press, pp. 97–109.

Barone, M. (2010) "America in an Age of Open Field Politics." *The American*. The Amercan Enterprise Institute. Available at: http://www.american.com/archive/2010/september/america-in-an-age-of-open-field-politics (accessed 10 August 2011).

Baumgartner, F.R., Berry J.M., Hojnacki, M., Kimball, D.C., and Leech, B.L. (2009) *Lobbying and Policy Change: Who Wins, Who Loses and Why*. Chicago: University of Chicago Press.

Baumgartner, F.R., Grant, J., McCarthy, J., Bevan, S., and Greenan, J. (2008) "Tracing Interest-Group Populations in the US and UK." Paper presented at American Political Science Association conference, Boston.

Baumgartner, F. R. and Jones, B.D. (2009) *Agendas and Instability in American Politics*, 2nd ed. Chicago: University of Chicago Press.

Bearnot, E. C. and Schier, S. E. (2012) "The Floating Voter in 2008 Elections." *The American Review of Politics* , 33 (Summer): 75–94.

Beckman, A. (2009) "The Volatile American Voter: Unstable Voting Behavior in American Presidential Elections, 1948–2004." Paper presented at American Political Science Association conference, Toronto.

Bell, L. C. (2002) *Warring Factions: Interest Groups, Money and the New Politics of Senate Confirmation*. Columbus: Ohio State University Press.

Berry, J. (1999) *The New Liberalism: The Rising Power of Citizen Groups*. Washington, DC: Brookings Institution.

Beutler, B. (2011) "Hoyer: Dems United Against Entitlement Benefit Cuts In Debt Fight." *Talking Points Memo*. Available at: http://tpmdc.talkingpointsmemo.com/2011/07/hoyer-dems-united-against-entitlement-benefit-cuts-in-debt-fight.php (accessed May 13, 2012).

Binder, S.H., Maltzman, F. (2009) *Advice and Dissent: The Struggle to Shape the Federal Judiciary*. Washington: Brookings Institution.

Bolton, A. (2011) "Reid Triggers 'Nuclear Option' to Change Senate Rules, End Repeat Filibusters." *The Hill*. Available at: http://thehill.com/homenews/senate/186133-reid-triggers-nuclear-option-to-change-senate-rules-and-prohibit-post-cloture-filibusters (accessed May 12, 2012).

Bond, J. and Fleisher, R. (1992) *The President in the Legislative Arena*. Chicago: University of Chicago Press.

—— (2000) *Polarized Politics: Congress and the President in a Partisan Era*. Washington, DC: Congressional Quarterly.

Brace, P. and Hinckley, B. (1991) "The Structure of Presidential Approval: Constraints Within and Across Presidencies." *Journal of Politics*, 53(4): 993–1017.

Brady, D., Galston, W. and Nivola, P. (eds.) *Red and Blue Nation*, vol. 1, Washington, DC: Brookings Institution.

Brudnick, I.A. (2011) "Congressional Salaries and Allowances." Washington, DC: Congressional Research Service.

Bryner, G. (1995) *Blue Skies Green Politics.* Washington, DC: CQ Press.

Burnham, W.D. (1970) *Critical Elections and the Mainsprings of American Politics.* New York: W.W. Norton.

—— (1991) "Critical Realignment Dead or Alive?" In B.E. Shafer (ed.) *The End of Realignment? Interpreting American Electoral Eras.* Madison, Wisconsin: University of Wisconsin Press, pp. 101–140.

Businessdictionary.com. 2011. Available at: http://www.businessdictionary.com/definition/professional.html> (accessed 29 July 2011).

Calabresi, S.G. and Yoo, C.S. (2008) *The Unitary Executive: Presidential Power from Washington to Bush.* New Haven, CT: Yale University Press.

Campbell, A., Converse, P. E., Miller, W. E., and Stokes, D. E. (1960) *The American Voter.* Chicago: University of Chicago Press.

Campbell, J.E. (2006) "Party Systems and Realignments in the United States, 1868–2004." *Social Science History*, 30(3): 360–86.

Canes-Wrone, B. (2001) "The President's Legislative Influence from Public Appeals." *American Journal of Political Science*, 45(2): 313–29.

Carmines, E.G. and Stimson, J.A. (1989) *Issue Evolution: Race and the Transformation of American Politics.* Princeton, NJ: Princeton University Press.

Carp, R.A., Stidham, R., and Manning, K.L. (2011a) *The Federal Courts.* Fifth Edition. Washington, DC: Congressional Quarterly Press.

Carp, R.A., Stidham, R., and Manning, K.L. (2011b) *The Judicial Process in America.* Eighth edition. Washington: Congressional Quarterly.

Carroll, M. (1980) "Koch Criticizes Ruling Backing Racial Quota for Federal Contracts; 'Never Give In' on Police Mayor Criticizes Contract System Decided by Race." *New York Times* Available at: http://select.nytimes.com/gst/abstract.html?res=F50E15F8385C11728DDDA00894DF405B8084F1D3 (accessed July 6, 2012).

Center for Biological Diversity. (2011) "Center Actions" Available at: http://www.biologicaldiversity.org/programs/public_lands/energy/dirty_energy_development/oil_and_gas/gulf_oil_spill/center_actions.html#drilling (accessed 29 July 2011).

Chaddock, G.R. and Parti, T. (2010) "Harry Reid: Senate Will Abandon Cap-and-Trade Energy Reform." *The Christian Science Monitor*, July 22, 2010.

Chanley, V.A., Rudolph, T.J. and Rahn, W.M. (2000) "The Origins and Consequences of Public Trust in Government." *Public Opinion Quarterly*, 64(3): 239–56.

Chayes, A. (1976) "The Role of the Judge in Public Law Litigation," *Harvard Law Review*, 89: 1281–1283.

CNN. (2011) "CNN Poll: Trust In Government At All Time Low." September 28, 2011. Available at: http://politicalticker.blogs.cnn.com/2011/09/28/cnn-poll-trust-in-government-at-all-time-low/ (accessed October 29, 2011).

Coffey, D.J. (2011) "More than a Dime's Worth: Using State Party Platforms to Assess the Degree of American Party Polarization." *PS: Political Science and Politics*, 44(2): 331–337.

Congressional Budget Office. (2012) "The 2012 Long-Term Budget Outlook."

Washington: Congressional Budget Office. Available at: http://www.cbo.gov/publication/43288 (accessed June 15, 2012).

Congressional Research Service. (2007) "Presidential Signing Statements: Constitutional and Institutional Implications." Available at: http://www.fas.org/sgp/crs/natsec/RL33667.pdf (accessed August 18, 2010).

Cook, B.J. (1996) *Bureaucracy and Self-Government: Reconsidering the Role of Public Administration in American Politics.* Baltimore, MD: Johns Hopkins University Press.

Cook, D.M. and Polsky, A.J. (2005) "Political Time Reconsidered: Unbuilding and Rebuilding the State under the Reagan Administration." *American Politics Research,* 33(4): 577–605.

Dalton, R.J. (2013) *The Apartisan American: Dealignment and Changing Electoral Politics.* Los Angeles: CQ Press.

Donovan, T. (2002) "Expanding Direct Democracy in the US: How Far is Too Far?" Paper delivered at The Democracy Symposium, Williamsburg, Virginia, February 16–18.

Donovan, T., Denemark, D. and Bowler, S. (2008) "Trust in Government: The United States in Comparative Perspective." In K. Hoover and T. Donovan (eds.) *Elements of Social Scientific Thinking.* New York: Thomson Wadsworth, pp. 173–197.

Downs, A. (1957) "An Economic Theory of Political Action in a Democracy." *Journal of Political Economy,* 65(2): 135–150.

Drucker, P. (1995) "Really Reinventing Government." *The Atlantic.* 275: 49–61.

Dungworth, T., and Pace, N.M. (1990) *Statistical Overview of Civil Litigation in the Federal Courts.* Washington: Rand Corporation and The Institute for Civil Justice.

Economist, The. (2012) "The Dodd-Frank Act: Too Big Not to Fail." February 18. Available at: http://economist.com/node/21547784 (accessed March 11, 2013).

Edwards, G.C. (2007) *Governing by Campaigning: The Politics of the Bush Presidency.* New York: Pearson Longman.

Edwards, G.C. III, and Wayne, S.J. (2006) *Presidential Leadership: Politics and Policymaking.* Belmont, CA: Thomson Wadsworth.

Eilperin, J. (2009) "In Shift, EPA Says Greenhouse Gas Emissions Are Threat to Public." *The Washington Post,* April 18.

Erickson, R.S., MacKuen, M.B., and Stimson, J.A. (2002) *The Macro Polity.* Cambridge: Cambridge University Press.

Falcone, M. and Walter, A. (2012). "Mood Swing: Mitt Romney's Loss Re-Examined." *The Note.* ABC News. Available at: http://abcnews.go.com/blogs/politics/2012/11/mood-swing-mitt-romneys-loss-re-examined-the-note/ (accessed November 15, 2012).

Farhang, S. (2010) *The Litigation State: Public Regulation and Private Lawsuits in the U.S.* Princeton, NJ: Princeton University Press.

Federalist Society. (2012) "About Us." Available at: http://www.fed-soc.org/aboutus/ (accessed May 31, 2012).

Feeley, M.M. and Rubin, E.L. (2000) *Judicial Policymaking and the Modern State.* Cambridge: Cambridge University Press.

Ferejohn, J. (2002) "Politicizing Law." *Law and Contemporary Problems,* 65(3): 41–68.

Fiorina, M. (1977) *Congress: Keystone of the Washington Establishment.* New Haven, CT: Yale University Press.

—— (1981) *Retrospective Voting in American Elections*. New Haven, CT: Yale University Press.

—— (1989) *An Era of Divided Government*. Boston: Harvard University Center for American Political Studies.

Fiorina, M., and Abrams, S. (2009) *Disconnect: The Breakdown of Representation in American Politics*. Norman: University of Oklahoma Press.

Fiorina, M., Abrams, S., and Pope, J. (2008) "Polarization in the American Public: Misconceptions and Misreadings." *The Journal of Politics*, 70(02): 556–560.

Fiorina, M. and Levendusky, M. (2006) "Disconnected: The Political Class vs. The People." In D. Brady, W. Galston and P. Nivola (eds.) *Red and Blue Nation*, vol. 1. Washington, DC: Brookings Institution.

Fisher, L. (1996) "The Judge as Manager." *The Public Manager*, 25(3): 7–13.

—— (2005) *Legislative Vetoes After Chadha*. Washington, DC: Congressional Research Service. Available at: http://www.loufisher.org/docs/lv/4116.pdf (accessed February 1, 2013).

—— (2010) "The Unitary Executive and Inherent Executive Power." *University of Pennsylvania Journal of Constitutional Law*, 12(2): 569–591.

Frendreis, J. and Tatalovitch, R. (2009) "Riding the Tiger: Bush and the Economy." In S.E. Schier (ed.) *Ambition and Division: Legacies of the George W. Bush Presidency*. Pittsburgh, PA: University of Pittsburgh Press, pp. 215–239.

Friedman, T.L. and Mandelbaum, M. (2011) *That Used to Be Us*. New York: Farrar, Strauss and Giroux.

Funk, C. (2001) "Process Performance: Public Response to Legislative Policy Debate." In J. Hibbing and E. Theiss-Morse (eds.) *What Is It About Government that Americans Dislike?* Cambridge: Cambridge University Press, pp. 193–204.

Gallup. (2011) "Americans Say Federal Gov't Wastes Over Half of Every Dollar." Available at: http://www.gallup.com/poll/149543/americans-say-federal-gov-wastes-half-every-dollar.aspx (accessed 29 October 2011).

Gallup. (2012) "Record-High 40% of Americans Identify as Independents in '11." Available at: http://www.gallup.com/poll/151943/record-high-americans-identify-independents.aspx (accessed 9 January 2012).

Gardner, T. (2011) "EPA Delays Carbon Limits on Oil Refineries." *Reuters*, November 21.

Ginsberg, B. and Shefter, M. (2002) *Politics by Other Means: Politicians, Prosecutors, and the Press from Watergate to Whitewater*. 3rd ed. New York: W.W. Norton.

Greenhouse, L. (2007) "Justices Say EPA Has Power to Act on Harmful Gases." *New York Times*. April 3. Available at: http://www.nytimes.com/2007/04/03/washington/03scotus.html?pagewanted=all&_r=0. (accessed February 1, 2013).

Gueron, N. (1995) "An Idea Whose Time Has Come: A Comparative Procedural History of the Civil Rights Acts of 1960, 1964, and 1991." *The Yale Law Journal*, 104(5): 1201–1234.

Hayes, C. (2012) *Twilight of the Elites: American After Meritocracy*. New York: Crown.

Hetherington, M. J. (1999) "The Effect of Political Trust on the Presidential Vote, 1968–96." *American Political Science Review*, 93(2): 311–326.

—— (2006) *Why Trust Matters: Declining Political Trust and the Demise of Political Liberalism*. Princeton, NJ: Princeton University Press.

Hetherington, M.J. and Rudolph, T. J. (2008). "Priming, Performance and the Dynamics of Political Trust." *Journal of Politics*, 70(2): 498–512.

Hibbing, J.R. and Theiss-Morse, E (1995). *Congress as Public Enemy: Public*

Attitudes Toward American Political Institutions. New York: Cambridge University Press.

—— (2001) "The Means is the End." In J. Hibbing and E. Theiss-Morse (eds) *What Is It About Government that Americans Dislike?* Cambridge: Cambridge University Press, pp. 243–250.

—— (2002) *Stealth Democracy: Americans' Beliefs about How Government Should Work.* Cambridge: Cambridge University Press.

Hill, S. (2005) "Divided We Stand: The Polarizing of American Politics." *National Civic Review*, Winter: 3–14.

Hirschl, R. (2008) "The Judicialization of Politics." In K.E. Whittington, R.D. Kelemen and G.A. Caldeira (eds.) *The Oxford Handbook of Law and Politics.* Oxford: Oxford University Press, pp. 119–141.

Horowitz, D.L. (1977) *The Courts and Social Policy.* Washington, DC: Brookings Institution.

Howard, C. (2006) *The Welfare State Nobody Knows: Debunking Myths About U.S. Social Policy.* Princeton, NJ: Princeton University Press.

Howell, W.G. (2003) *Power without Persuasion: The Politics of Direct Presidential Action.* Princeton, NJ: Princeton University Press.

—— (2005) "Unilateral Powers: A Brief Overview." *Presidential Studies Quarterly*, 35(3): 417–439.

Howell, W., Adler, S., Cameron, C. and Riemann, C. (2000) "Divided Government and the Legislative Productivity of Congress, 1945–94." *Legislative Studies Quarterly*, 25(2): 285–312.

Jacob, H. (1984) *Justice in America: Courts, Lawyers and the Judicial Process.* New York: Scott Foresman.

Johnson, B. (2011) "Small Ball in the Long Game: Barack Obama and Congress." In S.E. Schier (ed.) *Transforming America: Barack Obama in the White House.* Lanham, MD: Rowman and Littlefield, pp. 143–162.

Judis, J. and Teixeira, R. (2002). *The Emerging Democratic Majority.* New York: Scribner.

Kagan, R.A. (2001) *Adversarial Legalism: The American Way of Law.* Cambridge, MA: Harvard University Press.

Kaiser Family Foundation (2012) *Kaiser Health Tracking Poll August 2012.* Available at: http://www.kff.org/kaiserpolls/trackingpoll.cfm (accessed September 21, 2012).

Karmarck, E. (2007). *The End of Government . . . As We Know It: Making Public Policy Work.* Boulder, CO: Lynne Rienner Publishers.

Keele, L. (2007) "Social Capital and the Dynamics of Trust in Government." *American Journal of Political Science*, 51(2): 241–254.

Keith, B.E., Magleby, D.B., Nelson, C.J., Orr, E., and Westlye, M.C. (1992). *The Myth of the Independent Voter.* Los Angeles: University of California Press.

Kernell, S. (1978) "Explaining Presidential Popularity." *American Political Science Review*, 72(2): 506–572.

—— (1997) *Going Public: New Strategies of Presidential Leadership.* Third ed. Washington, DC: Congressional Quarterly Press.

Key, V. O. (1956) *American State Politics: An Introduction.* New York: Knopf.

King, A. (2012) *The Founding Fathers v. The People: Paradoxes of American Democracy.* Cambridge, MA: Harvard University Press.

Knuckey, J. (1999) "Classification of Presidential Elections: An Update." *Polity*, 31(4): 639–653.

Kraft, M. and Furlong, S. (2007) *Public Policy: Politics, Analysis, and Alternatives.* 2nd ed. Washington, DC: CQ Press.

Kurlowski, D. (2011) "Disappearing Intransitivities in the Party Identification Scale." Paper presented at Midwestern Political Science Association Conference, Chicago.

Ladd, E.C. (1997). "The 'No Majority Party' Realignment Continues." *Political Sciences Quarterly*, 112(1): 1–28.

Lawrence, D. (1997) *The Collapse of the Democratic Presidential Majority: Realignment, Dealignment and Electoral Change from Franklin Roosevelt to Bill Clinton.* Boulder, CO: Westview Press.

Lawrence, S.E. (1990) *The Poor in Court: The Legal Services Program and Supreme Court Decision Making.* Princeton, NJ: Princeton University Press.

Lee, F.E. (2012) "Individualism and Partisan Activism on the Senate Floor." In B.A. Loomis (ed.) *The U.S. Senate: From Deliberation to Dysfunction.* Washington, DC: Sage, pp. 110–131.

Leip, D. (2010) *Dave Leip's Atlas of US Presidential Elections.* Available at: http://uselectionatlas.org/RESULTS (accessed December 20, 2009).

Levey, N. (2012) "Obama Healthcare Law Not Yet Resonating with Public." *Los Angeles Times*, March 20.

Levi, M. and Stoker, L. (2000). "Political Trust and Trustworthiness." *Annual Review of Political Science*, 3: 475–507.

Lewis, D.E. (2008) *The Politics of Presidential Appointments: Political Control and Bureaucratic Performance.* Princeton, NJ: Princeton University Press.

Lewis-Beck, M.S., Jacoby, W.G., Norpoth, H., and Weisberg, H.F. (2008). *The American Voter Revisited.* Michigan: University of Michigan Press.

Lieberman, J.K. (1981) *The Litigious Society.* New York: Basic Books.

Lieberman, R.C. (2000) "Political Time and Policy Coalitions: Structure and Agency in Presidential Power." In R.Y. Shapiro, M.J. Kumar, and L.R. Jacobs (eds.) *Presidential Power: Forging the Presidency for the Twenty-First Century.* New York: Columbia University Press, pp. 274–310.

Light, P.C. (1995) *Thickening Government: Federal Hierarchy and the Diffusion of Accountability.* Washington, DC: Brookings Institution Press.

—— (1999) *The President's Agenda: Domestic Policy Choice from Kennedy to Clinton.* Baltimore, MD: Johns Hopkins University Press.

—— Interview by G. Ifill (2002) *Securing the Homeland.* PBS.

Lowi, T.J., Ginsberg, B., Shepsle, K.A., and Ansolabehere, S. (2010) *American Government: Power and Purpose.* New York: W. W. Norton.

Lublin, D. (2004) *The Republican South: Democratization and Partisan Change.* Princeton, NJ: Princeton University Press.

Mackenzie, G.C. (1996) *The Irony of Reform: Roots of American Political Disenchantment.* Boulder, CO: Westview Press.

MacKuen, M. B., Erikson, R., and Stimson, J. A. (1989). "Macropartisanship." *The American Political Science Review* , 83(4): 1125–1142.

Manchikanti, L., Caraway, D., Parr, A.T., Fellows, Hirsch, B and J.A. (2011). "Patient Protection and Affordable Care Act of 2010: Reforming the Health Care Reform for the New Decade." *Pain Physician*, 14: E35–E67.

Mann, T. and Ornstein, N. (2008) *The Broken Branch: How Congress Is Failing America and How to Get It Back on Track.* Oxford: Oxford University Press.

—— (2012) *It's Even Worse than it Looks: How the American Constitutional System Collided with the New Politics of Extremism.* New York: Basic Books.

Manzi, J. (2012) *Uncontrolled: The Surprising Payoff of Trial-and-Error for Business, Politics and Society.* New York: Basic Books.

Matheson, S.M., Jr. (2009) *Presidential Constitutionalism in Perilous Times.* Cambridge, MA: Harvard University Press.

May, P. (1991) "Reconsidering Policy Design: Policies and Publics." *Journal of Public Policy,* 11(2): 187–206.

Mayhew, D. (1974) *Congress: The Electoral Connection.* New Haven, CT: Yale Univesity Press.

Mayhew, D. (2005) *Divided We Govern: Party Control, Lawmaking and Investigations, 1946–2002.* 2nd ed. New Haven, CT: Yale University Press.

—— (2009) "Datasets for Divided We Govern (1991)." Available at: http://pantheon.yale.edu/~dmayhew/data3.html (accessed August 18, 2010).

McGhee, E. and Krimm, D. (2009) "Party Registration and the Geography of Party Polarization." *Polity,* 41(3), 345–367.

McQuaid, K. (1989). *The Anxious Years: America in the Vietnam-Watergate Era.* New York: Basic Books.

Milkis, S.M. (1993) *The President and the Parties: The Transformation of the American Party System Since the New Deal.* New York: Oxford University Press.

Milkis, S.M. and Rhodes, J.H. (2009) "Barack Obama, the Democratic Party and the Future of the New American Party System." *The Forum,* 7(1): Article 7. Available at: http://www.bepress.com/forum/vol7/iss1/art7/ (accessed June 2009).

Moe, R. (2001) *The President's Reorganization Authority: Review and Analysis.* CRS Report for Congress, Washington, DC: Congressional Research Service.

Moe, T.M. (2012) "Delegation, Control, and the Study of Public Bureaucracy." *The Forum,* 10(2): Article 4. Available at: at:http://www.degruyter.com/view/j/for.2012.10.issue-2/1540-8884.1508/1540-8884.1508.xml?format=INT Pages (accessed August 2012).

Naff, K.C. (2004) "From Bakke to Grutter and Gratz: The Supreme Court as a Policymaking Institution." *Review of Policy Research,* 21(3): 405–427.

Neustadt, R.E. (1991) *Presidential Power and the Modern Presidents: The Politics of Leadership from Roosevelt to Reagan.* New York: Free Press.

Nicholson, S.P., Segura, G.M. and Woods, N.D. (2002) "Presidential Approval and the Mixed Blessing of Divided Government." *Journal of Politics,* 64(4): 701–720.

Nye, J.S., Jr., Zelikow, P.D., and King, D.C. (1997) *Why People Don't Trust Government.* Cambridge, MA: Harvard University Press.

Olson, M. (1984). *The Rise and Decline of Nations: Economic Growth, Stagflation and Social Rigidities.* New Haven, CT: Yale University Press.

Ornstein, N. (2011) "Worst Congress Ever." *Foreign Policy,* July 19.

Ornstein, N., Mann, T., and Malbin, M. (2008). *Vital Statistics on Congress, 2008.* Washington, DC: The Brookings Institution Press.

Orren, K. (1991) *Belated Feudalism: Labor, the Law and Liberal Development in the United States.* Cambridge: Cambridge University Press.

Orren, K. and Skowronek, S. (1997) "Regimes and Regime Building in American Government: A Review of Literature on the 1940s." *Political Science Quarterly,* 113(4): 689–702.

—— (2004) *The Search for American Political Development.* New York: Cambridge University Press.

Oxford Advanced Learner's Dictionary. Available at: http://www.oxfordadvanced learnersdictionary.com/dictionary/swing-state (accessed August 5, 2011).

Palazzolo, D. (1992) *The Speaker and the Budget: Leadership in the Post-Reform House of Representatives*. Pittsburgh, PA: University of Pittsburgh Press.

Palmer, B. (2005) *Changing the Senate Rules: The "Constitutional" or "Nuclear" Option*. CRS Report for Congress, The Library of Congress, Washington, DC: Congressional Research Service.

Paulson, A. (2007) *Electoral Realignment and the Outlook for American Democracy*. Boston: Northeastern University Press.

—— (2009) "Party Change and the Shifting Dynamics in Presidential Nominations: The Lessons of 2008." *Polity*, 41: 312–330.

Pear, R. (2010) "Hoyer Defends Controversial House Procedure." *The New York Times*, March 16.

Pecquet, J. (2012) "Ryan Budget Cuts Medicaid By $810 Billion." *The Hill*. March 20.

Peterson, M. (1993) *Legislating Together: The White House and Capitol Hill from Eisenhower to Reagan*. Cambridge, MA: Harvard University Press.

Petrocik, J.R. (1974) "An Analysis of Intransitivities in the Index of Party Identification." *Political Methodology* , 1(3): 31–47.

—— (1987) "New Party Coalitions and the Nationalization of the South." *Journal of Politics*, 49(2): 347–375.

—— (2009) "Measuring Party Support: Leaners Are Not Independents." *Electoral Studies*, 28(4): 562–572.

Pfiffner, J.P. (2008) *Power Play: The Bush Presidency and the Constitution*. Washington, DC: Brookings Institution Press.

Pollard, K. (2008) "Population Research Bureau." Available at: www.prb.org/ Articles/2008/electiondemographics.aspx (accessed January 2010).

Pomper, G. (1967) "Classification of Presidential Elections." *The Journal of Politics* , 29(3:, 535–566.

Poole, K.T. and Rosenthal, H. (2007) *Ideology and Congress*. Piscataway, NJ: Transaction Publishers.

Prior, M. (2007) *Post-Broadcast Democracy: How Media Choice Increases Inequality in Political Involvelment and Polarizes Elections*. Cambridge: Cambridge University Press.

Rauch, J. (1999) *Government's End: Why Washington Stopped Working*. New York: Public Affairs.

Rohde, D. (1991) *Parties and Leaders in the Postreform House*. Chicago: University of Chicago Press.

Rosenberg, M. (2008) *Congressional Review of Agency Rulemaking: An Update and Assessment of the Congressional Review Act after a Decade*. CRS Report for Congress, Washington, DC: Congressional Research Service.

Rosenbloom, D.H. (2000) *Building a Legislative Centered Public Administration*. Tuscaloosa: University of Alabama Press.

Rourke, F.E. (1991) "The American Bureaucracy in a Changing Political Setting." *Journal of Public Administration, Research and Theory*, 2: 111–129.

Rudalvige, A. (2006) *The New Imperial Presidency: Renewing Presidential Power after Watergate*. Ann Arbor: University of Michigan Press.

Runkel, P.S. (1994) "The Civil Rights Act of 1991: A Continuation of the Wards Cove Standard of Business Necessity." *William and Mary Law Review*, 35(3): 1177–1239.

Sack, K. (2011) "Battle Over Health Care Law Shifts to Appellate Courts." *New York Times*, May 8.

Savage, C. (2009) "Obama Looks to Limit Impact of Tactic Bush Used to Sidestep New Laws." *New York Times*. Available at: http://www.nytimes.com/2009/03/10/us/politics/10signing.html (accessed August 18, 2010).

—— (2010) "Obama Takes New Route to Opposing Parts of Laws." *New York Times*, January 8.

—— (2012) "Shift on Executive Power Lets Obama Bypass Rivals." *The New York Times*, April 22.

Schattschneider, E.E. (1977) *Party Government*. Westport, CT: Greenwood Press.

Scherer, N. (2005) *Scoring Points: Politicians, Activists, and the Lower Federal Court Appointment Process*. Stanford, CA: Stanford University Press.

Schier, S.E. (2008) *Panorama of a Presidency: How George W. Bush Acquired and Spent His Political Capital*. Armonk, NY: M. E. Sharpe.

—— (2011) "Introduction: Obama's 'Big Bang' Presidency." In S.E. Schier, (ed.) *Transforming America: Barack Obama in the White House*. Lanham, MD: Rowman and Littlefield, pp. 1–20.

Schoenbrod, D. (1993) *Power Without Responsibility: How Congress Abuses the People Through Delegation*. New Haven, CT: Yale University Press.

—— (2006) "The EPA's Faustian Bargain." *Regulation*, Fall: 36–42.

Schultheis, E. (2012) "Exit Polls 2012: Split on Obamacare." *Politico*, November 6. Available at: http://www.politico.com/news/stories/1112/83427.html?hp=l4_b4 (accessed November 23, 2012).

Scott, R. and Hrebenar, R. (1984) *Parties in Crisis: Party Politics in America*. Vashon: Vashon Island Books.

Shepsle, K. (1989) "The Changing Textbook Congress." In J. Chubb and P. Peterson (eds.) *Can the Government Govern?* Washington, DC: The Brookings Institution, pp. 238–266.

Silverstein, G. (2009) *Law's Allure: How Law Shapes, Constrains, Saves, and Kills Politics*. Cambridge: Cambridge University Press.

Sinclair, B. (2006) *Party Wars: Polarization and the Politics of National Policymaking*. Norman: University of Oklahoma Press.

—— (2011) *Unorthodox Lawmaking*. 4th ed. Los Angeles: Sage/CQ Press.

Skocpol, T. (2004) *Diminished Democracy: From Membership to Management in American Civic Life*. Norman: University of Oklahoma Press.

Skowronek, S. (1996) *The Politics Presidents Make: Leadership from John Adams to Bill Clinton*. Cambridge, MA: Harvard University Press.

—— (2008) *Presidential Leadership in Political Time: Reprise and Renewal*. Lawrence: University Press of Kansas.

—— (2011a) *Presidential Leadership in Political Time: Reprise and Reappraisal*. 2nd ed. Lawrence: University of Kansas Press.

—— (2011b) "Taking Stock." In L. Jacobs and D. King (eds.) *The Unsustainable American State*. Oxford: Oxford University Press, pp. 330–338.

Smith, K. B., Greenblatt, A., and Mariani Vaughn, M. (2010) *Governing States and Localities*. 3rd ed. Washington, DC: CQ Press.

Squire, P. (1993) "Professionalization and Public Opinion." *The Journal of Politics*, 55(2): 479–491.

Stanley, H.W. (1988) "Partisan Changes: Dealignment, Realignment or Both?" *Journal of Politics*, 50(1): 64–88.

Stanley, H.W. and Niemi, R.G. (2010) *Vital Statistics on American Politics 2009–2010*. Washington, DC: Congressional Quarterly Press.

Stein, H. (2012) "Why Things Suddenly Stop." Available at: http://www.civicstrategies.com/resources/quotes.html (accessed June 20, 2012).

Stewart, R.B. (1975) "The Reformation of American Administrative Law." *Harvard Law Review*, 88(8): 1667–1813.

Stimson, J.A. (2009) "Public Policy Mood: 1952 to 2008." Available at: http://www.unc.edu/~jstimson/ (accessed June 8, 2009).

—— (2011) "Policy Mood." Available at: http://www.unc.edu/~cogginse/Policy_Mood.html (accessed May 28, 2011).

Sundquist, J. (1983) *Dynamics of the Party System: Alignment and Realignment of the Political Parties in the United States*. Washington, DC: The Brookings Institution.

Taylor, S. (2005). "Remote Control." *The Atlantic*. Available at: http://www.theatlantic.com/magazine/archive/2005/09/remote-control/4159/ (accessed July 29, 2011).

Teles, S.M. (2007) "Conservative Mobilization against Entrenched Liberalism." In P. Pierson and T. Skocpol (eds.) *The Transformation of American Politics: Activist Government and the Rise of Conservatism*. Princeton, NJ: Princeton University Press, pp. 160–188.

—— (2008) *The Rise of the Conservative Legal Movement: The Battle for Control of the Law*. Princeton, NJ: Princeton University Press.

Teixeira, R. and Halpin, J. (2012). "The Return of the Obama Coalition." *The Center for American Progress*. Available at: http://www.americanprogress.org/issues/progressive-movement/news/2012/11/08/44348/the-return-of-the-obama-coalition/ (accessed November 15, 2012).

Theriault, S. and Rohde, D. (2011) "The Gingrich Senators and Party Polarization in the U.S. Senate." *Journal of Politics*, 73(4): 1011–1024.

Trende, S. (2011) *Lost Majority: Why the Future of Government Is Up for Grabs – and Who Will Take It*. New York: Palgrave Macmillan.

Walsh, B. (2011) "Battle Brews Over EPA's Emissions Regulations." *Time*, January 3.

Weisman, J. (2009) "Signing Statements Reappear in Obama White House." *Wall Street Journal*, March 4.

West, W.F. (2004) *The Institutionalization of Regulatory Review: Organizational Stability and Responsive Competence at OIRA*. Working Paper, College Station: The Bush School of Government and Public Service, Texas A&M University.

Wilson, J.Q. (2010) *American Politics, Then and Now and Other Essays*. Washington, DC: AEI Press.

Wood, D.B. (2009) *The Myth of Presidential Representation*. Cambridge: Cambridge University Press.

Ziegler, J.C. (2003) "Historic Wyatt Case Ends." Alabama Department of Mental Health and Mental Retardation. Available at: http://www.mh.state.al.us/admin/downloads/MediaCenterDocuments/PR_31208_HistoricWyattCaseEnds.asp (accessed May 31, 2012).

Zmerli, S. and Newton, K. (2008) "Social Trust and Attitudes Toward Democracy." *Public Opinion Quarterly*, 72(4): 706–724.

Index

For Product Safety Concerns and Information please contact our EU
representative GPSR@taylorandfrancis.com
Taylor & Francis Verlag GmbH, Kaufingerstraße 24, 80331 München, Germany

* 9 7 8 0 4 1 5 8 9 3 3 0 5 *